T0314170

MARKETS, STATE, AND PEOPLE

MARKETS, STATE, AND PEOPLE

ECONOMICS FOR PUBLIC POLICY

DIANE COYLE

PRINCETON UNIVERSITY PRESS
PRINCETON AND OXFORD

Copyright © 2020 by Princeton University Press

Published by Princeton University Press
41 William Street, Princeton, New Jersey 08540
6 Oxford Street, Woodstock, Oxfordshire OX20 1TR

press.princeton.edu

All Rights Reserved

Names: Coyle, Diane, author.
Title: Markets, state, and people : economics for public policy / Diane Coyle.
Description: Princeton : Princeton University Press, [2020] | Includes index.
Identifiers: LCCN 2019019274 | ISBN 9780691179261 (hardcover)
Subjects: LCSH: Economic policy. | Economics.
Classification: LCC HD87 .C693 2020 | DDC 338.9–dc23 LC record available
at https://lccn.loc.gov/2019019274

ISBN (e-book) 978-0-691-18931-4

British Library Cataloging-in-Publication Data is available

Editorial: Sarah Caro, Charlie Allen, and Hannah Paul
Production Editorial: Kathleen Cioffi
Text and Jacket Design: Lorraine Doneker
Production: Erin Suydam
Publicity: Nathalie Levine and Kate Farquhar-Thomson
Copyeditor: Jennifer McClain

Jacket art: *The Ideal City*, c. 1470. Tempera on panel

This book has been composed in Sabon and Din Pro

Printed on acid-free paper. ∞

Printed in the United States of America

10 9 8 7 6 5 4 3 2 1

CONTENTS

PREFACE

Economics has a powerful influence on our lives, largely because it is so influential in shaping governments' decisions, and these decisions affect every area of human activity. The increasing power of economic thinking is reflected by the substantial increase in the number of economists employed by governments and public sector agencies in recent years. Many, perhaps most, policy decisions are justified on economic terms.

Whether there should be so much government influence on our lives is of course a matter of debate, and the partisan divisions over this question are about as wide as they have ever been. However, one of the points I make in this book is that any individual decision affects other people because we live in communities and societies. So even those who argue for "less" government need to consider how collective decisions get made. Traditionally, markets have been presented as an alternative: either the state or the market proves to be the best way of organizing a given economic activity or set of choices. But this is a misleading way of thinking about how societies can collectively use the available resources to achieve the best possible outcomes for their members. In every country and community, a mixture of private markets, government action, and non-governmental organizations determines economic outcomes. Good public policies recognize that sometimes these alternative modes substitute for each other, and sometimes they support each other. Regulations are the scaffolding necessary for markets to operate. Strong social norms may make regulation unnecessary and markets work better. Similarly, norms can make policies more effective—for instance, a small tax on plastic bags and a regulation limiting smoking in certain public places have proved powerful policy interventions because they operate in a context of changing social norms. What's more, markets and governments often "fail" in exactly the same circumstances, because of fundamentally difficult choices.

Markets, governments, and social norms or preferences are labels we give to different modes of organizing our society.

Another important element of public policy wisdom is the recognition that the "best" policies are not purely technocratic decisions, because they involve values and ethical considerations. This includes societal choice about what the "best" option means, because conflicts of interest are unavoidable in all economies. Economists rightly try to make their advice as evidence-based and objective as possible but should not over-claim. Part of the reason for the political confrontations we are currently seeing in many Western countries is pent-up anger about the repeated assertions that the judgment of "experts" must override everything else. Experts do know better about many things than the average citizen, or even the average politician, but there are trade-offs in terms of values as well as in terms of economic interests. There is a long tradition in economics of debating "social welfare" and social choices; it has been less prominent in recent times but is showing signs of reviving now.

A third point I emphasize here is that history and geography matter. So do ideas. Even if the right policies or approaches command consensus or can be identified with sufficient clarity, circumstances change. The economy changes its character over time, tastes and preferences change, crises occur—all of which means that there are big differences between the policy choices made in different countries and at different times. There is a mutual influence between events, economic ideas, and policy approaches, especially when the changes are significant. The Great Depression is an example of a crisis that profoundly changed economic thinking and political outcomes, and the 2008 financial crisis will prove to have been similarly decisive. Major technological shifts have a similar effect, and the continuing influence of digital technologies will also prove to change the way collective decisions ought to be and will be made in the future.

A book about economics for public policy could potentially cover a vast amount of territory. This one leaves out a lot, including some areas of policy such texts would traditionally cover, such as macroeconomic policies or the large literature on taxation. The focus here is on areas of applied microeconomics. It is a largely non-technical book so should be accessible to people who have not studied economics, so long as they skip the equations, but it also gives those who are or have been economics students a much broader perspective than they might get in the classroom on the issues policymakers face. Each chapter has an extensive set of suggestions for further reading, including more technical references. The examples are drawn from many different countries, although mainly the developed economies, as developing economies have distinct features and challenges. Having said that, I am a British economist and policymaker, so a good deal of the discussion about the historical ebb and flow of policy approaches is focused on the UK.

The first four chapters cover how societies organize the use of resources. Chapter 1 sets out the fundamental economics, including economists' approach to what is termed *social welfare*, or what it means to say there is a better economic outcome. Chapters 2, 3, and 4 consider the operation of markets; the choice about when to have the state engage directly in economic production or to regulate those markets where it is difficult for competition to occur; and the circumstances when non-market and non-state organization of economic activity can occur.

The second half of the book addresses a number of key current challenges to policy-making. One, discussed in chapter 5, is the challenge the discoveries in behavioral economics pose to how economists need to think about policy analysis. This is a lively area of research with many unresolved questions. The second, addressed in chapter 6, is the pressing problem of poverty in rich countries, the threat to middle-class jobs, and the discontent being caused by increasing inequality. These issues are the result of technological changes, globalization, and political choices; they help account for the current era of political turmoil throughout the West. A perennial challenge is the ubiquitous and all too common presence of government failure (the subject of chapter 7)—bad decisions with unintended or counterproductive consequences are a constant in public policy. The final chapter considers the role of evidence in shaping economic policies: how it is used in practice, how it should be used, and its limitations.

MARKETS, STATE, AND PEOPLE

CHAPTER 1

The State and the Market

This chapter sets the scene by considering one of the fundamental issues in public policy economics: What are the relative roles of the government and the private sector, or market, in the economy? Economic theory provides some tools for analyzing the question, so the chapter sets out some of the basics of what is known as welfare economics—in other words, the analysis of economic efficiency and the criteria for assessing whether something makes a society better off or not. (Readers who have previously taken microeconomics courses will be familiar with this.) The theory, taken literally, implies that competitive markets will deliver the highest social welfare; but there are two pitfalls in taking too simplistic a view of economic theory, based as it is on some strong assumptions. One pitfall is concluding that the more markets can be relied on the better; in fact, there are pervasive "market failures." The opposite one is concluding that it is possible for the government to work out how to correct all market failures; for government failure is widespread too. In fact, practicing economists use the theory as a framework for analyzing policy problems rather than as a guide to solving them. Besides, when it comes to policy choices, economic analysis alone is not enough, or there would be none of the familiar political debate about the proper roles of state and market. So the chapter also discusses the way political or historical events and economic thinking influence each other, helping to explain the variations in government interventions in the economy over time and across countries. It concludes by looking, in the light of this context, at the examples of specific types of market failure: externalities and public goods.

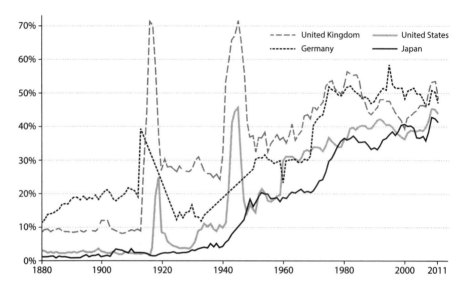

Figure 1.1. Total government spending, including interest government expenditures, as percentage of GDP. *Source*: IMF Fiscal Affairs Departmental Data, based on graph at https://ourworldindata.org/public-spending.

Governments intervene in the economy in many ways. For instance, government spending is a reasonably high share of national income in all developed economies, between 28.7% (Ireland) and 57% (Finland) in 2015, while the size of this expenditure relative to the economy has trended up over time, as well as moving up and down in business cycles (figure 1.1). The spending goes on many services: defense, the legal system, police, education, health, pensions, local government services, roads and infrastructure, state pensions, welfare or social security benefits, subsidies for certain activities or industries, and more. Almost as much (although usually less, as budget deficits are the norm) is raised in revenue through a wide range of taxes, licenses, and charges. All these ways of raising revenue affect the choices individual households and businesses make because they affect people's incentives. Some of the taxing and spending is intended to redistribute money from rich to poor. The excess of expenditure over revenue is paid for by money borrowed in the financial markets, and this government borrowing can affect interest rates paid by private sector borrowers for their loans.

To focus just on the government's taxing and spending is to miss a huge part of its intervention in the economy, though. Governments also write and enforce laws and regulations that govern how businesses are run and how consumers are protected. Competition policy aims to stop businesses from growing too powerful at the expense of consumers, or regulators. Employment law is intended to protect workers from exploitation or discrimination. Government bodies enforce technical and safety standards. Professionals of many kinds are required to hold licenses to operate their practices, in the interest of consumer protection. Therefore, governments can affect when and how people work, who businesses employ, what we can buy and the prices we pay, how goods are manufactured, what information has to be handed over to the authorities, and much more. Box 1.1 lists many of the ways the government influences the economy. It is not easy to measure the scope of all these kinds of intervention, or compare countries, but examples such as the length of the rule book for financial services or the tax code in many countries suggest it has been steadily increasing. In any case, the government is deeply involved in economic activity.

Sometimes economic policies seem intrusive, and people often react in unanticipated ways to specific government actions. High taxes are never popular and have in the past been far higher than now. In 1966 the highest (marginal) rate of income tax was 91% in the United States and 98% in the United Kingdom. No surprise the Beatles wrote their song "Taxman" (on the 1966 album *Revolver*) complaining about the tax burden. Swedish pop star Abba's Björn Ulvaeus revealed (in a 2014 book) that they wore such outrageous costumes because the cost of their clothes could be set against their tax due as long as the outfits could not be worn in everyday life. "In my honest opinion we looked like nuts in those years. Nobody can have been as badly dressed on stage as we were," he wrote. Businesses constantly complain about the burden of regulation, but also constantly call for more government investment in research or in infrastructure such as bridges and roads or subsidies for innovative products. Sometimes policies are entirely counterproductive while other policies are astonishingly effective: see box 1.2.

Box 1.1. Examples of the scope of government involvement in the economy

Spending on services such as health, education, housing, defense, policing, pensions, waste collection, lighting, parks, social services, roads, justice, prisons, and much more

Taxation/licensing—multiple taxes, fees, auctions

Subsidies and tax incentives for specified activities

The "welfare state"—benefits, pensions, income redistribution

Regulation—of many activities

Competition policy—merger control, market investigations, antitrust

Public ownership, and also privatization of public corporations, contracting out of public activities, private finance initiatives

Shaping markets—legal frameworks, takeover rules, intellectual property law

Granting patents, copyright

Setting technical standards

Persuasion and "choice architecture"—public health information campaigns

Investment (infrastructure, research)

Box 1.2. Policy failures and successes

The Cash for Clunkers scheme was introduced in the US in 2008, intended to boost the revenues of the struggling auto manufacturers by encouraging Americans to trade in their old cars for environmentally cleaner new models. It cost $3 billion in subsidies of up to $4,500 to people who traded their "clunker" for a new fuel-efficient auto. In theory, the program would hit two targets: a stimulus for the manufacturers and a contribution to combating climate change and pollution by getting older gas-guzzlers off the road.

(*continued on next page*)

(*continued from previous page*)

However, the program led to people bringing forward the purchase of a new car—and trading down to a cheaper model, due to the weak state of the economy at the time. The scheme actually reduced the industry's revenues by an estimated several billion dollars compared to what they would have been without it. The new cars were less damaging environmentally, but as a "green" policy Cash for Clunkers was not cost-effective. It was without question a policy failure.*

On the other hand, small taxes on plastic carrier bags seem like a highly effective policy. Even when low, they dramatically reduce the quantity of single-use bags shoppers use, many of which otherwise end up as landfill. The taxes also raise revenues for the government in an uncontroversial way. In Washington, DC, a 5 cent tax reduced the use of carryout bags by 60%. Ireland introduced a 22 (euro) cent tax in 2002, which almost eliminated their use. A 5 pence charge in the UK reduced usage by 85% and encouraged the government to propose doubling the fee to 10 pence. The aim of the charges is to reduce this non-biodegradable source of waste, often harmful to wildlife, and the policy is highly effective in this respect. However, the substitute canvas and other bags have an environmental impact, too, in their production and disposal; there may be trade-offs even between environmental aims.**

* Mark Hoekstra, Steven L. Puller, and Jeremy West (2017), "Cash for Corollas: When Stimulus Reduces Spending," *American Economic Journal: Applied Economics* 9, no. 3: 1–35.
** The UK's experience (https://www.gov.uk/government/news/plastic-bag-sales-in-big-seven-supermarkets-down-86-since-5p-charge) is similar to Ireland's (https://www.dccae.gov.ie/en-ie/environment/topics/waste/litter/plastic-bags/Pages/default.aspx) and to US cities such as Washington, DC (https://doee.dc.gov/sites/default/files/dc/sites/ddoe/documents/0%20BL%20Survey%20Overview%20Fact%20Sheet.pdf).

In traditional public economics courses, government activities are divided into three "branches": stabilization, allocation, and distribution. The first of these concerns macroeconomic policy, aiming for a high and stable level of employment and steady growth and inflation. This book does not cover macroeconomic stabilization. Nor does it cover much of another staple of traditional courses, the structure of taxation and sources of tax revenues, which are at the heart of fiscal policy analysis. Instead, the focus here is on allocation and distribution: What is produced, how, and by whom? And how is what is produced distributed among different members of society? The fundamental issue here is therefore the collective use and consumption of resources by large numbers of individuals in society— how is the economy organized? Economics poses these as questions of efficiency and equity (or, in other words, fairness). Often economists focus on the efficiency questions, acting as if they can be analyzed in isolation from judgments about distribution or fairness, but it is impossible in practice to draw any policy conclusions without making value judgments. Almost any policy change creates winners and losers.

The starting point here is therefore to ask how a society can organize production and consumption—the economy—in the best way. This might seem to be a factual kind of question, but in many countries it is of course politically contested. People have conflicting views at any moment in time, and the modes of economic organization societies choose vary at different points in history and in different countries.

Which activities should be done by the government, which by the market, or in some other way? (And, by the way, what do we mean by "the government" or "the market," and what other ways are there? These questions will be explored further.) If the government is involved, what is the best way for it to try to achieve some socially desirable outcome: public ownership, public provision of services, regulation, taxes, subsidies, or some other policy instrument? (And is it clear what outcome is desired, or are there competing, even conflicting, aims?) The way economists have answered these questions has changed considerably over time. This is due to significant events, such as financial crises or wars, and because politics responds to events. It is also because economic thinking changes, as ideas respond to events and to political trends, too. Tracking changes in economic thinking is important because the reasons for change illustrate some fundamental dilemmas in determining public policies. It is also important because a key message in this book is that, on many policy issues, economics does not have answers that are right for all time. The right answer is, ultimately, it depends—on context and on political choices. At the same time, economic analysis can provide analytical and empirical insights to inform these contingent choices. The aim of public policy economics is to combine this technical rigor with sensitivity to the specific context.

Social Aims

Evaluation of success and failure in policy has to begin with its ultimate aims. Societies are driven by different aims or values at different times. Some of these, such as patriotism, national power, or honor, have little relation to economics, and might even damage the economy. The aims where economists can contribute something to the discussion are *efficiency*, *equity* or *fairness*, and *mutual insurance against life's uncertainties*; and perhaps also *social cohesion* or *civic participation*, and *freedom*.

These aims can conflict with each other. Clearly, some of them are not only economic but also ethical questions. Economics has tended to assume that answers to the ethical or political questions, requiring value judgments, can largely be separated from answers to the purely technical economic ones. The assumption is not always justified, although it is surely desirable to conduct economic policy analysis in as impartial a manner as possible.

One important potential trade-off between social aims, the one most often discussed in economics texts, is between efficiency and equity. If the government wants to redistribute income from rich to poor by taxing the former, it can bring about a more equal society but perhaps at the cost of discouraging some people from working as hard, or discouraging some investment, and so shrinking the size of economic output and incomes compared to what they would otherwise have been. The tax causes some loss of efficiency. But many other things influence effort and output. So alternatively, it might be that a very unequal society discourages work effort by the poor—why bother to be productive if most of the gain goes to someone else? In which case, there is no simple trade-off between efficiency and equity.

Efficiency and equity are two key rationales for much state intervention in private economic activities ("the market"):

- *efficiency* whenever either individual or *market failures* occur— "failures" meaning sub-optimal decisions because of externalities, natural monopolies, public goods, or simply non-rational choices (all explored below);
- *equity* whenever enough people in society have a preference for redistributing resources—redistribution that can be either monetary payments or the provision of public services, such as education, health, or housing.

Much of the analysis in public policy economics sets aside the distribution question to start with, asking: For a given income distribution, what is the most *efficient* way for society to use its resources? What will deliver the greatest *social welfare*? This book starts the same way, returning to distributional questions in chapter 6. Framing the analysis like this also begs the question about the efficiency of government intervention. Chapter 7 focuses on government failure. While there are many examples throughout the book (as in life) of government policies gone wrong, one of the themes is that there are inherent difficulties in organizing an economy to achieve broad and possibly conflicting aims, and in some contexts both government and market solutions will "fail." Another theme, following from this, is that it is a mistake to think of "the government" and "the market" as alternatives. Societies have a range of organizational structures involving a mixture of private and collective choices, the latter sometimes taken by "official" public sector bodies and sometimes by "unofficial" community agreement; chapter 4 explores this further.

The rest of this chapter covers the question of the appropriate roles of the government and the private sector (state and market) in the economy, the main issue in so much political debate about economic policies. On certain assumptions, economic theory justifies the competitive market as the "best" way of organizing production and consumption. The next sections consider what "best" means and what assumptions lead to the presumption in favor of markets. It is worth emphasizing here that although economists working on public policy have this theoretical equipment at the back of their minds, all are aware that it provides no more than a useful framework for organizing their thoughts. No one thinks consumers and producers behave in reality as they do in these abstract models. Critics of economics often mistakenly think practitioners take the abstract theory at face value, whereas public policy economics in practice is firmly rooted in empirical reality. With that warning in mind, the next sections introduce the theoretical basics of what is referred to (somewhat confusingly) as *welfare economics*.

Efficiency

The first question is the criterion for preferring one way of organizing production and consumption in the economy over another: What does it mean to say an activity is *efficient*? The specific meaning used in economics is known as *Pareto efficiency* (after the Italian economist Vilfredo Pareto, 1848–1923).

> An allocation of resources is *Pareto efficient* if nobody can be made better off without somebody else becoming worse off.
> A *Pareto improvement* is a change that makes some people better off without making anyone else worse off.

This requires a definition of "worse off" or "better off." The criterion used is each individual's own evaluation of their welfare. *Social welfare* must then in some way be the aggregate of the welfare of the individuals in the society—a question discussed below. For now it seems reasonable to agree that a change helping someone and harming no one is an improvement.

Note that a Pareto improvement might—or might not—lead to a Pareto efficient outcome; but if the economy is at a Pareto efficient point, there is no possibility of a Pareto improvement. What's more, the criterion is agnostic about the distribution of resources; even in a very unequal society, it insists that it is not an improvement to make one rich person worse off even if many poorer people are better off.

Pareto efficiency is related to key concepts in microeconomic theory. The annex to this chapter sets out some of this background, which is covered in all the standard microeconomics textbooks; it will be familiar to anybody who has already studied economics, and rather mysterious to anybody who has not yet become familiarized with some of these nuts and bolts of economic theory. It does not help that different textbooks give slightly different definitions. Here I try to make the ideas as intuitive as possible.

Pareto efficiency consists of the following:

- *Productive efficiency*: Given the kind of resources available (such as land or minerals, labor, machines) and their relative prices, and given the state of technology, is output as high as it can be? Is the economy operating on its *production possibilities frontier*?
- *Allocative* (or *consumption* or *exchange*) *efficiency*: Given the production of different goods and their relative prices, are the goods produced going to the people who most value them? Are people on their highest possible *indifference curve*?

The definition used sometimes focuses on allocative efficiency alone, sometimes both allocative and productive; and sometimes it adds a third element:

- *Product mix* (or *output*) *efficiency*: Do the goods being produced correspond to the goods people want to buy, or is there another combination of goods produced with the same resources that would make people better off (put them on a higher indifference curve)?

Together the three components cover how effectively resources are turned into products, whether the products correspond to people's preferences, and whether, through exchange, they go to the people who value them most. If any of the three is not satisfied, then at least one person could be made better off (through use of resources in production, mix of goods being produced, or exchange of products) without making anyone else worse off. This seems reasonably intuitive as a concept of efficiency.

It is important to note that the terminology can mislead people into thinking Pareto efficiency is only a technical concept. After all, it is silent on questions we would think of as ethical issues, particularly the distribution of resources. This is correct in the case of productive efficiency but not entirely when it comes to allocative efficiency, which assumes that "better" means satisfying people's preferences, whatever they are (and also that it is possible to aggregate up from individual preference satisfaction to *social welfare*). "Efficiency" sounds like it is only about *positive* questions, matters of fact; but Pareto efficiency is *normative*, involving a value judgment in assuming the satisfaction of individual preferences is the right criterion for assessing economic policy outcomes.

Pareto Efficiency and the Competitive Market

Equipped with the notion of Pareto efficiency and a set of assumptions, it is possible to prove two fundamental theorems of welfare economics.

The first theorem states that if a competitive market equilibrium exists, then it is Pareto efficient. Otherwise people would be able to undertake exchanges that increased their utility—so it could not have been an equilibrium to start with. The competitive prices measure the (marginal) increase in welfare for one more unit of each good. As long as market exchange is possible, people can trade with each other until all the potential improvements in their welfare have been captured. This theorem is the underpinning of the instinct in favor of competitive markets as a benchmark, although this depends on the validity of the assumptions, which are discussed further below.

The second theorem says that given an initial allocation of resources, there is a set of competitive prices that support the Pareto efficient outcome. It implies that efficiency can be achieved by the price mechanism in competitive markets, and can be separated from the question of the preferred distribution of resources: exchanges at market prices will deliver a Pareto efficient outcome, whatever the distribution. If society wants to redistribute resources to begin with, the competitive market can again deliver a Pareto efficient outcome.

The theorems rely on certain assumptions, however; some are obvious, others subtler (box 1.3).

To list these is to see that they often do *not* hold in reality, and economists are well aware of this. Even Paul Samuelson, who did more than anyone to embed the grand theory sketched above in the way economics is learned and practiced, was explicit about this: "The above does not happen in real life." The Pareto efficiency approach and welfare theorems nevertheless hold powerful sway in the worldview of economics in offering a conceptual framework for thinking about why, in any particular real-world context, competition and market exchange are *not* the social welfare–maximizing approach. The theorems organize ideas rather than dictating recommendations. The nature of government interventions is assessed in light of how these correspond to the way reality departs from the

---

Box 1.3. Assumptions for welfare theorems to hold

Consumers and producers are rational and self-interested
They have fixed preferences
There is perfect competition with no economies of scale and no barriers to entry (or exit)
Individuals have full information, and it is symmetric (the same) for all
Goods are rival—if I consume or use it, you can't
Private and social benefits are equal
Private and social costs are equal
There are complete markets (including markets for all future goods)
Goods are owned and able to be exchanged—there are property rights and effective contract law

assumptions. And even though there is limited hope in reality of a Pareto improvement in public policy—as there are so often losers as well as winners—the evaluation of public policy is often made in terms of specific market failures as departures from Pareto efficiency. Otherwise economists would constantly need to make explicit judgments about the distributional questions, something they understandably hesitate to do.

Departures from the assumptions behind the welfare theorems also form the organizing principle for the rest of this chapter, and the book. First, though, there are some other issues relating to the theorems to touch on: the problem of the "second best" world, questions of distribution, and how to aggregate individual welfare into social welfare.

The Second Best Theorem

One issue is how useful the Pareto efficiency criterion is when the economy is not in a competitive equilibrium, and there are multiple market failures or departures from competition and free exchange. The *second best theorem* (proved by Richard Lipsey and Kelvin Lancaster in 1956) shows that a change that would be a Pareto improvement in a first best world will rarely be so in a second best world. For instance, if European tariffs on high-cost imports from the US are abolished, making their purchase price lower, but there are still tariffs on imports from low-cost Asian producers, then Europeans switching to buying American goods produced at higher cost will not increase social welfare. Another example is a monopolist polluting the atmosphere. Ending the monopoly—removing one market failure—makes another market failure, the pollution externality, worse because prices will fall and output will increase in a more competitive market.

The second best theorem makes formally the important point that it is not possible to take a pick-and-mix (or *partial equilibrium*) approach to evaluating society's economic welfare, considering policy changes in isolation. For example, imperfect information often leads to *moral hazard* in insurance markets: if I have insurance on my house, I might not take enough care about fire safety, with more careful householders subsidizing my insurance premium. One solution might be to subsidize the price of smoke alarms. However, that fixes a problem in one market but creates a distortion in another, leading to more-than-efficient production of smoke alarms relative to, say, bicycle lights. Ideally, there should be a policy to correct for that distortion, but the real-world analysis of such connections is challenging to say the least. These complexities gave rise to a *third best* theory, which says that as governments cannot have all the empirical evidence they need to make general equilibrium assessments, they should just address the problems they do know enough about.

Again, the second best theorem is a formal exercise, but one that underlines a key message of this book, which is that neither "the market" nor "the government" is the solution to economic problems. The second best theorem explains why in any context where one thing diverges from Pareto efficiency, the competitive market outcome for everything else need not be the most efficient. However, it also explains why so many government policy interventions have unintended consequences, a key form of "government failure." In both cases, there is a failure to take on board this lesson that everything in the economy is connected.

Distributional Questions

The definition of Pareto efficiency puts questions of distribution or fairness to one side. As it requires that nobody be made worse off, the initial distribution of resources is a given. The second welfare theorem formalizes the separation between distribution and efficiency. It implies that if the initial distribution is undesirable a society should make a lump-sum redistribution, and then the market process of exchange at prevailing prices will bring about a Pareto efficient outcome. This led economists to argue for a principle of compensation (first discussed in 1939 papers by John Hicks and Nicholas Kaldor, and so sometimes referred to as Kaldor-Hicks compensation). If a particular policy would make someone worse off, could the winner simply pay the loser a suitable amount in compensation?

The answer (pointed out almost immediately in a 1941 journal article by Tibor Skitovsky and several times subsequently) was no, because the amount of compensation required would need to be valued at the prevailing prices for the goods in the economy, and a policy change would change these relative prices. Should compensation be calculated at winners' prices or losers' prices? Depending on the choice, a policy and its reversal could *both* look like Pareto improvements. It depends whose perspective you take. This debate about deep issues in theoretical welfare economics makes little difference to practical policy questions, which quite often involve compensation to losers—such as payments to households having a new rail track laid at the end of their garden, or to private shareholders being bought out if a company is nationalized. However, it underlines the point that the theory is for all practical purposes a framework for organizing concepts.

Social Welfare

There is also the question of how to aggregate from individuals' welfare to society. Is it possible to calculate aggregate social welfare by adding up individuals' utilities? Kenneth Arrow's famous 1951 impossibility theorem proved it is not possible to aggregate individual preferences into social preferences without breaching some reasonable-seeming assumptions—including the Pareto efficiency criterion. Social welfare can be defined, however, by allowing interpersonal comparisons of welfare, for example. (There is more detail in the annex to this chapter.)

In this case, the government, or its economists, can define a social welfare function incorporating specific value judgments about distribution. A simple one would be basic utilitarianism, the arithmetic sum of individual utilities. The aim is to maximize the total sum of individual utilities; as long as there are enough gainers, or the gains are large enough, losses to other individuals are acceptable. As Mr. Spock put it, sacrificing his life for others in *Star Trek II: The Wrath of Khan*, "The needs of the many outweigh the needs of the few. Or the one." Other options would include giving different weights to the utility of different groups or putting a floor on the outcome for any individual. Typically, the judgments economists express about social welfare (i.e., whether a policy is desirable or not) have a social welfare function implicitly in mind, and it is also typically a utilitarian or consequentialist one. For example, cost-benefit analysis, widely used in policy appraisal, weighs costs borne by some people against benefits gained by others. Utilitarianism is woven into the fabric of economics, as indeed is indicated by the use of "utility" as the criterion for judging policy success or failure.

Market Failure and Government Failure

As already noted, in practice a polite veil is drawn over the theoretical issues with welfare economics, but the theory shapes a useful conceptual framework for analyzing market failures. The competitive market benchmark means economic policies are typically often evaluated in terms of specific market failures corresponding to failures of the assumptions for the fundamental welfare theorems (box 1.4).

This framework for considering the rationale for policy interventions is used in this book because it helps to clarify what kinds of policy might be best suited to a particular problem. However, the "market failure" approach can often fall into one of two opposing traps. The first is to assume, perhaps because of the terminology or the elegance of the economic proofs, that market failures are exceptional, and there is therefore a presumption in favor of "free markets." Yet the assumptions are an idealized benchmark and clearly never hold in practice, as practicing economists are well aware. On the other hand, this does not mean that there should be an opposite presumption in favor of the government correcting (frequent) market failures by some kind of intervention. For "government" consists of people who might have their own motivations or incentives, and who are acting as "agents" for the rest of the population—questions chapter 7 returns to. Economists have often underestimated the limits on state capacity in analyzing policy

---

Box 1.4. Market failures

Assumption	*"Market failure" when it does not hold*
A1 Consumers and producers are rational and self-interested	"Non-rational" choice, social influence
A2 They have fixed preferences	
A3 There is perfect competition with no economies of scale and no barriers to entry (or exit)	Natural monopoly
A4 Individuals have full information, and it is symmetric (the same) for all	Information asymmetries
A5 Private and social benefits are equal; private and social costs are equal	Externalities
A6 There are complete markets (including for all future goods)	Adverse selection; tragedy of the commons
A7 Goods are owned and able to be exchanged—there are property rights, and people obey the law	Transaction costs
A8 Goods are rival—if I use it, you can't	Public goods/free riding

---

choices. Hence, as well as frequent market failure, there is also frequent government failure, and it is just as important not to contrast market failure against an idealized perfect state as the other way around.

In fact, markets and governments often fail in the same contexts and for the same reasons. This is why the structures of economic organization have varied so much over time and between countries.

It is why different societies end up with different mixes of "state" and "market," and there is never either a pure state-run or a pure free market economy.

The Historical Ebb and Flow of "Market" and "State"

Earlier, this chapter referred to the links between historical events, political trends, and economic ideas. Having now set out the basics of the theoretical economic framework to provide a classification of policy challenges, this section briefly locates this modern framework in its broad historical context. Later chapters also include relevant economic history. This is a UK- and to some extent US-centric account, not only because I am British but also because US and UK economists and universities have been so dominant in the discipline, meaning the experience of those two countries has had a disproportionate effect on economics. However, although the historical narrative is different for other countries, the issues and analytical principles are more universal.

The dominant view in economics concerning the role of government has shifted over time. In *The Wealth of Nations* (published in 1776), Adam Smith was advocating a greater role for market exchange because there were then many government restrictions on activity, favoring established interests, at a time when the economy was on the cusp of the huge technological and social changes of the Industrial Revolution. He set the dial in favor of markets being the preferred means of coordinating economic activity in society—hence the first welfare theorem is sometimes described as the invisible hand theorem. But modern free market advocates have often caricatured his views, omitting his emphasis on the importance of ethical values and social bonds in making markets function effectively.

Thanks to Smith and other classical economists, as economics was formalized in the late nineteenth and early twentieth century, and the theoretical welfare economics framework described above developed, the role for government came to be seen as fixing market failures in some specific ways. If you could identify an externality or a natural monopoly, then the government could in theory calculate how to fix it, although preferably in a way that would distort private choices as little as possible. For example, in his 1920 book *The Economics of Welfare* Pigou recommended a flat rate tax to raise the private cost of selling alcohol until it matched the social cost (of rowdy behavior, crime, illness). This approach is how alcohol is still taxed in many countries (see box 1.5).

Box 1.5 Pigouvian taxes on alcohol

Applying a Pigouvian tax on alcohol, to correct for externalities associated with drinking, is appealing but involves practical difficulties, including how to measure the size of the externalities and the appropriate tax rate. One challenge is that the ideal tax rate will vary between individuals, and ought to be much higher for heavy drinkers. For instance, in the US only 7% of the population are frequent binge drinkers, but they account for around 75% of the costs of excessive alcohol use. A "second best" policy would set a tax equal to the average external marginal cost across all drinkers. However, if heavy drinkers tend to choose different drinks than light drinkers (say, whiskey rather than wine), a better policy would set a higher tax on the form of alcohol preferred by the heavy drinkers. One study found that in the UK heavy drinkers indeed prefer drinks with a higher alcohol content, and are also more than three times as likely as light drinkers to switch to a cheaper type of drink (rather than drinking less) when the price goes up.* Using these differential preferences and these differential *price elasticities of demand*, it is possible to show there would be a big increase in social welfare from introducing higher taxes on high-strength spirits. The researchers also point out that this is a second best world (i.e., the optimal Pigouvian alcohol taxes could have distributional consequences); that the alcoholic beverage industry might have some monopoly power; and that government regulation is an alternative to using Pigouvian taxation.

* R. Griffith, M. O'Connell, and K. Smith (2017), "Design of Optimal Corrective Taxes in the Alcohol Market," IFS Working Paper No. 17/02.

Before the twentieth century, state capacity was more limited than it is now. Governments collected taxes, fought wars, and administered some justice, and perhaps set some standards for weights and measures. But beyond these basics most policies (including enforcement of justice, or policing of standards, but also poverty relief) operated at the local level if at all. This limited capacity is still the reality in many low-income economies. In the industrialized economies, though, the early part of the twentieth century saw a big expansion in the role of government. The Wall Street crash of 1929 and the Great Depression, combined with the steady expansion of the vote from the mid-nineteenth century on, led to growing demands for the government to manage the economy, given the dramatic demonstration of how badly things could go if left to the market.

Indeed, central planning looked rather attractive at that stage—more rational and efficient—to some economists on both left and right of the political spectrum. From the communism of the USSR to the corporatist economic policies of fascist Germany and Italy, there were many examples in the early 1930s of increasingly extensive state involvement in production and allocation. A vigorous debate took place among economists at this time, known as the "socialist calculation" debate, which explored whether a centrally planned economy could substitute for the competitive market, delivering as much social welfare. Some economists who opposed socialism on the grounds that it would reduce liberty nevertheless thought socialism would prove a more attractive and successful option than capitalism—famously, Joseph Schumpeter in his 1942 book *Capitalism, Socialism and Democracy*. On the other hand, Friedrich Hayek argued that the market is a means of decentralized information processing far superior to any possible centralized approach. In a famous 1945 article, he argued that prices are a uniquely elegant way of summarizing information and coordinating the choices of many individual consumers and producers with different preferences, or facing different costs and conditions of supply. It is impossible for any centralized planning authority to handle so much information, he argued—probably even now with vastly greater computer power and online information—but the market discovers and coordinates so that the myriad everyday goods and services are available to consumers when they want them.

This period also saw the development of national accounting in the form still in use today, in parallel with John Maynard Keynes's macroeconomics in his famous book *The General Theory of Employment, Interest and Money*. Measurement of total economic activity had begun before the Second World War with the efforts of Simon Kuznets and Colin Clark, and became imperative during the war so governments could know what resources were available for wartime production and what consumption sacrifice their populations would have to make. The construction of national accounts—including GDP/GNP—continued in the postwar era, becoming an international standard. As well as the creation of this key data, macroeconomic management was also made possible by the work on business cycles (pioneered by Ragnar Frisch) and macroeconometric models (by Jan Tinbergen and his followers). All of this important intellectual activity in economics, which later made possible macroeconomic management and the postwar welfare state, had poignantly overlapped with the rising tide of tragedy and conflict from the mid-1930s to mid-1940s.

The demands of the Second World War, when wartime needs had priority, followed by the scale of reconstruction required after the conflict ended, involved governments ever more heavily in economic planning. Many Western economies, such as France and the Netherlands, and also Japan set up planning agencies after the war in part to manage their use of the generous Marshall Plan funds provided by the United States to rebuild their damaged economies. These countries still have a strong legacy of state involvement in the economy.

Through the 1940s and into the 1950s, the scope of government economic intervention in most of the rich industrialized economies grew. The welfare state expanded, including state pensions and unemployment insurance. The state undertook house-building programs and funded more public services, such as education and health. Governments intervened more in production, nationalizing industries or individual firms, to a greater or lesser degree. The post office and communications had been government-owned in most countries from the early twentieth century or even earlier, governments always having a particular interest in what citizens were saying to each other. Many municipalities either provided utilities such as gas and electricity, water and sewage services, and local transport themselves, or privatized these essential services very early, too. However, across Europe (but not the US) the big wave of nationalization of business occurred in the 1940s through the 1970s. The UK government, for instance, nationalized car manufacturer British Leyland in 1973 and aircraft and shipbuilding companies as late as 1977.

The dominant philosophy regarding ownership of the means of production, and more broadly the economic role of the state, changed after the late 1970s. This was partly political, driven by the election of Margaret Thatcher in the UK and Ronald Reagan in the US, but events played a role. Economic thinking evolved alongside the political changes.

The ideas of market-oriented economists like Hayek had gradually become more influential over time because some of the problems with government ownership or production were growing more apparent. Thirty years of extensive state ownership in the European nations provided many examples of government failure. Chapter 3 looks at this in detail. For now it is enough to note that the profit motive in a competitive market gives private firms a strong incentive to keep costs down and to innovate. The postwar experience of nationalized industries showed they were indeed not as efficient or as innovative as private sector equivalents. Partly due to strong public sector unions or professional bodies, too, many services were run more in the interest of producers than consumers. Managers in the government sector are not held accountable by the profitability of their enterprise, and tend to get bailed out by finance ministries if they are losing money.

Right-wing politicians and think tanks promoted Hayek's approach for ideological reasons. Yet in academic economics at the same time the leading areas of research emphasized individual rational, maximizing behavior in line with the invisible hand theorems described above. What's more, one increasingly influential branch of economics, public choice theory, rightly insisted it was essential to take into account the motives and incentives of public policymakers and public sector employees. Earlier economic analysis assumed "the government" was benevolent and objective, acting in a disinterested manner to maximize social welfare. But public choice theorists (such as James Buchanan) argued that the lens of economic analysis should be applied to the incentives public sector officials and workers face and assume that, like anyone else, they respond to those incentives, acting in their own interest. This could be financial (promotion, or even corruption), or it could be growing their bureaucratic empire or getting re-elected.

Events in the 1970s helped make this case. It was a troubled decade for all the advanced economies, with OPEC increasing the price of oil dramatically, inflation trending up at the same time that many countries experienced a recession, and a sense by mid-decade that there was a crisis of capitalism. In the UK, the decade saw a growing number of strikes and pay increases and an upward wage-price spiral, culminating in the so-called Winter of Discontent in 1978–79, when a Labour government presided over rubbish piling up in the streets, power cuts, and even the dead lying unburied because of strikes by municipal workers. Mrs. Thatcher, elected in 1979, and Mr. Reagan, in office from 1981, adopted Hayek's arguments for the market and the public choice arguments against government intervention. The collapse of communism in 1989 seemed to set the seal on their economic philosophy. Soviet communism was revealed to have been an economic as well as a political and moral disaster. The fall of the Berlin Wall in 1989 underlined the point in a dramatic way: East Germans, free for the first time since the Second World War to cross the border to the west, came face-to-face with the reality that they were poorer, with less choice of shoddier products, than their compatriots in West Germany.

The 1990s and 2000s were decades of strong economic growth, technological innovation, and financial market booms. Some important low-income countries, above all China, embraced market economics and the philosophy of liberalization. This choice helped China achieve the biggest reduction in poverty the world has ever experienced. But the pendulum—in politics and in economic thinking—will swing again, and might already be doing so. The Great Financial Crisis of 2008 was not a good advertisement for the market. For one thing, real median personal income declined by about

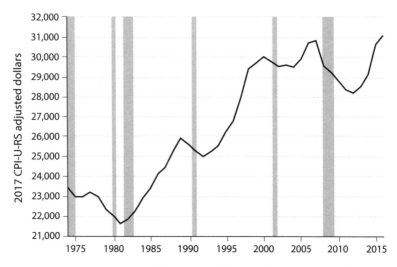

Figure 1.2. Real median personal income in the United States. Shaded areas indicate US recessions. *Source*: US Bureau of the Census.

a tenth in the US during and after the crisis, the biggest proportionate fall since the 1970s crisis (figure 1.2). Incomes also stagnated or declined significantly in many other member countries of the Organization for Economic Cooperation and Development (OECD), including those affected by the subsequent Euro area crisis.

In recent years, attention has also focused on the dramatic increase in inequality since 1980; although the rise in inequality occurred mainly in the 1980s, the fact that living standards have not improved for many people in most Western countries since (at least) 2008 has done a lot to undermine support for "free markets" (in quotes because it is an abstraction that does not exist in reality). Chapter 6 returns to the question of distribution. The discontent being expressed in elections in many countries recently is prompting some politicians to think more favorably again about state involvement in the economy. Meanwhile, in economic thought the tide some time ago turned toward emphasizing the failures of the list of assumptions set out above, with much research now looking at externalities, information asymmetries, or "non-rational" decision-making.

The moral is that the boundary between state and market has constantly ebbed and flowed, with events, political trends, economic ideas, and policy choices inextricably linked, evolving together.

Externalities and Public Goods

The swing of the pendulum can be illustrated by looking at some of the most frequently encountered market failures: the existence of externalities (assumption A5 of the fundamental theorems in box 1.4 does not hold) and public goods (when A8 is not valid). Although the analysis seems straightforward, views about what policies best tackle these market failures can vary, and for illuminating reasons.

An *externality* exists when one person's or firm's choice affects others in such a way that private and social costs or benefits diverge. Examples include pollution or CO_2 emissions from a factory, affecting the air everyone breathes and the climate; my disturbing the neighbors by holding a noisy party; a radio station whose transmissions interfere with those of another station; learning a skill that makes it more likely employers who want to hire skilled workers will locate in town; getting your children vaccinated, increasing the likelihood of "herd immunity" in the area as well as improving their own resistance to disease; joining a social network so it becomes more interesting or useful to other members. The fact that we live in societies or communities, not as hermits, means that externalities are pervasive.

One way for the government to tackle externalities is to use taxes or subsidies to equalize the private and social costs and benefits. In figure 1.3, the supply curve shows the private marginal cost of a product. As mentioned earlier, Alfred Pigou introduced the idea of a lump-sum tax (the same amount per unit of output)—known as a Pigouvian tax—to increase the private cost to equal the social cost and reduce the amount of the good consumed. It is not straightforward to calculate what the best tax rate might be, but the principle applies to "sin taxes" on alcohol and tobacco, or to a carbon tax.

A *public good* is one whose consumption is non-rival (one person consuming it does not stop others doing so too) and also non-excludable (people cannot be prevented from consuming it) (figure 1.4). Examples of public goods include clean air, street lighting, national defense, the police and justice system, public parks, roads, and public transport. Some of these are non-excludable (street lighting and defense, for example). They are sometimes referred to as

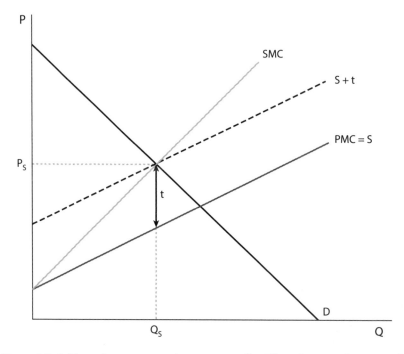

Figure 1.3. A Pigouvian tax correcting an externality. There is a negative external-ity, so social marginal cost (SMC) exceeds private marginal cost (PMC, the supply curve S). The Pigouvian tax t raises the supply curve to the point where it meets SMC. The price is higher and quantity produced and consumed lower than with-out the tax.

pure public goods. Others are excludable, although the providers might not bother to control access to them. For example, a park can be fenced in and an entry fee charged, but most towns and cities provide at least some free access to green spaces and playgrounds. Non-rival goods with limited access like this are sometimes called *club goods*: once you have paid a fee to join the club, consumption is non-rival (table 1.1). Conversely, although public goods are nor-mally non-rival, they can become congested; roads are an example where for the most part nobody is excluded (toll roads excepted), but beyond a certain point the amount of traffic means my driving limits your ability to travel.

Public goods will be under-provided by the market: at any given quantity produced (where supply equals the first person's demand,

(a)

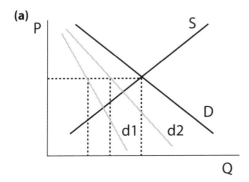

(b)

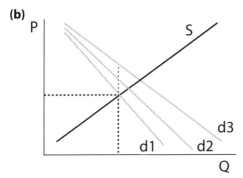

Figure 1.4. Private (a) and public (b) goods. Private goods are rival in consumption, and market demand is the (horizontal) sum of individual demand curves. Public goods are non-rival, so once the first individual demand is met, others can free ride, consuming the same output.

in figure 1.4b), additional demand could be satisfied with no adverse effect on previous users or consumers. This non-rival character means it can be difficult to finance public goods (box 1.6). There is a great temptation to *free ride*, in other words, use them without paying for them. This is why many public goods are tax-financed or at least partly subsidized or provided by the state.

The idea that the government must provide all public goods, because otherwise the free riding problem will mean they are under-

Table 1.1. Types of Goods

	Rival	*Non-rival*
Excludable	Private goods (e.g., clothes, food)	Club goods (e.g., toll roads, entry fees)
Non-excludable	Commons (e.g., fish in the sea)	Public goods (e.g., national defense, streetlights)

Box 1.6 Public goods

Public goods are non-rival (zero marginal cost of additional consumption). There is a problem of "free riding": people consuming for free the output others have paid for. Financing public goods is therefore often difficult. The classic policy is to pay for public goods from tax revenues. Textbooks often say public goods are also non-excludable—but this is misleading as excludability can take many forms, including legal enforcement. Many public goods are excludable, by various means—park gates, road tolls, license fees, spectrum licenses—and are then often called club goods. A lot of digital goods are (privately provided) public goods because of their zero marginal cost and non-rivalry, but can be excludable (passwords). If free riders are not excluded, their providers (for example, newspapers) face the problem of how to finance them now.

---

supplied, has been challenged, however. There are examples of public goods being financed in different ways. Lighthouses were often used as an example of a pure public good because their warning light is visible to any passing ship. Historically, however, the payment of harbor dues often financed lighthouses. Although some ships were surely free riders, any whose captain wanted to put in at the nearby port would be contributing to the cost. Some pro-market economists argue this shows private funding of a public good is often possible; examples like these are considered club goods because they are financed by a subscription-type arrangement. What is notable about this example, however, is that local authorities or institutions arranged the financing of this non-rival good. It was not exactly a free market outcome, but rather a collective arrangement—just not one involving a decision by a government official and funded by general taxes. So the debate about whether public goods must be publicly provided, or whether instead the private sector can provide them, is partly a question of what "private" means.

Another example of collective but not government provision of a non-rival good is the investment in Britain's nineteenth-century road system. This public good was organized by "turnpike trusts"— bodies composed of local dignitaries who had the right to collect tolls and the responsibility to maintain stretches of road. These were privately organized entities but supported by the government in terms of their legal basis. In a way, they foreshadowed the public-private partnerships of the late twentieth and twenty-first century. The private provision of roads is more common in some countries than others (box 1.7). Chapter 4 looks more closely at collective institutions that are neither private nor public.

It is worth mentioning, too, some special cases of public goods, known as *merit goods* and *experience goods*. Rather than being under-supplied, these goods are under-demanded. Merit goods are those considered to be good for people although they do not realize it. Party political broadcasts (note that in countries other than the US paid political advertising on television is generally restricted or banned) are one example. Nobody wants to watch them, but it is good for voters to be informed about rival parties' policies. Experience goods are those people do not know whether they will enjoy or benefit from until they try them—novels, movies, music, and other cultural experiences are obvious examples. Some such goods might require policies to encourage their use—for example, getting more reluctant people to try taking part in sports (to help tackle obesity), which leads them to discover they enjoy the activity.

There is less of a difference between public goods and externalities than it seems at first sight. To say goods are non-rival is equivalent to saying social benefits exceed private benefits. Public goods are a special case of externalities.

The same point could be made of natural monopoly industries (i.e., assumption A3 is not valid—see box 1.4), discussed further in chapter 3. Some products are referred to as *natural monopolies*, with increasing returns to scale due to high fixed costs (economies of scale in supply) or network externalities (economies of scale in demand), because there tends to be just one (or at most a small number) producing them. (Strictly, an industry is a natural monopoly when average cost declines over the entire range of output levels.

Box 1.7. Private road provision

There is great variation between countries in the private sector's role in what could be seen as a classic public good, namely, major roads or highways. In Europe, thirteen nations (mainly small ones such as Estonia and Liechtenstein) have no toll roads, and eight charge only for crossing certain bridges or tunnels. (The latter group include the Netherlands and also Sweden, whose famous 8 km Oresund Bridge—state-owned—between Malmö and Copenhagen was featured in the TV series *The Bridge*.) Among those countries with tolls, the UK has very few—one motorway and a small number of ferry or bridge crossings)—while others such as France and Italy have extensive toll road networks. Across the Atlantic, the United States has many privately owned and run roads and bridges and has recently been privatizing state-owned and -run ones—to take one instance, the Indiana Toll Road is now operated by an Australian-Spanish consortium on a 75-year lease. Such roads can be run by the government or one of its agencies, or entirely by a private operator, or privately financed and operated with a government guarantee of minimum revenues, or in some form of public-private partnership. There is a trend at present toward public-private partnerships to share risks and also overcome tight government budgets.

Crossing the Oresund Bridge. Photograph by Luc De Cleir/Pexels.

One firm producing all output is the least-cost solution. If the government doesn't provide these products itself (as many do with highways or water and sewage systems), it regulates them strictly (all utilities are regulated). Increasing returns to scale are also a special case of an externality, because when one firm increases its production other firms in the industry can benefit from the increased scale of the market.

Pigou and Coase

The "Pigouvian" way of thinking about social welfare involves the government identifying a market failure, such as the presence of externalities or public goods, and correcting it with a specific policy, such as a tax or subsidy. Other direct policy approaches to either correct externalities or provide public goods include allocating licenses (to control radio spectrum used for broadcasts and telephony, or to constrain individuals from flying drones near airports); government provision of services, such as health and education (to encourage take-up of vaccinations or other public health measures, or increase demand for educational qualifications to the benefit of employers and other workers); and regulation (to limit activities such as noisy late-night parties or dumping waste in rivers), enforced either through fines or legal action. This interventionist perspective on government actions to solve specified market failures held sway for much of the twentieth century, and of course all these types of policies are still widely deployed by many governments.

There is an influential alternative way of thinking about externalities in general and the special case of public goods in particular. This approach, associated with Ronald Coase, helped tilt policy in the direction of market solutions to market failures such as externalities and public goods.

Coase pointed out that in theory externalities are reciprocal. Take the noisy late-night party, a negative externality for the neighbors (presumed not to be invited). That could equally be seen as the stick-in-the-mud neighbors imposing their desire for quiet as an externality on people wanting to have a bit of fun. The example Coase gives in a famous 1960 paper is cattle straying onto the neighboring farm and eating the crop. The intuitive presumption is that the cattle rancher should be fined through police or courts, but this is because we are assuming the farmer has an inviolable property right to the fruits of his land. Coase asked, What if the benefit of fatter cows to the rancher outweighs the lost revenue from the corn? Why should the rancher and the farmer not privately negotiate a payment that would effectively mean the rancher renting the right for his cattle to eat corn? This could be a mutually beneficial deal. Similarly, if a factory pollutes a stream and kills the fish, we should ask whether the value of the dead fish is more or less than the cost of lost production if the factory has to stop polluting. There is theoretical symmetry in all externalities. They become asymmetric in practice when a property right is assigned to one party, and even then a private deal may be possible depending on the transaction costs of reaching the deal.

Coase therefore went on to say that if people could negotiate freely, and if transaction costs were not too high, they would sort out the allocation of the costs by themselves through market transactions, with no need for the government to step in and fix the "externality" with a Pigouvian tax or regulation. Many market-oriented economists took this to heart and have argued that there is far less of a case for government policy than implied by the assumption that market failures need fixing. Indeed, there are big variations between countries in the extent of taxes and subsidies on different products or the provision of public goods, so this is self-evidently a matter of debate.

However—as his Nobel Prize speech makes clear—Coase recognized that people would often *not* be able to negotiate, because the transaction costs of doing so are too high. What are the transaction costs? Essentially, the time and effort needed to find out the information for the transaction to go ahead. Is it easy to identify who the straying cows belong to (or which factory dumped the toxins in the river)? Could the corn farmer be lying about how much of his crop was damaged—is it easy to monitor what is happening? Are there few enough people involved that negotiation is feasible (since in life there are rarely just two parties)? It is also sometimes the case that property rights are unclear. When two airline passengers fought over the use by one of a "knee defender," preventing the other from tilting his seat backward, it might have been the case that the transaction costs of negotiating a fee with your neighbor for the right to recline—$5? $50?—are too high; but it is also surely the case that it is not clear who owns the right to the space in dispute. It is not clear, unfortunately, whether your ticket entitles you to the bit of space in front of you—which would justify your use of a knee defender—or the bit of space behind you—which would entitle you to recline your seat (although one imagines that the kind of person who would use a knee defender might imagine themselves entitled to both).

Nevertheless, the Coaseian approach has had great impact on some economists and underpins the school of economic thought emphasizing the role of the legal system in resolving externalities, or rather the disputes to which they give rise. Courts had long been the means of handling civil claims based on common law (economic torts), but the influential school of law and economics deriving from Coase's arguments emphasizes the allocation of property rights (property law) and the efficient resolution of disputes (contract law).

Coase's work underlines two key points, fundamental to public policy economics. One is the importance of the clear definition and assignment of property rights. In his example, the farmer has a property right to the land and its produce, although the rancher might be able to make him an offer that makes it worth letting the cattle eat the corn. Similarly, in the Vittel case in box 1.8, the property rights belonged to the landowners. In other circumstances, like the knee space in an airplane, a Coaseian negotiation might not be possible if it is not clear who owns the property in question.

Mostly, we take the prevailing assumptions about property rights as part of the natural order of things, yet they are entirely determined by the political and legal system, as well as by custom. For instance, when you buy a meal in a restaurant, you assume that you are buying the food, and renting the space to sit there for an hour or two, but not that you can walk out with the plates and glasses you use. The law enforces the norm, as the restaurant could call the police were you to do so. Technology often disrupts assumptions about property rights, however. The claims so often made in today's

Box 1.8. A Coaseian bargain in practice

The mineral water Vittel is bottled from springs in the Vosges region of France. From the 1970s, farming in the region became more intense and the quality of the natural spring water started to deteriorate. The presence of nitrates in the water threatened the business, but Vittel's owner, Nestlé, successfully negotiated with the forty farmers involved to pay them compensation to change their farming practices and limit the runoff that was threatening water quality. A study of the negotiation concluded that there were some important reasons for its success. There were relatively few farmers involved, and Vittel itself had bought some land upstream. Research had established that it would be more cost-effective for the company to improve upstream land management than to build a new filtration plant, so it was willing to compensate the farmers with income support, equipment subsidies, and technical training.

C. Déprés, G. Grolleau, and N. Mzoughi, "On Coasean Bargaining with Transaction Costs: The Case of Vittel," Centre d'Economie et Sociologie appliquées à l'Agriculture et aux Espaces Ruraux, Working Paper No. 2005/03, https://www2.dijon.inra.fr/cesaer/wp-content/uploads/2012/11/WP2005_3.pdf.

economy to "intellectual property" are always contentious (because, consisting of ideas, it is a public good, non-rival in consumption, costless to copy). Digital technology has made possible vast new swathes of intellectual property and a sort of gold rush to lay claim to it. Although it has sometimes been controversial, the law and economics approach inspired by Coase gives a useful perspective on the importance of intellectual property in increasingly intangible and digital modern economies, and the relative paucity of pre-existing norms and case law about ownership of intellectual property. Chapter 4 returns to these questions.

Coaseian bargaining, solving through negotiation or legal action the problems created by externalities, also requires the transaction costs involved to be not too high. These include the time it takes to negotiate with all the parties involved, and the difficulty of finding out all relevant information and monitoring everyone's actions. In principle, people boarding a flight could negotiate with the people in front of and behind them to figure out who values the space more, but in practice the hassle would be too great. In his Nobel Prize lecture, Coase himself said he thought the transaction costs would often be prohibitive. He added, though: "If we move from a regime of zero transaction costs to one of positive transaction costs, what becomes immediately clear is the crucial importance of the legal system."

The presence of transaction costs is thus key in determining what arrangements a society makes for producing goods and services, and allocating resources to different uses. For instance, as discussed in chapter 7, it is relevant to the question of whether the public sector should undertake an activity or contract it out to private providers (or for that matter whether a private business should keep an activity in house or contract it out to a supplier). Is it possible to spell out in a contract or service agreement exactly what a private provider has to deliver, and monitor whether or not the contract is being fulfilled? For some activities—such as payroll, or waste collection—this is straightforward. It is hard for others, especially where there are information asymmetries—for example, it is difficult to monitor the quality of many services, such as health provision or social care, and the temptation for the supplier to cut costs (having bid for a competitive contract) will be strong.

Thinking about transaction costs also underlines that the world is not neatly and comprehensively divided into markets and government. Indeed, the idea of a "market" is somewhat ill defined in economic theory (never mind a "free" one). Microeconomic theory concerns individual consumers and producers. Yet there are plenty of organizations that are neither a private profit-making business nor a government entity. Unions, mutuals, collectives and cooperatives, parent-teacher associations, voluntary groups, non-profit corporations—all engage in some economic activities, often alongside either government bodies or private firms, or both. There is a rich array of organizations involved in collective economic outcomes, and all need to be taken into account in public policy. Much of the insight in economics into why activities are organized in one way rather than another depends on transaction costs and asymmetries of information. In another classic paper, Coase used the transaction cost approach (rather than assuming all the activities occur through market exchange) to explain why firms exist; this approach has formed the basis for much subsequent work looking at the organization of businesses and industries, and also at economic institutions in general.

Conclusion

This chapter has described the approach economics takes to assessing public policies: Do they contribute to social welfare (in the very specific sense used in economics, encompassing Pareto efficiency)? Despite the word *efficiency* and despite putting to one side distributional considerations as well as other ethical criteria, such as freedom or national pride, this is a normative standard. It takes preference satisfaction, or individual utility, aggregated in some way, as the criterion for assessing social welfare. No economist takes the standard welfare economic theorems as a realistic description, and yet this framework has set the benchmark of a competitive market as the way to think about government and market interaction. Even so, there has been considerable debate ever since Adam Smith as to the shape and scope of public policies. The next chapter looks in more detail at the government-market relationship and in particular the balance between competition and government regulation.

Annex to Chapter 1

This annex briefly describes—in non-technical form—the microeconomic theory underpinning welfare economics. Standard microeconomics textbooks (such as H. Varian, *Microeconomic Analysis*) present the technical detail. *An Introduction to Modern Welfare Economics* by P. O. Johansson focuses on the theory of welfare

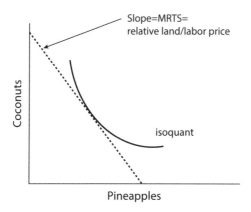

Figure 1.5. Production: isoquants.

economics in far more detail than here, in a non-technical fashion. There is a vast specialist literature on welfare economics and social choice. For those interested in how economic thought in this area has changed, Roger Backhouse surveys the evolution of welfare economics in a recent paper, "The Origins of the New Welfare Economics" (http://www.ier.hit-u.ac.jp/extra/10.Backhouse.pdf).

Here, consider a simple Robinson Crusoe economy, where the producers and consumers are the same two individuals, Robinson and Friday; there are two production factors, land and labor, and two products, coconuts and pineapples. Starting with production, *isoquants* are curves describing the mix of land and labor needed, given the production technology, to produce each output. Figure 1.5 shows the isoquant for coconuts, and there is a similar one for pineapples. Isoquants are assumed to have nice mathematical properties and are drawn as smooth curves.

Productive efficiency requires the rate land and labor substitute for each other in production be equal for both coconuts and pineapples. Otherwise more of at least one of the crops could be produced by changing the mix of inputs. This rate (known as the *marginal rate of technical substitution*, MRTS) is equal to relative factor prices, or the price of land relative to labor. The *Edgeworth box diagram* draws the two sets of isoquants with origins in opposite corners from each other (figure 1.6).

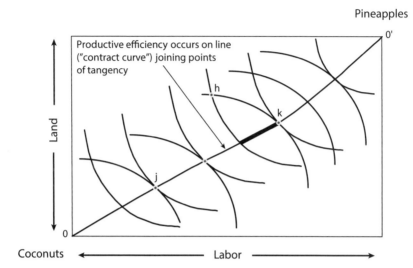

Pineapples

Productive efficiency occurs on line ("contract curve") joining points of tangency

Land

Coconuts ← Labor →

Figure 1.6. Productive efficiency.

The curves represent isoquants showing a constant level of output of coconuts (origin at the bottom left corner) and pineapples (origin at top right corner), respectively, for varying combinations of land and labor. Productive efficiency occurs when the two sets of isoquants are tangent to each other and the tangent is equal to the marginal rate of technical substitution (and to the factor price ratio). Otherwise it would be possible to produce more of at least one output for given levels of land and labor. The line joining the points of tangency is known as the *contract curve*. Suppose the economy is starting at a point off the contract curve, such as h, which represents an initial combination of land and labor use. Any move from h toward the heavily shaded segment of the contract curve (known as the *core*) is more efficient—a Pareto improvement.

An analogous story can be told for consumption (figure 1.7). The preferences of Robinson and Friday can each be represented by indifference curves, tracing the mixes of coconuts and pineapples that deliver them a constant level of utility.

There is also an analogous Edgeworth box diagram representing allocative efficiency (figure 1.8). For any initial level and distribution of the products, the two individuals can increase their utility by

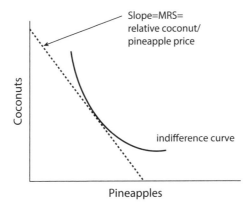

Figure 1.7. Consumption: Friday's indifference curves.

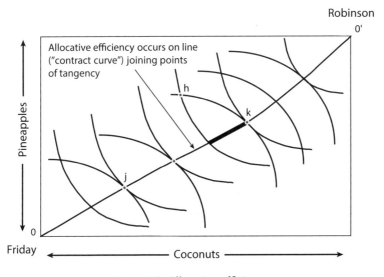

Figure 1.8. Allocative efficiency.

trading with each other, exchanging coconuts for pineapples, to the point where the *marginal rate of substitution* (MRS)—the number of pineapples per coconut they will trade—is equal for both of them.

In figure 1.8 the curves represent indifference curves showing a constant level of utility for Friday (origin at the bottom left corner) and Robinson (origin at top right corner), respectively, for varying combinations of coconuts and pineapples. Allocative efficiency occurs when the two sets of indifference curves are tangent to each other and the tangent is equal to the marginal rate of substitution (and to the relative price of pineapples and coconuts). Otherwise it would be possible increase at least one person's utility given the output of the two foods by exchanging coconuts for pineapples. Suppose the initial endowment of coconuts and pineapples is point h. Then at least one of them can be made better off by trading coconuts for pineapples until a point on the core is reached, the part of the contract curve lying between the two people's initial indifference curves. At a Pareto efficient point, this also equals the marginal rate of technological substitution of coconuts for pineapples in production.

Finally, the product mix efficiency requirement says that the rate at which coconuts can be turned into pineapples (the marginal rate of transformation, or slope of the production possibility frontier) must also equal the marginal rate of substitution in consumption.

This chapter also touched on the question of how to aggregate from individual outcomes to social outcomes. Arrow's impossibility theorem establishes that for any general possible sets of preferences, there is no way of aggregating individual utilities into social welfare while satisfying all of the following assumptions:

Pareto efficiency—nobody can be made better off without at least one other becoming worse off

Independence of irrelevant alternatives—an individual's preference between alternatives A and B is not affected by the introduction of C (so if I prefer apples to coconuts, introducing grapes does not make me prefer coconuts to apples)

Non-dictatorship—if people in the society have different preferences, there is no individual whose preferences always prevail

Unrestricted domain or universality—individuals' preferences can be specified over all the goods available

A large technical literature on social choice has probed the theorem, and a comprehensive presentation of the results is the expanded (2017) edition of Amartya Sen's classic, *Collective Choice and Social Welfare*. Sen argues in particular that aggregation can be sensibly achieved if the aggregate social welfare function does not need to

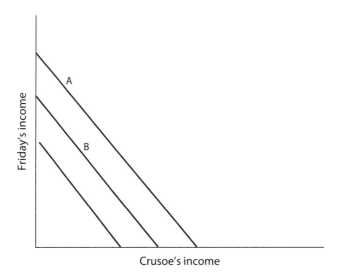

Figure 1.9. Strict utilitarian social welfare. In strict utilitarianism, people's incomes are perfect substitutes: more A is better than less B no matter what the distributional implications.

rank comprehensively *all possible* collections of individual preferences, but can confine its attention to specific issues.

Public policy economics assumes a social welfare function does exist, often implicitly and usually a variation of utilitarianism. However, different perspectives on equity can be represented by different *social welfare functions*. For example:

Rawlsian maximin SWF = min $(u_1, u_2, \ldots u_n)$

Strict utilitarian SWF = $\sum(u_1, u_2, \ldots u_n)$

Moderate egalitarian SWF = $\sum(u_1, u_2, \ldots u_n) - \lambda \sum[(u_1, u_2, \ldots u_n) - \min(u_1, u_2, \ldots u_n)]$

These could be represented on a social indifference map; for instance, figure 1.9 shows the strict utilitarian set of social indifference curves.

As pointed out earlier, the often complicated theoretical apparatus of welfare economics does not stop public policy economists from a pragmatic, more or less utilitarian, approach to social welfare in their empirical work.

Further Reading

Technical Follow-Up

Ethan Bueno de Mesquita (2016), *Political Economy for Public Policy*, Princeton University Press, chapters 1–3.

Lee Friedman (2002), *The Microeconomics of Public Policy Analysis*, Princeton University Press.

Bruce C. Greenwald and Joseph E. Stiglitz (1986), "Externalities in Economies with Imperfect Information and Incomplete Markets," *Quarterly Journal of Economics* 101, no. 2 (May 1): 229–264.

P. O. Johansson (1991), *An Introduction to Modern Welfare Economics*, Cambridge University Press.

Kevin W. S. Roberts (1980), "Possibility Theorems with Interpersonally Comparable Welfare Levels," *Review of Economic Studies* 47, no. 2: 409–420.

Amartya Sen (2017), *Collective Choice and Social Welfare*, expanded ed., Penguin.

Hal Varian (2014), *Intermediate Microeconomics: A Modern Approach*, 9th ed., W. W. Norton.

Classics

Kenneth Arrow (1951), *Social Choice and Individual Values*, Wiley.

Ronald Coase (1960), "The Problem of Social Cost," *Journal of Law and Economics* 3: 1–44.

Ronald Coase (1937), "The Nature of the Firm," *Economica* 4: 386–405.

Friedrich A. Hayek (1945), "The Use of Knowledge in Society," *American Economic Review* 35, no. 4: 519–530.

R. G. Lipsey and Kelvin Lancaster (1956), "The General Theory of Second Best," *Review of Economic Studies* 24, no. 1: 11–32.

Paul Samuelson (1947), *Foundations of Economic Analysis*, Harvard University Press, chapter 9.

Joseph Schumpeter (1942), *Capitalism, Socialism and Democracy*, 5th ed., Harper. (1976 edition, George Allen and Unwin.)

On the Scale of Government Intervention in the Economy

Wilfred Beckerman (1986), "How Large a Public Sector?" *Oxford Review of Economic Policy* 2, no. 2: 7–24.

On Welfare Economics

Sam Bowles, Alan Kirman, and Rajiv Sethi (2017), "Friedrich Hayek and the Market Algorithm," *Journal of Economic Perspectives* (Summer).

Francis Spufford (2011), *Red Plenty*, Faber. (A novel comparing the planned economy USSR and the free market USA in the 1950s.)

On Historical and Political Forces

Daron Acemoglu and James Robinson (2013), "Economics versus Politics: Pitfalls of Policy Advice," *Journal of Economic Perspectives* 27, no. 2: 173–192.

Diane Coyle (2015), *GDP: A Brief but Affectionate History*, revised ed., Princeton University Press.

Wayne Leighton and Edward Lopez (2012), *Madmen, Intellectuals, and Academic Scribblers: The Economic Engine of Political Change*, Stanford University Press, chapters 1–3.

On Externalities and Public Goods

Ronald Coase (1991), Nobel Prize lecture, "The Institutional Structure of Production," http://www.nobelprize.org/nobel_prizes/economic-sciences/laureates/1991/coase-lecture.html.

Ronald Coase (1974), "The Lighthouse in Economics," *Journal of Law and Economics* 17, no. 2 (October): 357–376.

Tyler Cowen, "Public Goods," http://www.econlib.org/library/Enc/PublicGoods.html.

Timothy Tayor, "Pigouvian Taxes and Bounties," http://conversableeconomist.blogspot.com/2017/03/pigouvian-taxes-and-bounties.html.

CHAPTER 2

Making Markets Work

REGULATION AND COMPETITION

This chapter considers how policies can try to make markets work better, in the sense of greater economic efficiency as defined in chapter 1: How can greater productive and allocative efficiency be achieved in contexts where there are market failures, such as increasing returns to scale (natural monopoly) or information asymmetries (i.e., assumptions A3 or A4 from box 1.4 fail)? The alternatives are, broadly speaking, establishing competition in the market or regulating the market—or, more often, both. The chapter starts by considering how to interpret the social welfare criteria of chapter 1 in the context of a specific market, and sets out the rationale for considering competition to be generally the most effective means of increasing social welfare. The chapter discusses the principles and practice of competition policy, and also its limitations in the context of market failures. Regulation can be an alternative to competition in such circumstances, although there is often a trade-off between them as greater regulation makes it harder for newcomers to compete. There is an upward ratchet in the extent of regulation over time, not least because it can often seem the most attractive option in political terms in high-profile markets. When this occurs, technological innovation is often the most effective route for introducing new competition, and there are recent examples of tech entrants disrupting some highly regulated markets (such as taxis and finance). However, the new technology markets bring their own challenges to competition policy, and in many countries the digital giants are coming under increasing scrutiny.

All markets exist in a framework created and sustained by the government. The rule of law is fundamental: Can people have confidence that their contracts will be enforceable, that they will have some redress if the products or services they buy are faulty or do not live up to their description, and that property rights are respected and enforced? However, in most economies the role of the government in the operation of markets is far more extensive. Most countries, including many low-income ones, have competition policies enforced by a specialist agency, to prevent large companies from gaining and exploiting monopoly power; and there is everywhere a great deal of regulation, ranging from quite basic ones (such as technical standards, rules on weights and measures, and basic safety requirements) to complex ones concerning everything from employment conditions to product labeling.

Particularly difficult policy choices exist in those markets characterized as *natural monopolies*. A natural monopoly is an industry where there are economies of scale such that the producer's average costs are declining: the more output is produced, the lower the cost of each unit on average. In the purest cases, the lowest-cost way to produce is to have just one firm in the market. Examples include sectors requiring expensive investment in infrastructure, such as the electricity grid, water supply, and rail networks. In many European countries, these kinds of sectors were nationalized in the postwar era, so there was a state-owned and -run monopoly, many of which were subsequently privatized in the 1980s and 1990s (public ownership and production is considered in more detail in the next chapter). Establishing competition in industries such as electricity, water, rail, and telecommunications when they are in the private sector has turned out to be problematic, however. An example considered in this chapter is electricity, an old and well-understood technology, yet one that is socially difficult to provide: many low-income countries do not have a stable electricity supply at all, while even the most advanced economies sometimes experience power cuts, and often get complaints about prices and service. Where the electricity industry is privately owned, it is dominated by a small number of companies, and consequently heavily regulated; it is impossible for the state to leave provision of such a fundamental utility entirely to the market.

However, regulation can also be a problem, as it is often counterproductive and a barrier to competition. It is hard for new entrants to break into a market when there are lots of regulations to satisfy, but much easier for a large incumbent to satisfy all the regulations. How much and what to regulate presents its own inherent dilemmas—revisited in later chapters—for the regulatory burden adds to costs and prices even though it has other benefits. The difficulty in establishing a balance between competition and regulation in some old network industries, such as rail, telecoms, or energy, has a modern parallel in new network industries, such as online search and digital platforms, also subject to increasing returns to scale. This chapter looks at what kinds of public policies may be required in these digital network sectors too.

Why Does Competition Matter?

Andy Grove, the former chief executive of Intel, called his 1998 memoir about the then-dynamic young computer chip industry *Only the Paranoid Survive*. Businesses generally dislike competition, to the point of paranoia, as it reduces their profit margins and dents their hopes of a quiet life. Economists love competition. The fundamental welfare theorems described in the first chapter explain why: markets enable allocative and productive efficiency. Competitive market prices efficiently convey information about consumer preferences and conditions of supply. Consumer choice forces companies to produce at least cost and to provide good quality or innovative products and services. So competition should mean lower prices, higher quality, and more innovation. Profits should be reasonable ("normal") but no higher. Competition should be good for people in their capacity as workers, too, because the more firms competing in an industry and therefore in the job market, the more choice of potential employers they have. What's more, productivity growth (and therefore the rise in living standards over time) is higher in economies where the force of competition is greater, because businesses are kept on their toes and inefficient ones go bankrupt. Monopoly power, when there are just one or a few big firms, means the reverse of all these good things. (When there are a few big firms, this is an oligopoly rather than a monopoly. There is an extensive literature on oligopolies, important in practical competition policy applications. For simplicity, the focus here is on the pure monopoly case.)

The first welfare theorem states that a competitive equilibrium is Pareto efficient. It applies in the context of the economy as a whole—it is a *general equilibrium* concept. To translate the finding into the context of a particular market or industry, we need a *partial equilibrium* version (while trying to keep in mind the second best problem). In any particular market, economic welfare is defined as

$$
\begin{array}{ccccc}
\text{TS} & = & \text{PS} & + & \text{CS} \\
\text{Total} & = & \text{Producer surplus} & + & \text{Consumer surplus} \\
\text{surplus} & & \text{(profits)} & & \text{(value consumers put} \\
& & & & \text{on the product above} \\
& & & & \text{the price they pay)}
\end{array}
$$

Total surplus is at a maximum in a perfectly competitive market (table 2.1). In figure 2.1 this is where price P^{PC} is equal to the marginal cost of production, shown as the horizontal supply curve. The producer is earning only "normal" profit, so producer surplus is shown as zero, while consumer surplus is the area above the price paid and below the demand curve—which shows what consumers would have been willing to pay. So in this perfect competition case TS = CS = areas A + B + C.

In a perfect monopoly, the monopolist equates marginal revenue and marginal cost. So in figure 2.1 (using the same marginal cost curve for the purposes of comparison), PS = B, the monopoly profit, while CS = A (consumers are now paying price P^M for quantity Q^M). TS = areas A + B, which is smaller than in the perfect competition case. There is a *deadweight loss*, area C. The size of the deadweight loss due to monopoly depends on the elasticity of demand (the more *price inelastic*, or less responsive to price changes, is demand, the greater the deadweight loss) and also the structure of

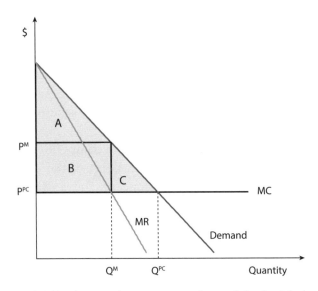

Figure 2.1. Producer and consumer surplus, and deadweight loss.

Table 2.1. Allocative and Productive Efficiency under Perfect Competition

Consumer surplus	Producer surplus
Price is equal to marginal cost of production	Firms make zero or "normal" profit at this price
All consumers with a willingness to pay higher than this market price benefit	If price were higher, profits would temporarily be higher but there would be new entries; if lower, firms would make losses and exit the market

costs (deadweight loss is lower the less steeply average and marginal costs decline with output).

So moving from monopoly to competition increases welfare, and the perfectly competitive equilibrium is Pareto optimal. (Note the move is not a Pareto improvement, though; as the monopolist loses out, the size of the producer surplus declines.)

Total surplus is maximized under perfect competition, but this is a textbook benchmark; in real life the question is about the degree of competition—there is a spectrum, as illustrated in figure 2.2.

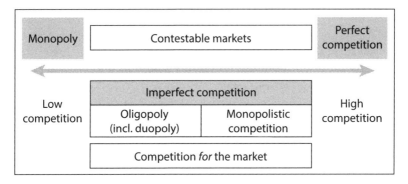

Figure 2.2. Competition spectrum.

Monopoly power can also cause additional efficiency losses, beyond those shown in figure 2.1. One source is known as *rent seeking*: big firms spend a lot of money on lobbying to protect their market power (more on this in chapters 4 and 7). This can be thought of as limiting the scope for a market to become more competitive.

Another source of inefficiency concerns how market power affects costs over time in the industry. Without the threat of competitors winning over customers, production might be less efficient than otherwise, and fail to innovate. The use of new technologies will be lower, and marginal costs will be higher, in a lazy monopoly than in an alert (or paranoid) competitive business. This is known as *x-inefficiency*. Consumer surplus is lower than in the competitive case, but so is producer surplus.

Principles of Competition Policy

All the OECD economies, and many developing countries, have a set of laws and rules to implement a *competition policy*. The authorities in the European Union and United States are particularly influential in shaping the economic analysis of competition policy as they are large jurisdictions and have legal powers to fine or alter the business structures and practices of very large companies. The policy framework in any jurisdiction has to implement in real life the theoretical presumption in favor of competitive markets.

One practical question is whether the distribution of total surplus between producers and consumers is a matter of policy concern. Competition law in different countries can refer to different aims. In some cases, the aim is maximizing total surplus, or profits plus consumer surplus, as implied by the theory. Other jurisdictions (including the EU and US) opt to focus on consumer surplus alone, on the grounds that producers that come to the attention of the competition authorities have market power by definition, so it is the consumers who need protection. In the US, the legal tradition takes "consumer welfare" as the standard, ever since the publication of an influential 1978 book, *The Antitrust Paradox*, by jurist Robert Bork. Some economists and legal scholars have criticized "consumer welfare" as an imprecise term, and have debated whether it is better to aim at total surplus (the welfare of buyers and sellers in the market, regardless of the distribution between them) or consumer surplus (the welfare of buyers). In practice, the distinction is not always pressing: there are relatively few markets competition authorities are asked to scrutinize where increasing the producer surplus (at the expense of consumers) is likely to increase total surplus. Even where a merger will clearly improve productive efficiency (for example, where there are economies of scale), there is no reason to expect anything other than a decrease in allocative efficiency as the merged firm will not have a strong incentive to pass on the efficiency gains to its customers through lower prices. Common sense, the law, and politics all tend to emphasize consumer interests.

An additional point, following from noting the importance of innovation in market economies, is that any assessment of the economic efficiency of competition in any market should involve dimensions other than price. Quality, range of choice, service standards, and innovation are all relevant, although in practice many competition authorities focus on price because it is easier by far to observe and quantify.

A second issue, harder to deal with in practice, is how to take into account what will happen in the future. The standard microeconomic analysis (as in figure 2.1) looks at static (productive and allocative) efficiency, but in real life firms need to invest and innovate: *dynamic efficiency* also matters. It is probably far more sig-

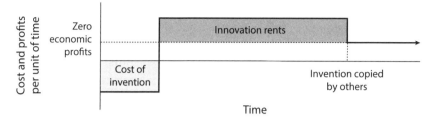

Figure 2.3. Innovation rents from a patent.

nificant for long-term economic welfare. Sometimes innovation concerns the processes of production and the organizational and commercial arrangements of businesses. This *process innovation* over time reduces the cost of producing outputs, shifting down long-run average and marginal costs and shifting out the supply curve; in the simple case in figure 2.1, this would be the marginal cost curve shifting down over time. *Product innovation* involves producing better goods and services, or altogether new products. Constant innovation, of both kinds, both incremental and radical, is exactly how businesses win and retain customers: competition *is* innovation. This is the argument famously made by Joseph Schumpeter, who referred to it as *creative destruction*; it is sometimes described as the Austrian School. Businesses need to make a profit to invest in new techniques and products, however.

If there is perfect competition, other firms will copy innovations, and the innovator will after a short while get no profit from its efforts. Some monopoly profit is needed for a while at least to create the incentive to bother in the first place. The Austrian School emphasizes this trade-off between short-run static efficiency and long-run dynamic efficiency, and the role of monopoly profits. The patent system is intended precisely to create legal temporary monopolies over innovative products to offer a strong enough profit incentive (known as *innovation rents* in this context) to innovate (figure 2.3). Businesses in research-intensive areas, such as pharmaceuticals and high tech, are particularly likely to take out patents.

However, patents are rare in other industries, and particularly in services; and they rarely cover process innovations (with some well-known exceptions, such as Amazon's One Click).

What industry structure most encourages innovation by rewarding it with enough profit? Probably not one with cut-throat competition between many small producers. There is no settled welfare economics analysis of these dynamic issues, though. Competition authorities at present decide the questions on a case-by-case basis when they are scrutinizing mergers or markets. But—as described in box 2.1—the emergence of dominant firms, such as Google and Facebook, in some digital markets is making this a matter of pressing concern to competition authorities. It is particularly worrying if it is the case, as some economists suggest, that the economy is evolving in the direction of having more winner-take-all or superstar markets because of the rising share of services and intangible or digital products.

Box 2.1. Winner-take-all economics

The idea of winner-take-all markets, sometimes referred to as superstar markets, is gaining prominence because many newer services and products in the rich economies seem to have the characteristic that one, or a few, will dominate the market. The idea was first made prominent in a 1981 article by Sherwin Rosen.* The idea is that technological changes are making it easier for one firm (or one person in a labor market, such as a movie actor) to capture most of the revenues in a market. There are technology-enabled economies of scale so the more of a market one firm can supply, the lower the marginal cost and price—in many digital markets this is more or less zero. On the demand side, in the case of services that are experience goods (you don't know what they are like until you buy and experience them), consumers are likely to choose the provider they know. In some digital markets, there are also strong network effects that mean every new consumer increases the utility for all existing consumers. For example, the more of your family and friends are on Facebook, the better a service it is for you.

* Sherwin Rosen (1981), "The Economics of Superstars," *American Economic Review* 71, no. 5: 845–858.

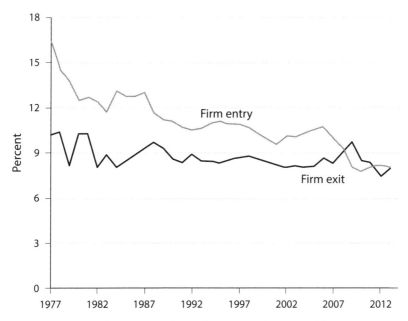

Figure 2.4. Entry and exit rates of new firms, United States, 1977–2013. *Source*: Council of Economic Advisers, 2016 Economic Report to the President.

Some economists counterargue, against the Austrian view, that *any* period of market power makes businesses less likely to continue innovating; any innovation rents tend to reduce the desirable paranoia among corporate executives. The empirical research on the links between competition, market power, and productivity tends to support the view that greater competition increases an economy's productivity. The OECD has looked at the evidence across its member countries, while in the US the 2017 Economic Report to the President from the Council of Economic Advisers suggested that increased concentration in many sectors of the economy, and a slowdown in the rate of creation of new businesses because of barriers to entry in some markets, help explain why productivity growth in the US has been so slow for the past decade. Figure 2.4 shows the declining rate of both entry and exit (the latter being more important for productivity growth) of businesses.

There is also more recent evidence in both the US and some European countries of greater concentration in many sectors of the

Box 2.2. Evidence of increasing concentration?

If broad economic trends, such as the growth of digital and service industries, imply a move toward markets dominated by a few large firms, this should manifest itself as rising concentration in many countries; whereas if there is rising concentration in just some countries, this may be linked to differences in the application of competition policy. The reality is probably a bit of both. It is difficult to find comparable data across different countries. MIT economist John Van Reenen looked at the significant increase in concentration ratios for the top four and top twenty firms in several sectors of the US economy, including services. He argued it reflected the superstar phenomenon rather than a weakening of competition policy.

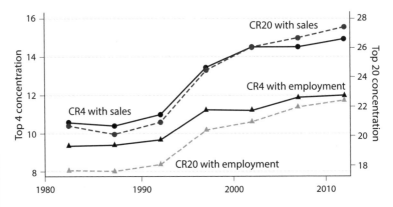

Average concentration: Four-digit industries in services.

John Van Reenen, "Increasing Differences between Firms: Market Power and the Macroeconomy," paper presented at the Federal Reserve Bank of Kansas City's annual Jackson Hole conference, August 2018, https://www.kansascityfed.org/~/media/files/publicat/sympos/2018/papersand handouts/jh%20john%20van%20reenen%20version%2020.pdf?la=en.

economy, as measured, for example, by *concentration ratios* (the proportion of market share in terms of total employment or revenue accounted for by the biggest firms in the market), or more generally by the share of national income going to profits rather than workers' incomes (box 2.2). However, the pattern differs between countries, due to differences in both the structure of the economy and the way competition policy is applied.

Competition Policy in Practice

Competition policy is, in most countries, the responsibility of specialized government agencies charged with

- policing mergers between big companies or that involve a large share of a given market, and deciding whether or not they can go ahead, and if so under what conditions;
- investigating markets where a large company seems to be abusing a dominant position, or whole markets that do not seem to be serving consumers well;
- monitoring for the existence of price-fixing cartels and prosecuting them;
- enforcing regulation to protect consumers in sectors where there is no or inadequate competition, such as electricity or rail;
- ensuring consumer protection laws and regulations are being observed and responding to complaints; and
- policing government subsidies for particular businesses to ensure they are not limiting or distorting competition in certain markets ("state aid").

The exact institutional arrangements differ between countries and legal jurisdictions in terms of how these functions are divided, as does the terminology used. For example, the US has two government agencies—the Federal Trade Commission (with responsibility for protecting trade across state borders) and the Department of Justice are the lead agencies—and individual state governments may also bring anti-trust cases before the courts. In Europe, the European

Commission has responsibility for applying competition law when more than one member country is involved, set out in the Treaty on the Functioning of the European Union, while the member countries have national agencies in addition.

These authorities, at least in the OECD member countries, are usually independent expert bodies, given independence because politicians are more vulnerable to lobbying by big businesses that want to take over competitors or make it hard for new entrants in their markets. This is a change from twenty or thirty years ago, when in many countries politicians (rather than independent experts or judges in court) made the decisions, and were especially vulnerable to the claim from incumbents with market power that stopping a merger from going ahead would lead to job losses. Competition policy is similar to monetary policy in this respect, having become more technocratic over time because of the adverse effect of short-term political pressures on decisions. Competition policy is also, and partly as a result, very legalistic. Lawyers and economists work closely together on the side of both the competition authorities and the businesses they are scrutinizing. The legal framework and terminology differ between jurisdictions, although the economic approach is common. However, there are always contexts in which competition decisions involve politics, so there are usually specific exclusions for matters of national security. Even where national security is not the issue, politicians express strong views about some takeover bids, such as foreign bids for symbolic domestic companies. For instance, in 2005 the French authorities blocked a takeover bid for food and drink producer Danone by PepsiCo; it was seen as unacceptable for one of France's premier global success stories to fall to American capitalism.

Competition authorities can therefore approve (or not) planned mergers or takeovers, and in some jurisdictions can also consider the effectiveness of competition in important markets, such as banking, electricity supply, mobile phone operators, or airports—all examples of market inquiries in the UK in recent years. Sometimes official investigators get evidence of *cartels*, the term for active collusion by companies to fix prices or carve out a market between them. This is rare, not only because it is a criminal offense (box 2.3)

Box 2.3 Cartel-busting by the US Department of Justice

One particularly high-profile busting of a cartel came in 1996 when the FBI, thanks to a whistle-blower, got evidence of a criminal conspiracy among agri-businesses to fix the price of lysine, an input into animal feeds. The lead company, Archer Daniels Midland (ADM), paid $100 million in fines in the US and over $50 million in the EU, Canada, and Mexico. The events were considered exciting enough to be made into a popular book by Kurt Eichenwald and then a film, *The Informant*, starring Matt Damon. The Department of Justice also recorded the real-world meetings, and these videos can be searched for online. In a further twist, the cooperating witness from ADM, Mark Whitacre, who gave his consent to the recordings, lost his non-prosecution protection agreement with the government when it was later learned that he had embezzled over $10 million from ADM—some of it while he was cooperating with the government.

---

but because, even without the weight of the law, cartels are often unstable; individual members have an incentive to cheat on the agreement as long as it is hard for other members to monitor their production. The OPEC oil producers' cartel is one exception that proves the rule, and even though it has lasted since 1960, there is cheating by individual producers, while agreements about how much each member can produce have had to be renegotiated frequently.

What Does a Competition Inquiry Involve?

The analysis the competition authority carries out usually involves the following steps (although again the terminology may differ in different jurisdictions):

Define the scope of the relevant market.
The boundaries of the market for a given product are determined by figuring out which goods or services consumers could switch to if a monopolist increased the price of the

product above the competitive level. This process is known as the SSNIP test (standing for a "small but significant non-transitory increase in price"). This *market definition* exercise involves estimating the elasticity of substitution between the product in question and "nearby" products. These judgments can be tricky. Is a bar a good substitute for a coffee shop if you can buy coffee and other non-alcoholic drinks there? How close do grocery stores need to be to each other for one to be a good alternative to another?

Assess how competitive the market is.

One way to start this is to look at the market share of the biggest companies, and how it has changed over time; sometimes a rule-of-thumb threshold, such as a share over 25%, is taken as cause for concern. Another rule of thumb is to consider the *Herfindahl-Hirschman Index* (HHI). The HHI measures concentration by calculating the sum of squares of the market shares of the N firms in the industry, normalized to the range 0 to 1 (sometimes for reasons of practicality in an inquiry only the fifty biggest firms are included):

$$\text{HHI} = \frac{\Sigma_{i=1}^{N} s_i^2 - 1/N}{(1 - 1/N)} \quad \text{when } N > 1$$

and

$$\text{HHI} = 1 \qquad \text{when } N = 1$$

where s_i is the revenue share of firm i

Again, a rule of thumb is used to decide how concerned to be: anything over 0.25 would be considered a sign of a very concentrated market.

These kinds of rules are a first step. A merger inquiry or market investigation will then look in greater detail at the way the businesses and consumers behave, including, for example, reading board papers and management accounts, carrying out consumer surveys, looking at the history of entry and exit in the market, visiting the companies, carrying out econometric work to estimate demand and supply conditions, considering the profitability of the businesses over time, and taking written and oral evidence from all interested parties.

Assess the barriers to entry.

How easy is it for new entrants to break into the market and compete for the pool of customers? This question has become particularly important in some digital markets, where—for reasons discussed below—one or a very few companies might dominate the market, but the identity of the dominant company changes from time to time. This is referred to as *competing for the market* or *contestability* rather than *competing in the market*. For instance, MySpace used to be the dominant social media platform until Facebook knocked it from that position; Facebook and Google would now claim they are vulnerable to firms with better technologies winning their markets, although many competition experts are skeptical about this claim. *Entry barriers* can include, for example, economies of scale (and therefore the need to have deep pockets to finance entry), scarce skilled labor, consumer inertia, technological advantages, or the existence of burdensome and costly regulations that either add to the scale barrier or require special know-how or approval by another regulator.

Decide the counterfactual.

Working out the counterfactual if a merger were not to go ahead can be the trickiest part of a competition inquiry. What would happen if the merger under scrutiny did not happen? What is the likely alternative outlook for the market? Would the firm being taken over go out of business, in which case the merger wouldn't make any difference to the outcome? Alternatively, would a potential new entrant decide to compete if there is no merger creating a rival too powerful to take on?

What are the theories of harm?
Last but far from least, what consumer harm will come about? Will prices be higher or innovation and investment reduced? If a digital giant has an almost complete monopoly but is providing an excellent free service to consumers, does the market power matter? Merging firms often claim that the efficiencies, synergies, or economies of scale they can achieve will benefit consumers, but the obvious question then is what incentive they have to pass on the benefits to consumers in the absence of stronger competition.

If the competition authority decides there is a competition problem (a "substantial lessening of competition" in UK and US terminology or "abuse of dominance" in the EU), they normally have a range of *remedies* they can impose. These include

- Fines
- Blocking the merger or (if already completed) requiring it to be undone
- "Structural" remedies, such as divestment of part of a business
- "Behavioral" remedies, for example, treating customers in a particular way—such as giving them extra information or making it easier for them to switch to a rival

Cartels, if proved, are typically a criminal offense and can involve the possibility of prison.

Other Factors Affecting Competition

Although competition is generally considered to increase economic welfare, sometimes economic policies deliberately restrict competition. There are various rationales, some good (that is, welfare-enhancing in the sense described earlier in this chapter), some bad (table 2.2).

Table 2.2. When Policies Restrict Competition

	Market power is	
	Deserved	*Undeserved*
Concession	Competitive, well-designed auction (e.g., spectrum auction, drilling license)	Unpaid-for legal monopoly (e.g., tax farming)
Intellectual property	Major innovation (e.g., patents)	Obvious, non-novel innovation (e.g., 70-year post-mortem copyright)
Utility regulation	Investment in new infrastructure	Lucky cost and demand conditions

Valid reasons for limiting competition (in other words, reasons likely to enhance economic welfare) are

- Protection of intellectual property with a temporary monopoly in the form of a patent or copyright (although this protection can be overly generous—see below).
- Concessions or licenses when there is a natural monopoly, preferably awarded by a well-designed competitive auction (for instance, for oil exploration, a rail franchise, or access to radio spectrum). An auction amounts to a competition for the market.
- Utility regulation, as an incentive/reward for investment and universal service provision in the case of essential natural monopoly sectors, such as electricity.

At times, though, there have been many examples of government-awarded limitations on competition that do not enhance economic welfare:

- Legal monopolies that have not been paid for, but given as a reward to a crony (such as tax farming)—historically common but now vanishingly rare in the rich economies.
- Patents or copyrights awarded for obvious, non-novel innovations or for too long a period (see box 2.4).
- Lucky cost or demand conditions (for instance, rail franchises benefiting from unexpectedly high demand).

Box 2.4. Does copyright protection go too far?

In 1998 the US extended copyright protection (in what is known as the Sonny Bono Act) from fifty to seventy years after the death of the author—and longer for "corporate" copyrights—thanks to lobbying by corporations such as Disney. In some cases, copyright protection in the US can last for 95 years from publication or 120 years from creation. Many other countries followed the US in extending their copyright terms to seventy years after death as well. But no author is going to be incentivized to write new works from beyond the grave, while for companies a century of protection for their copyrighted works does not seem to strike a good balance between the economic aims of incentivizing investment on the one hand and on the other maximizing public enjoyment of creative works or others' ability to mash up existing ideas for their own purposes, as creative people have always done. Should Katy Perry really have been forced to pay Flame $2.8m because one riff in her *Dark Horse* sounded like one in his *Joyful Noise*? The earlier term extension meant that a bumper crop of older works became free from copyright protection on January 1, 2019, including the Cecil B. DeMille film *The Ten Commandments*, novels by Agatha Christie, Edgar Rice Burroughs, and P. G. Wodehouse, and the classic song "Yes, We Have No Bananas" (https://law.duke.edu/cspd/publicdomainday/2019/). Without the term extension, *Lawrence of Arabia* and "Blowin' in the Wind" would also have become copyright-free in 2019, but they will now have to wait another twenty years.

The degree of competition in the economy depends on other areas of policy too. One important issue is whether unsuccessful firms are allowed to go out of business. As the next chapter discusses in more detail, governments have often been unwilling to allow this to happen because politicians hate headlines about job losses and will be tempted to subsidize important although failing firms. This happened frequently in the past with support for "national champions" whose very insulation from competition in their home market tended to make them inefficient. Airlines are a good example, as until very recently many rich countries felt it important for the "national carrier" to survive. However, it is a constant temptation and all governments sometimes do it. As pointed out in chapter 1, the Obama administration in the US bailed out the big auto manufacturers after the financial crisis in the Car Allowance Rebate scheme (Cash for Clunkers). France, another large automaker and exporter, bailed out Renault and PSA Peugeot Citroën in 2009 too, in that case through providing cheap loans.

The other issue, which is absolutely pervasive, is how heavily the economy is regulated. All markets are regulated to some extent, and without regulation no market could operate: consumers need confidence in weights and measures or safety standards, for instance. Yet the more regulation there is, the harder it is for new entrants to get into the market and grow. Even setting up a local café can involve multiple regulatory hurdles (box 2.5), although individually they all seem very reasonable.

Box 2.5. Regulations on cafés and restaurants in the UK

Registration with local authority 28 days in advance

Licenses for some activities (e.g., hot food after 11 p.m., alcohol, street stands)

Premises regulations, including separate sinks for food and humans

Food safety regulations

Hygiene regulations

Minimum and maximum temperatures for food

Health and safety regulations for employers

Training regulations for food handling

Written records of all food supplies, including batch numbers, use by & best before dates

Value added tax (VAT) registration

Displaying prices and VAT

Displaying 14 food allergens on menus

Labeling GMO food

Financial record keeping

Employers' taxes, pension contributions, and maternity pay

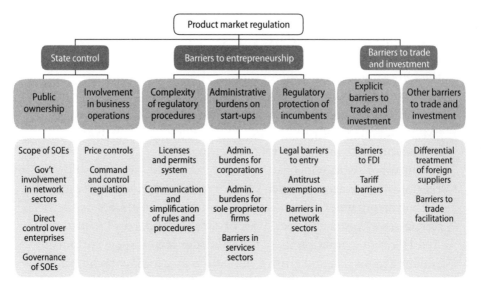

Figure 2.5. Scope of regulation of goods in OECD countries.

The balance between competition and regulation can be hard to strike, particularly for markets with one or both of two market failures: increasing returns to scale and asymmetric information.

Regulatory Policy

All businesses complain about red tape—the regulations the government forces them to implement. These take a wide range of forms; figure 2.5 illustrates possible types of regulation that apply to physical goods in OECD member countries. Typically, services are even more heavily regulated. Governments also use regulations on businesses as the means to deliver a range of social policies, such as sick pay and maternity pay or minimum wages.

All regulation tends to reduce competition. It curtails new entry into the market by making it more costly and time consuming to set up and run a business. The burden of regulation constrains economic growth (box 2.6). Some of the regulation may be unnecessary: competition could often be enough to make sure consumers get good-quality products and services at the best possible price.

Reducing the amount of regulation protects consumers better by increasing competition when it is easy to monitor quality and when businesses want to win repeat customers. In these circumstances, competition makes some kinds of regulation (such as safety standards or rules about weights and measures) less necessary or beneficial. Many businesses fall into this category, one would think. One bad haircut or meal will stop people from returning to that salon or restaurant. If a brand of consumer goods is always breaking down, word of mouth and the media will soon make it known. This is another area (like the treatment of externalities, discussed in chapter 1) where the courts could perhaps handle consumer protection. This is the basis of *tort law*, the US and UK body of civil law that allows people to get redress for negligence. On the other hand, it is unreasonable to expect individuals to take legal action against a business except for egregious cases where many aggrieved customers can cooperate in a class action; it is easy to demand that politicians "do something" about a scandal, so regulations tend to accumulate.

Box 2.6. Regulation and new entry

While some regulation is essential, countries differ greatly in the extent to which they regulate their economy. A study of the link between the regulatory burden and entrepreneurial activity in nine member countries by the OECD found a negative impact of regulation on new entry into manufacturing and service sector markets.* The study found that administrative burdens, regulation of products or services especially in technological sectors, and restrictions on hiring and firing employees all contributed particularly strongly to the adverse effects on productivity and industry growth. In countries where it is costly to lay off employees, there is a corresponding reluctance by firms to hire workers in the first place. Such countries, including France and Spain, tend to have high rates of youth unemployment in particular, as young people are untested in the labor

---

(continued on next page)

(*continued from previous page*)

market and employers do not want to risk taking on someone inexperienced whom they would find hard to dismiss. In France, more regulations kick in for firms with fifty or more employees, such as the requirement to organize and fund works councils, report more detailed statistics to the government, and face more barriers to laying off or firing workers. Another study found France has a spike in the number of particularly productive firms with forty-eight or forty-nine employees; the authors estimate that the regulatory burden dissuading them from growing to fifty and beyond imposes a social welfare cost equivalent to 3.4% of GDP.**

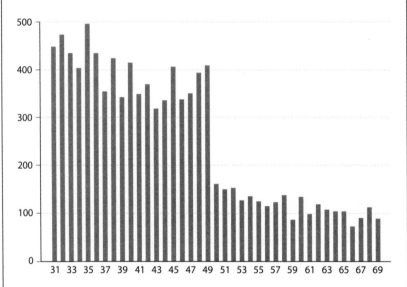

Number of firms by employment size in France. *Source*: Garicano et al.

* Stefano Scarpetta et al. (2002), "The Role of Policy and Institutions for Productivity and Firm Dynamics: Evidence from Micro and Industry Data," OECD Economics Department Working Paper No. 329, OECD Publishing, Paris.

** Luis Garicano, Claire Lelarge, and John Van Reenen (2016), "Firm Size Distortions and the Productivity Distribution: Evidence from France," *American Economic Review* 106, no.11: 3439–3479.

There are countless examples of government regulation of economic activity. Here are just a few:

- Authorization of banks and other financial services firms
- Food hygiene rules and certification for cafés and restaurants
- Mandatory criminal record checks of employees
- Compulsory fire extinguishers in hotels and restaurants
- Minimum guarantees for electronic and other manufactured products
- Rules of origin for food products
- Controls on prices or rents
- Licenses for many professional occupations
- Technical standards for products or buildings

There are many more.

Individually, each may seem reasonable, but the scope of their application has steadily increased. For example, food safety rules for formal businesses are being gradually imposed on voluntary activities, such as fund-raising for places of worship or children selling homemade lemonade in the park without a street traders' license. Regulators regulate and so have no incentive to reduce their scope. For politicians, there is an upward ratchet: it is always easy to call for some new rule after a bad news story, and nobody wants to take the risk of repealing a regulation and then getting the blame if something later goes wrong.

In any case, many of the things people buy are not so straightforward, particularly as the economy has become increasingly complex and based on services rather than physical goods. Even in these cases, though, it is not always completely obvious that regulation does effectively protect consumers. Take the example of financial services products, unsurprisingly under increased regulatory scrutiny after the 2008–2009 crisis. Are bank customers better protected by more regulation or by new competition? It seems obvious that ordinary consumers can never be as well informed about the risks and returns on investment products as the professionals marketing them, so regulation of the information provided or what the financial provider can do with clients' money seems inevitable, particularly post-2008, when so much unethical behavior by the finance industry was revealed. But what about ordinary current or checking accounts? Here too there are information gaps, created by banks that do not inform customers about the charges they will pay if they overdraw or take out cash overseas, nor let customers know what they could earn in interest if they move their funds to savings accounts. This information could be figured out, but it is complicated, and few people want to spend much time thinking about their banking arrangements. Everyday banking has also become more regulated over the years, to try to encourage more switching by customers and therefore more effective competition. The financial crisis has also led to higher limits for deposit guarantees in many countries, with the guarantee schemes paid for by a levy on banks.

The trouble with this well-meaning regulation is that it is making it harder for new competitors to enter the market. Technology is enabling a wave of "fintech" start-ups offering retail banking services. It will be all the harder for them to challenge the incumbent big-name banks if they have to comply with costly and extensive regulations (box 2.7).

Incumbents in many sectors might grumble about red tape, but they do appreciate the way regulation can protect them by acting as a barrier to entry. Often, in sectors such as telecoms or electricity, big businesses hire lawyers and policy experts to engage in constant discussion with their regulators and with politicians— these authorities are highly prone to *regulatory capture*. This term refers to the way agencies meant to regulate an industry in the interest of the public end up serving the interests of the industry they are supposed to be regulating. One specific concern is the revolving door, whereby people switch jobs between the watchdog and the regulated firms. Big companies usually hire public affairs consultants—lobbyists—to present their case to their regulator; lobbying is a major industry in itself. In a complex market, much of the expertise and knowledge about what is happening lies with the companies—there are some insurmountable asymmetries of information. Even if a regulator is sincerely dedicated to the wider public interest, it is human nature to be sympathetic to people one deals with all the time.

Box 2.7. Assisting competition in UK financial services

The rule book for the UK's Financial Conduct Authority (FCA) would stand two meters high if printed out, according to its chief executive. Well aware of the trade-off between competition and regulation, the FCA has an innovation team dedicated to helping start-ups get off the ground without overly onerous regulation, in a "regulatory sandbox."* Start-ups can apply to enter the sandbox to test products and services without the full regulatory burden. The UK's Competition and Markets Authority is hoping its mandating of "open banking" standards will also enable tech start-ups to enter the market.** Large banks and building societies (like savings and loans) are required to make customer information available in a standardized format to third parties, if requested to do so by the customer. New entrants can exploit the API (application programming interface, allowing the creation of apps by third parties) to offer financial services. It is still to be seen whether new entrants can eat into the market power of the small handful of big banks, however, as the experiment is in its early days.

* https://www.fca.org.uk/firms/regulatory-sandbox.
** https://www.openbanking.org.uk/wp-content/uploads/What-Is-Open -Banking-Guide.pdf.

The Rising Tangle of Red Tape

The political choice as to which point to choose in the unavoidable trade-off between relying on competition and relying on regulation has shifted over time. The political turn away from the state and toward "free markets" around 1980, described in chapter 1, brought about much more emphasis on relying on competition. Governments often talk about reducing red tape, and this was especially the case in the era of privatization, often accompanied by deregulation of those industries and of others such as finance. The decline in the scope of product market regulation was most pronounced from

1998 to 2008, according to an OECD study, and was most prevalent in its member countries other than the US and UK (which were relatively lightly regulated to start with, by comparison, having relied more heavily on civil law).

However, regulation has probably increased steadily in services, now accounting for 75%–80% of most Western economies, and certain areas of regulation have expanded, such as environmental. One key form of regulation in services is *conduct regulation*, governing who can provide a service and what they can/must/cannot do. Many professions also regulate entry through *occupational licensing*. The information available on the extent of this requirement in the US indicates that it has spread to cover around 30% of the workforce, up from just 5% in the 1950s (figure 2.6). The 2015 Economic Report to the President, which investigated the issue, states: "There can be an obvious disconnect between the strictness of licensing regulations and the potential harm to consumer safety. For example, Michigan requires 1,460 days of education and training to become an athletic trainer, but just 26 to be an emergency medical technician (EMT). In fact, across all states, interior designers, barbers, cosmetologists, and manicurists all face greater average licensing requirements than do EMTs." A wide range of professions, including auctioneers, scrap metal recyclers, barbers, manicurists, eyebrow threaders, and tour guides require state licenses, and the report found there is up to a 15% price gap between services in states that do and do not require licenses; and no evidence of quality improvements.

A natural political mechanism tending to increase the amount of regulation is the desire of politicians to be seen to do something when a problem hits the news. Incumbents in the industry sometimes support these moves. They too want to be seen as responsive to problems and, what's more, are well aware that the harder it is for potential rivals to enter the industry in the future, the better it is for them. So an upward ratchet in regulation, and decrease in competition, over time is not surprising. There is little empirical appraisal (such as cost-benefit analysis; see chapter 8) of proposed new regulations. It takes an act of political will of the kind demonstrated by Mrs. Thatcher and Mr. Reagan to hold back the tide.

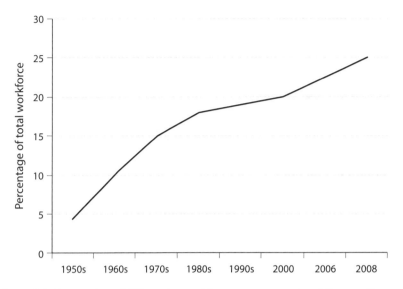

Figure 2.6. Proportion of US workers with a state occupational license. *Source*: CEA 2015, https://obamawhitehouse.archives.gov/sites/default/files/docs/licensing _report_final_nonembargo.pdf.

However, there is another mechanism that can restore competition: technological disruption. This is exactly what is happening in many sectors of the economy now, from finance to travel accommodation to taxis. Some economists argue in a slightly disparaging way that new digital entrants to these markets are engaging in *regulatory arbitrage*, in other words, specifically picking the markets where there is heavy regulation. The implication is that the new disrupters are trying to evade well-intentioned regulations. The other way of looking at it is that they have spotted the most obvious opportunities to serve consumers better because the heavy regulatory burden favors the incumbent producers at least as much as the consumers it is supposedly protecting. Taxis are a good example of this debate, as described below.

So political choices can shift reliance on regulation to bring about welfare-improving effects. Technology is a more powerful influence still in getting the economy to a less regulated, more competitive point on the trade-off, and one that is introducing new competition into a number of markets now.

The Regulation-Competition Trade-Off

The strong economic welfare benefits of competition described at the start of this chapter presume the absence of other market failures. Several market failures can justify regulation.

The most important is the presence of *information asymmetries* (assumption A4 fails—see box 1.4). These are widespread. Examples include—as well as financial services—any professional services, medical products and services, the content or origin of food products, and the performance of electronic products. The appropriate regulatory response is often a requirement on the producer to provide accurate and relevant information, or to satisfy minimum product standards.

However, where people are prone to making *non-rational choices* (assumption A1 fails), information alone will not be enough, or at least how it is presented needs to be regulated too. Work in behavioral economics (chapter 5) has underlined how difficult most people find it to calculate the expected future return on a financial product, for instance. Or people might intend to eat healthily but be unable to resist the temptation to buy desserts, justifying some regulation of sugar content in food products or at least labeling the product so that consumers can be aware of how bad it is for their health.

In some markets, it might be nearly impossible to sustain competition because they feature *natural monopolies* (assumption A3 fails). Chapter 3 looks at these sectors of the economy, as they have often been state-owned and -run, and when privatized require extensive regulation.

The policy conclusion is that where it is possible, competition probably serves consumers and economic welfare better than regulation; and if regulation is necessary for the above reasons, policy-makers should be clear about which kind of market failure they aim to address, and tailor the appropriate regulatory interventions. As the regulatory burden accumulates, it serves incumbent producers increasingly well at the expense of consumers. The authorities become increasingly prone to capture by the industries they are supposed to be regulating. Technological disruption might then be the best hope of tilting the balance back in favor of consumers.

The remainder of this chapter looks in more detail at three aspects of markets: the importance of information asymmetries in preventing competition from working well and so requiring regulation; technological disruption as a force for increased competition; and why natural monopoly markets always require heavy regulation.

Information Asymmetries

The absence or presence of information asymmetries can make all the difference to how a market functions. One of the most famous economic models, George Akerlof's "market for lemons" model, captures the key insight into how the fact that one party has more information than another can prevent a market from working at all. (It is also an example of how a very simple and apparently unrealistic model can illuminate a profound insight—economists are often criticized for using abstract models not at all like the real world, but this one is a terrific demonstration of why that criticism is often misplaced.)

The model makes the following assumptions:

- Secondhand cars are either low or high quality—the former are known as "lemons"
- Only the seller knows the quality of the car she is selling (this is the information asymmetry)
- The seller has a minimum price she is willing to accept
- The buyer has a maximum price he is willing to pay

Think about the buyer's decision first. She does not know whether the car on sale is a lemon or a good car. The price she is willing to pay reflects the risk (λ) that it is a lemon. Suppose the buyer is willing to pay $5,000 for a good car but just $2,500 for a lemon. And suppose the seller is prepared to accept $4,500.

The equilibrium price reflects the risk, as shown:

$$P = (1 - \lambda) \times \$5,000 + \lambda \times \$2,500$$

If the risk of the car being a lemon is too high (20% or more in this example), the price the buyer is willing to pay will not be as high as the lowest price the seller is willing to accept (as $0.8 \times \$5,000 + 0.2 \times \$2,500 = \$4,500$).

In fact, *only* the sellers of a lemon will accept the buyer's offer if the probability of a car being a lemon is sufficiently high. When this occurs, over time people wanting to sell good cars will withdraw from the market, leaving only lemons available, which buyers do not want to purchase. This process is known as *adverse selection*—in the extreme, the market can collapse as ultimately only lemons are offered for sale. Even though everyone would be better off if trades take place, there can end up being no sales occurring because of adverse selection.

Of course as a tale about second-hand cars, the market for lemons model is unrealistic because in real life these get bought and sold a lot. The point of the model is to highlight the role of the various mechanisms for accommodating the information asymmetry. Here are some examples:

- Second-hand car dealers can build a reputation for fair dealing through investing in showrooms, offering mechanical inspections, promising money-back guarantees and so on.
- Buyers can pay for their own inspection of vehicles.
- Sellers can pay for an annual service and keep the records to show potential buyers.
- Regulation can require annual mechanical tests for vehicles over a certain age

In the second-hand car market, the market itself largely solves the problem by the provision of additional information, including documentation of regular vehicle servicing, dealers' warranties, and even their investment in showrooms to reassure potential customers (just as banks use branches to convey an impression of their solidity). But there is a role for regulation too, such as mandatory testing of older vehicles. In all markets where there are information asymmetries, there will be a mixture of market solutions (including the potential for legal claims) and regulation.

Many markets can experience adverse selection. The phenomenon often features in insurance markets: if the risk of a claim, and therefore the premium, is too high, only people who are bad risks will want to buy insurance, but the insurer will be reluctant to sell it to them. For instance, people who know they have a medical condition are the most likely to want to purchase health insurance, which insurers will want to price reflecting the probability that willing purchasers will be more likely to need to claim. Information asymmetries generally make it unlikely that the market can achieve economically efficient outcomes without some policy intervention. Governments make some forms of insurance mandatory to provide, such as third-party coverage for drivers. Insurers seek as much information as they can about individuals' risk profiles, and lacking that charge different premiums to different categories of people, such as very high drivers' insurance premiums for young men.

Technological Disruption

The taxi market should be one in which competition can work effectively. There are no obviously insuperable information asymmetries, nor barriers to entry. In many cities, there appear to be some competing taxi firms. However, taxi markets are heavily regulated, and the number of licenses is often tightly restricted. These regulations are the main barrier to entry, and a very effective one at that. Often the individual drivers are not themselves the licensees, but rather rent access to a license or medallion, and to a vehicle, from either cab companies or investors.

Regulation of taxis is not without a rationale, and much of it dates back many decades:

- To protect passenger safety, personal and mechanical, through record checks on drivers, compulsory insurance, regular vehicle tests, and so on
- To prevent price gouging of customers by regulating fares
- To provide universal service requirements (for instance, in London the "black cabs" cannot turn down any rides within a 7-mile radius of the city center, although they can and often do turn down longer trips)

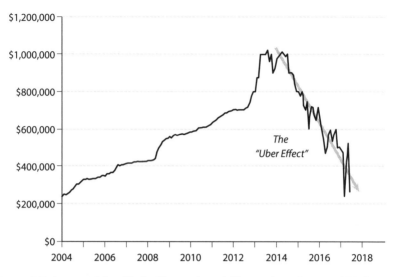

Figure 2.7. Average New York City taxi medallion prices. *Source*: AEI, https://www.aei.org/publication/schumpeterian-creative-destruction-the-rise-of-uber-and-the-great-taxicab-collapse/.

These regulations might perhaps be justified in terms of market failures such as asymmetric information. After all, taking a taxi is an experience good: if you turn up at the airport in a strange city, you do not know if your driver is safe or how much you should pay to get to your destination. Yet all too often there has been over-regulation. After all, how does a local official know how many licenses or medallions to issue? They do not, and the number only rarely increases. In New York City, for instance, there were fewer taxi medallions on issue in 2013 than in 1932 (13,000 versus 16,000). There is strong pressure from incumbent medallion or license holders not to increase the number, and to keep taxis in short supply, and passengers waiting. The reason is that medallions can be traded, and are bought as investment assets by people who then rent out the license to operate the taxi.

Similarly, when prices rather than quantity are fixed by officials, there is no reason to expect them to be set at the market clearing level, and under- or over-supply often results.

The price of medallions is clear evidence of the market distortion. This topped $1 million in NYC in 2013 (figure 2.7), having risen more by then than the S&P 100 share price index or the price of gold. In many taxi markets, regulation creates market power and gives incumbent license holders a *monopoly rent*. The cost to consumers is an absence of taxis when they want one, or a long waiting time; and what's more the opportunity cost of people's time has been going up as real earnings increase. Many regulators have become aware of the malfunctioning of taxi markets, and various governments or local authorities have tried to deregulate taxis at various times (box 2.8). These efforts have rarely been successful, as taxi drivers and license owners are a well-organized and vocal lobby group, skilled at deploying the consumer safety arguments, which is after all a perfectly valid concern. Yet it is clear that new entry into the market would decrease the value of their asset, the license or medallion, and possibly also the ongoing earnings of drivers, so they have an economic incentive to protest against new entry.

The remarkable success of taxi license holders and drivers in preventing competition in their markets made it vulnerable to tech-

---

Box 2.8 Taxi deregulation in Ireland

One rare effort that did succeed, at least in part, was taxi deregulation in Ireland in 2000. One of the clever things about the Irish deregulation was that, rather than directly expand entry into the market by issuing new licenses, the existing drivers were given a second license, which they could and did sell. Their property right in their initial license was recognized, although it was diluted. This reduced the political opposition to deregulation. The evidence is that the number of taxis increased, passenger waiting times decreased, and service quality improved. The dire adverse effects that had been predicted by opponents of the liberalization did not materialize. There was, however, a small decrease in the earnings of incumbent drivers, and the new drivers who bought those second licenses then became just as determined to keep out further new entrants. The deregulation led to a protracted political and legal battle, including claims for compensation from the incumbent drivers.

nological disruption, however. Platforms such as Uber and Lyft have used their technology to present themselves as a matching app (like online dating) rather than as new taxi companies, and they have successfully entered many cities, albeit with many regulatory disputes over what licensing conditions they must meet. Taxi drivers everywhere are protesting against Uber in particular (and assessing the economic welfare effects of its entry into the market is complicated by the fact that it has such a nasty corporate culture). The matching algorithms bring together people who want a ride with drivers. There are set rates for fares depending on time and distance (which rise in surge pricing at certain peak times). The fare is shared between drivers, costs such as insurance and the software platform, and the platform's margin.

In principle, all parties—drivers, passengers, and the platform—benefit. Drivers can earn more because the algorithm finds them more rides (in particular, in the "backhaul" journey returning from one passenger's destination having picked up another customer). People can drive in marginal time, perhaps just a few hours a week, to make a bit of extra money, and they do not have to pay for a taxi license or rent a medallion (although some do lease cars). There is some evidence that this has provided a route into formal work for people who have found it hard to get employment, such as ethnic minority drivers from the dismal *banlieues*, or suburbs, of big French cities. A study by Boston Consulting Group (commissioned by Uber) found that one in four jobs created in Paris in 2016 was due to ride-sharing companies. Unemployment in France is relatively high, and Paris and other French cities have fewer conventional taxis per head of population than cities like London or New York. On the other hand, the study found the average Uber driver in Paris worked 52 hours a week and earned 1,400 euros per month, just below minimum wage.

Passengers wait less and pay less; Uber's and Lyft's rates are lower than alternatives, perhaps partly because they have a lower regulatory burden but partly because the drivers can get more passengers and so will accept a lower rate per mile. The GPS tracking can offer some safety protection—and there is no evidence the new entrants are less safe than conventional taxis—and the apps limit price gouging at least as well as do the regulatory alternatives. Besides, if safety is a real concern, regulators can directly require Uber and Lyft to do more prior checks, rather than ensuring safety indirectly through issuing a limited number of licenses.

How can both drivers and passengers gain (as well as there being a margin for the platform)? To the extent they do, the answer is that better matching delivers a pure efficiency gain (more rides for drivers, less waiting for passengers); and as the demand for taxi rides seems to be price elastic in most cities, demand overall has increased. There is also some evidence that certain areas are better served by Uber or Lyft drivers (where licensed cab drivers are reluctant to go because the high cost of their licenses mean they want to concentrate on high-margin (i.e., short) trips with a better chance of getting a return fare); and that becoming a driver offers a route into the formal labor market for some groups previously marginalized, such as women who only have a few hours spare a week because of caregiving duties, or members of minority groups who find it hard to get other jobs. What's more, the new competition in the market seems to have improved the quality of service provided by existing cab companies, many of which are now developing their own apps. However, as figure 2.7 also illustrates, the new entrants have hit incumbents hard. Investors in New York City yellow cab medallions have experienced a huge decline in the value of their asset, and many have gone bankrupt. Drivers without the benefits of the matching app have seen their incomes from driving decline.

Uber is particularly controversial because of its corporate behavior. Some people also object to surge pricing at busy times (although it is no different in principle from peak pricing for electricity use or differential prices for airline seats or hotel rooms), and Uber has had to limit this in emergencies, after several terrible misjudgments. Yet the alternative is a shortage of taxis at busy times, as the supply of Uber drivers does seem to increase when there is surge pricing.

Some concern has been expressed, too, about Uber's long-term intentions. Does it aim to monopolize the markets it enters over time? This is not inevitable as the inherent barriers to entry are not high (as Uber itself has discovered, facing new competitors). Has it contributed to urban congestion? Perhaps, to the extent that it is substituting for public transport, cycling, or walking; and if so, there is an environmental external cost. Is it making the rates paid and conditions less attractive to drivers, having lured them in? If so, this will be limited by the fact that it needs drivers—it has no business if there are not enough of them to meet demand, for a matching app requires a balance between customers and drivers. And many drivers have other options, including returning to the cab companies many of them switched from in the first place.

Uber and Lyft have, though, been unambiguously bad for one group: the incumbent license or medallion holders. This group has concentrated lobbying power, including bringing public pressure to bear by snarling up city centers with driver protests. To the extent they have been successful, this is another example of regulatory capture of regulators by those they are supposed to regulate in the interest of consumers. Various cities around the world have introduced restrictions on Uber in particular. Incumbent taxi drivers often claim the newcomers are unfair competitors; why, they ask, should they be subject to extra regulations when Uber is not? One possible answer is that their regulatory burden should be reduced. Another is that they should try to improve their service by adopting better technology themselves. A third is that if things are so tough for them they could switch to become Uber drivers. The lack of appeal these potential courses of action seem to have for them is a clue that the real objection is to competition that is leaving them worse off by reducing their market power: What kind of competition would they consider to be "fair"?

Restrictive regulations limiting entry in the past in effect conferred a property right on incumbent taxi license or medallion holders, who sometimes invested in medallions (sometimes on borrowed money) on the basis of a stream of future rents. In the US, taxi medallion holders have indeed argued explicitly that their ownership should entitle them to compensation. The question is whether anybody can really have a legal right to monopoly power and the consequent monopoly rents. As discussed above, there are some such legal rights, in the form of patents and copyrights; and although these are in principle temporary, incumbents such as the recording and movie industries have lobbied so effectively against digital new entrants that (1) copyright terms have been repeatedly extended and (2) many governments have introduced laws that require internet service providers to report illegal downloaders of music or movies to the police. Copyright protection is now so long term that it is quasi-permanent. But permanent legal monopolies are hard to justify in terms of economic welfare.

Some other markets where digital platforms have made big inroads, increasing competition, are also heavily regulated: Airbnb in accommodations and peer-to-peer lending platforms, such as Upstart and Funding Circle in the finance sector, for example. Matching platforms have the potential to increase the efficiency of the market—and to do so in a Pareto-improving way—because their improved matching of buyers and sellers is equivalent to increasing the liquidity of the market and increasing the number of potential trades. The platforms use both the improved physical technology of broadband, GPS, and smartphones and the improved intellectual technology of market design models encoded in their algorithms. *Market design* is a thriving area of economic research, which has found applications ranging from government bond auctions or spectrum auctions to transport planning and matching donor kidneys to recipients (box 2.9). For all the controversy associated with the prominent big platforms, the potential improvement in economic efficiency from these technologies—smartphones, pervasive broadband, and algorithms—could be significant.

Box 2.9. Matching markets

Economist Al Roth won the Nobel Prize (along with Lloyd Shapley) for his work on algorithms for acceptance markets. The best known is the *deferred acceptance* rule, which can be used in applications ranging from school admissions to marriage markets. Suppose there is a set of men M (with a typical man m ∈ M) and a set of women

---

(continued on next page)

(*continued from previous page*)

W (w ∈ W) and the aim is to match them in w,m pairs. Each woman has strict (complete and transitive) preferences over the individual men and vice versa. A man is acceptable to a woman if she prefers him to being unmatched. A matching is a set of pairs (w,m) such that each individual has an acceptable partner. It is also stable if there is no alternative (w,m) pair, each of whom would prefer each other rather than their current partner.

So if

Ajay prefers Rosie to Priya
Bob prefers Priya to Rosie
Rosie prefers Ajay to Bob
Priya prefers Bob to Ajay

there is one unique, stable matching (Rosie, Ajay), (Priya, Bob).

The deferred acceptance algorithm starts by having each woman propose to the highest man in her ranking; the men can reject or tentatively accept the offer. Each rejected woman then makes an offer to the next man in her ranking. This continues until there are no more rejections or offers, and the tentative matchings are implemented. The algorithm produces a stable, one-to-one matching: proposers are rejected by their higher-ranking choices so have reached the best partner they can attain; recipients are only tentatively matched until they reach the best offer they can attain.

Roth and other market designers have deployed this algorithm in many real-world contexts, such as medical internship applications and school choices. These are not markets in the sense that no prices are set or money paid. But they match demand and supply in the most efficient way possible. The theories also look at how to make sure the algorithms incentivize participants always to reveal their true preferences rather than to choose strategically. The deferred acceptance algorithm is not strategy proof, as the receiving party has an incentive to game it by turning down acceptable offers given the chance of getting a better offer in the next round. Acceptable is a less demanding standard than the best of all possible worlds.

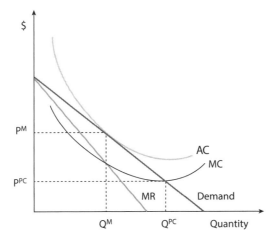

Figure 2.8. Natural monopoly.

Natural Monopolies: The Example of Electricity

A *natural monopoly* refers to a context where average costs are declining over the relevant range of output, and marginal costs are lower therefore than average costs (figure 2.8). One firm producing all the output is the least-cost solution. However, there is no allocative efficiency with only one producer—no competition in the market. Prices are higher under a monopoly than in the competitive market (P^M instead of P^{PC}) and quantity similarly lower. The final example in this chapter, prefiguring the next chapter, concerns the balance of regulation and competition in a natural monopoly sector: the provision of electric power.

Electricity generation, distribution, and transmission form a natural monopoly because there are large economies of scale. It will always be lowest cost to have just one set of physical cables running from generators to homes and businesses, and even in power generation the economies of scale are such that the scope for vigorous competition is limited. Whatever the ownership structure and organization in the electricity business—and these vary widely between countries—it is difficult to establish competition in an industry with such large economies of scale (assumption A3 from box 1.4 fails). It is also difficult to regulate. The electricity sector is one of the most politically sensitive and contested across the globe.

The electricity market has many distinctive features:

- Electricity cannot be stored easily—matching supply to demand is harder than in other markets because it has to happen at every instant, including those times when everybody turns on the oven or the TV at the same time. (This is the *peak loading* problem, the same as Uber faces shortly after midnight on New Year's Eve.)
- It is lethally dangerous and requires a good deal of technical expertise and extensive safety measures.
- The economies of scale are very large. Power stations are expensive to build (up to tens of billions of dollars for a nuclear station), and the investment is expected to last for fifty years or more.
- There is a natural monopoly in the transmission (high power lines from power stations to the grid) and distribution (lower voltage lines from sub-stations to premises) network. The least-cost means of distributing power is to have just one network of cables and transmission towers, sub-stations and wires. The network has a physical geography too. For instance, a network with a few big power stations is completely different from one with many wind farms or solar farms.
- There are important negative externalities in production—pollution, greenhouse gas emissions, and neighborhood disamenities, such as the buzzing of transmission towers or the whirring of turbine blades.
- Electricity is a necessity, with a low price elasticity of demand.
- There are equity considerations; in the UK, energy bills account for 6% of average household spending, 15% for low-income households.
- Energy is special as well, in that it is fundamental to the rest of the economy—power cuts are much worse than excess capacity, so society needs more capacity than the sum of individual investment decisions would provide, as collective insurance.

Hence there are several potential market failures as well as some important non-efficiency considerations. The difficulty of providing a consistent electricity supply is demonstrated by the fact that many advanced economies, such as the US, Sweden, Denmark and Italy, have at times experienced significant blackouts, while some low-income countries struggle to provide a reliable electricity supply at all. Focusing on the advanced economies, the market is characterized by a small number of large companies. Often they are vertically integrated too—that is, the same company owns the power stations, the high-voltage transmission cables, and the low-voltage distribution network, or two out of these three supply chain links.

These features make for a complicated public policy problem. Governments have several conflicting aims, in addition to an economically efficient electricity industry:

- affordability—ensuring that people on low incomes do not have to spend too much money on heat and light;
- security of supply—limiting the amount of oil or gas needing to be imported from potentially unattractive trading partners; and
- emissions—reducing pollution and especially the emission of CO_2 and other greenhouse gases.

The first aim points to keeping prices down, the other two require investment and therefore prices high enough to generate a return on the necessary finance.

In many countries, a lot of investment in power stations and networks took place in the postwar decades. This was only partly reconstruction. Those decades of rapid economic growth in the late 1940s to late 1970s (so impressive in retrospect that they are referred to in French as *les trente glorieuses*) induced an even faster growth in demand for energy. Subsequently, the oil shocks of the 1970s, and the shift away from manufacturing to services, led to a big drop in the energy intensity of economic growth. The energy ratio (energy used per unit of GDP) in the OECD member countries had dropped to 57% of its 1970 level by 2001. For this reason, by the 1990s many countries appeared to have plenty of electricity generating capacity. Compared to earlier decades, there has subsequently been relatively little investment in conventional power stations; investment in renewable sources has increased more recently, but the generating capacity it provides is still relatively small. So for some countries there is an energy gap, and electricity has to be imported.

The UK is one of these, for instance, importing about 10% of its energy. The UK's traditional generating capacity is aging and declining. Coal-fired power stations are mostly being phased out: the equipment needed for them to meet tough modern CO_2 emissions targets makes them too expensive. Nuclear power stations provide about a fifth of the UK's electricity; they are low in carbon emissions and provide the *baseload* supply (the constant minimum level needed to keep the system running) because they have to run all the time. But they are nearing the end of their life, and the decision to invest in new nuclear has only recently been made. Renewables have been heavily subsidized as their small scale to date has made them uneconomical. Although their share is rising fast, in a country like the UK sun and wind are not consistent and least available when energy demand is highest—winter. (In California, by contrast, sun and wind are more consistent, and demand is high in the summer for air conditioning.) Gas, much of it imported from continental Europe, has been plugging the gap. Unfortunately, imports are vulnerable to geopolitics. Russia, for instance, is a big gas exporter.

However, the distribution mix varies a lot by country depending on geology and geography (which affects the scope of generation from low-carbon renewable sources, such as wind, solar, tidal, and hydropower), and on political choices. Germany turned away from its own nuclear power after the 2011 Fukushima nuclear disaster in Japan, but filled the gap at first with highly polluting lignite coal as well as more renewables, and with power imported from neighboring France, three-quarters of whose electricity is generated by nuclear plants. In the United States, the fracking boom has tilted the energy generation mix strongly toward gas.

Different countries have a different legacy of past investment choices: power stations are big investments that last for decades, with limited scope to improve their technology over time. So far renewables technologies have been too costly to replace conventional power stations, although their costs are now falling rapidly. But the amount of electricity a wind farm can generate is small compared to, say, a gas-fired station, so a lot of investment will be needed in both renewables and a new distribution network (because renewables generation occurs in small amounts at many sites rather than in large amounts at a few sites).

The organization of the industry also varies greatly between countries. In some cases, such as France, the industry is still majority-owned by the state, in others it is wholly in private hands. The structure of the market in the latter case differs too—for example, do generators have to sell their electricity into a wholesale market or are they fully vertically integrated and able to sell direct to customers? How is the setting of prices regulated? How are emissions obligations enforced and who pays for the subsidies to renewables? These varying market structures reflect different choices made about costly long-term investments in a natural monopoly. In Western European countries, private power companies were nationalized in the postwar period, and the state-owned electricity companies invested substantially in capacity, including in then new technologies such as nuclear. As the next chapter describes, they were among the state-owned corporations privatized from the 1980s on. However, the industry has continued to be subject to a good deal of government regulation and intervention because of its natural monopoly characteristics and its fundamental importance to the rest of the economy.

In the UK, the privatization in stages from 1989 on of the state-owned Central Electricity Generating Board created three private generating companies, National Power, PowerGen and Nuclear Electric (later British Energy), and the privately owned but regulator-controlled National Grid. There have since been multiple changes of ownership and structure. Now the National Grid combines electricity and gas transmission; there are six big companies that generate electricity, supply gas, and market energy to retail customers, and a number of smaller suppliers. But the transmission network has separate owners. There are many small companies entering the market, and going bankrupt, too, in some cases. There have been several major reforms to the regulatory framework, and there is a growing body of regulation governing how the companies operate. A two-year Competition and Markets Authority investigation from 2014 to 2016 into the market concluded that the companies were not making excess profits but that "vulnerable" (low-income) customers were unlikely to switch to better price deals. It imposed new requirements on the "Big Six" large generators. Subsequently, politicians from across the spectrum have called for additional regulation, and a price cap is likely to be imposed on certain kinds of customer deals. In sum, this is not a market that is working well.

The next chapter describes how prices were regulated after privatization, recognizing that this was necessary in a natural monopoly: prices could only rise by a regulator-determined amount. This was aimed at forcing gains in efficiency and also making sure the efficiency gains got passed on to consumers. Prices paid for electricity indeed declined, but that meant no investment for a couple of decades in the electricity infrastructure. Now, twenty years later, the companies need to invest in new power stations and pay the financing costs on that private investment—delivering a much higher rate of return to shareholders than the 5% a year return previously required by the Treasury. In a modest success, however, the UK's CO_2 emissions have declined modestly, although not enough to hit the government's environmental targets. Meanwhile, despite the ever-increasing detail of the regulation, and government intervention in supposedly private decisions, such as the new generation of nuclear projects, and multiple reforms of the market structure, there is no explicit acknowledgment of the reality that the state will never leave energy to the market.

Many countries struggle with organizing the electricity market; the UK is not unique, although it has been a pioneer in trying new models. In Australia, for example, the vast geographic scale of the grid and surges in demand for air conditioning during ferocious heat waves have led to power cuts. The industry was privatized and restructured in the mid-1990s, switching from a state-level pattern to a national (wholesale) electricity market. There are three federal regulators, with different responsibilities, issuing detailed and inflexible rules that give the private generators little incentive to respond to changes in demand. Like most other advanced economies, there is also a trend toward renewables, with the investment that requires. Prices have been rising, power outages occur from time to time, and significant new investment is required. California, too, has had a particularly fraught experience with electricity deregulation (box 2.10).

Box 2.10. California's electricity restructuring disaster

In the early 2000s something had clearly gone wrong with the electricity market in California, which had been deregulated in the mid-1990s following the example set by the United Kingdom. The generation of electricity was deregulated, as was the retailing of electricity to customers through resellers—energy service providers. In between were the transmission and local distribution by utility companies, which bought from the generators in markets vulnerable to price spikes because of the inherent variability of demand for electricity, and sold power to the retail providers, at prices that remained regulated and politically sensitive. In mid-2000, prices in the wholesale market jumped to more than twice as high as any previous month. This meant big profits for the power generators and financial disaster for the utilities that had to buy wholesale power for sale to businesses and households. In March 2001 Pacific Gas and Electric, the state's largest utility, went bankrupt. The state of California took over and spent $1 billion a month through 2001, paying average prices ten times higher than a year earlier. It was easy for economists to conclude the generators were exercising monopoly power. In addition, though, the structure of the market was bound to cause problems. In 2001 the federal authorities allowed California to introduce price caps in the wholesale market, and the California regulators increased retail prices. A 2002 study of the California experience concluded: "Those states and countries that have not yet started down the road of electricity deregulation would be wise to wait to learn from the experiments that are now occurring in California, New York, Pennsylvania, New England, England and Wales,Norway, Australia and elsewhere."* A market with a natural monopoly cost structure, inelastic but volatile demand, and supply that is also very inelastic in the short run is not an easy one in which to enable competition or apply regulation.

* Severin Borenstein (2002), "The Trouble with Electricity Markets: Understanding California's Restructuring Disaster," *Journal of Economic Perspectives* 16, no. 1: 191–211.

Recognizing that the context varies so much, the challenge is to think about how energy policy can deliver efficiency, maximizing economic welfare. Given the combination of natural monopoly and conflicting policy aims, it is not surprising that this market rarely seems to work well in terms of *any* of the aims. Are there policies that would help achieve greater social welfare? The answer is possibly yes, if the trade-offs are acknowledged. Policy needs to tackle the different aims of energy policy separately.

For it is not possible to have both a higher and a lower electricity price simultaneously. There are other ways lower-income households might be compensated for higher electricity prices, such as using the benefit or welfare system to ensure they have enough income to pay their bills.

Setting aside the affordability question, the point that society cannot function if energy supply fails, combined with the desirability of large but risky investments, could lead to the conclusion that electricity supply is too important to be left to the market and competition will not work because of the natural monopoly features. A return to a centralized model, organized by the government even if the assets are in private hands, could deliver greater economic efficiency and also support non-economic aims, such as security of supply. But it would require safeguards against the old inefficiencies that led to privatization in the first place (see chapter 3 for more).

An alternative is to place more confidence in the ability of new technologies to enable competition in this market, as they already have in others. Investment in renewables can take place in smaller amounts than investment in a new conventional power station. Individual households and businesses can install their own photovoltaic cells and wind turbines, and feed the excess into the grid. Perhaps a new digital platform will enable a more efficient wholesale market with many suppliers and many customers. This competitive vision would still require a suitable regulatory framework and would still have natural monopoly components, so it is not a no-brainer, but it is not impossible.

The worst place to be is the one many countries have found themselves in—falling between the two stools of state control and a competitive market, with frequent confusing and even contradictory policy changes, because of the failure to acknowledge that this is a case where governments will never be able to "leave it to the market."

Natural Monopolies: Digital Platforms

The concept of a natural monopoly has traditionally been applied to network utilities, such as electricity, water supply, rail systems, and fixed-line telephony. However, many digital businesses have identical economic characteristics—if anything, they are even more like natural monopolies (box 2.11).

There are high fixed costs and low marginal costs (zero in many cases). For instance, developing an operating system or search algorithm takes a lot of time and engineering skill up front, but when completed it can serve more and more users at almost zero cost. There are powerful *network effects* reinforcing the cost structure. The more people use one social network or one search engine, the more valuable it is to each one of them. In some cases, the lowest production cost and highest consumer utility occur when only one or two companies serve the entire market.

There are many examples of digital markets captured by one dominant product. Google had 88% of all online searches in late 2017. Facebook had 2.2 billion active users (excluding its other platforms, such as Instagram and Messenger), compared to just under 1 billion on the next biggest social media platform, China's WeChat. Microsoft had an 85% share of all desktop operating systems. However, the identity of the dominant player in each market has shifted over time. In 2002 Microsoft's Internet Explorer accounted for 96% of all web browser usage but had declined to 15% by 2017, when Chrome was far in the lead (49%) and Firefox had a sizable market share too (13%). Before Facebook became the dominant social media platform in 2008, MySpace was by far the

---

Box 2.11. Network effects and multi-sided markets

Network effects (or network externalities) mean that a user of a network gains more benefit from it the more other users there are. The increase is non-linear and accelerates: if two people are using a phone network, there is one possible link. Metcalfe's law states that the value of the network rises with the square of the number of users (the number of connections is $n*(n - 1)/2$ for n users). Network effects can be considered as demand-side economies of scale, rather than the traditional supply-side economies of scale discussed in the context of natural monopolies.

Network effects can be direct, as with the phone network, or indirect, when one group of users benefits from there being more members of another group of users, as in many digital platforms. As a customer of restaurants, I benefit the more restaurants list with the booking app, and the restaurants benefit the more diners use the app.

When there are indirect network effects, the market is described as two-sided or multi-sided. It is difficult to apply to them the standard competition policy approach described earlier in this chapter, because even when there are strongly competing digital platforms, they often charge a price lower than marginal cost to one group of users (often the consumers). This price structure, where one side subsidizes the other, is a key characteristic of multi-sided platforms. Think of the restaurant booking app or many accommodation sites: the consumer does not pay (although of course the suppliers' costs get reflected in the prices they ultimately charge). Market definition is much harder too, as platforms tend to extend across many activities. Which "market" is Google in?

---

leading one. Given these examples of turnover in the identity of the dominant player, the digital giants argue that they compete *for* the market (rather than *in* the market), and are vulnerable to a new entrant with better technology.

However, competition authorities are not convinced that the size and market share of the digital giants is benign, or that the potential for new entrants is enough to ensure competitive pressure and economic efficiency. Microsoft's Internet Explorer only started to lose share in the browser market after the European Commission forced Microsoft to unbundle IE from its desktop operating system so it would be easier for consumers to choose their browser. An earlier tech giant, IBM, only started to lose market share in PCs when the US competition authorities had taken action against it. The European Commission recently announced it intended to fine Google over its anticompetitive behavior in non-neutral display of search results (Google is appealing the decision).

Although competition for the market is indeed competition, having a dominant position makes it possible for incumbents to raise the entry barriers for potential new competitors. One common way of doing so is by bundling together a range of products and services so consumers are reluctant to switch to a newcomer unless the new entrant can offer the same array of services. It is much harder (and more expensive) to enter a market along a broad front than a narrow one. Bundling is common in both digital and communications services. For instance, people might use one platform for search, news, entertainment, social media, chat or messaging, and shopping. Similarly, consumers increasingly buy a package of mobile and fixed telephone, broadband, and TV together. Another form of barrier is known as *envelopment*, whereby a platform uses its large customer base to move into other markets—such as Google into online maps or Uber into food delivery.

Dominant digital platforms also often observe that they provide an excellent and compelling service to consumers, who in fact benefit from their dominance because of the importance of direct and indirect network effects. This is obviously true. What is unknown is how that value compares to the potential adverse effect on competition, and economic efficiency, from the new entry that does not happen or the diminished incentive the incumbent has to innovate. Appropriate competition policy for digital platforms is a hotly debated question as the digital platforms grow (box 2.12).

Box 2.12. Enforcing competition in digital markets

Competition authorities around the world—apart from the US, to date—have become increasingly active against giant digital companies such as Google, Facebook, and Amazon. With the group sometimes including Microsoft or Netflix or Apple, various acronyms have been coined to describe the group: FAANGs or GAFAM. The European Commission has been at the forefront, for example, fining Google 4.3 billion euros (roughly $4.8 billion) in 2018 for using its Android mobile platform to illegally favor Google search, and 2.42 billion euros (around $2.7 billion) in 2017 for using its dominance in search to favor its own shopping service.

Australia's competition regulator, the Australian Competition and Consumer Commission, is taking steps to counteract near monopoly positions or excessive market power of certain tech giants, especially Google and Facebook, following an investigation on the impact of digital platforms on the advertising and news industries. According to the report, Google accounts for 98% of searches from mobile devices, while 68% of Australians access Facebook on a monthly basis. The regulator aims to force Google to unbundle its Chrome internet browser from mobile phones and other devices. It also seeks to establish a watchdog to monitor how large digital platforms, such as Google and Facebook, rank and display advertisements and news content in light of concerns regarding abuse of market power.

The French competition authority concluded in a 2018 inquiry that there were competition concerns in the online advertising market (dominated by Google and Facebook), with action likely to follow. In Germany, the competition authority—the Bundeskartellamt— proposed amendments to competition law enforcement that would enable it to pursue concerns about the way online pricing algorithms operate. In the UK, a government-commissioned, wide-ranging expert inquiry into competition in digital markets is likely to result in new enforcement actions.

Although the US authorities have not yet followed suit—perhaps unsurprising as these are all successful US companies—debate has

(continued on next page)

(continued from previous page)

been raging in academic and legal circles in the United States as to whether the consumer welfare standard established by Robert Bork (described earlier in this chapter and also referred to as the Chicago School of anti-trust) is appropriate for digital market where prices are often zero. At a zero price, this kind of standard cannot identify any problems due to lack of competition, but many critics of the digital giants point to their adverse effects, for example, on political discourse or in freezing out new entry. Economists broadly argue that economic analysis is sufficiently flexible to take these aspects into account; but some legal scholars have begun to argue for a return to the trust-busting policies of the early twentieth century, when President Theodore Roosevelt broke up giant corporations, most prominently Standard Oil in 1911.

Conclusion

This chapter has described the policy tools available for trying to increase social welfare in markets where there are market failures such as information asymmetries or natural monopoly. Competition, where it is possible, will likely increase efficiency; competition policy based on economic analysis is standard in many economies. Regulation is the alternative principal tool for addressing market failures. Although all markets require regulation—making the idea of a "free market" an unrealistic abstraction—there is often a trade-off between competition and regulation. Competition is not easy to enforce in many contexts in modern economies, where the markets are complicated, involving advanced technologies, and where information asymmetries and increasing returns to scale are pervasive. It is often easier for politicians and regulators to turn to regulatory instruments, although (as chapter 7 describes) these interventions are often themselves ineffective, costly, or even counterproductive; bad regulation is one of the most common forms of "government failure." The next chapter continues the analysis of the regulation of natural monopoly markets, looking at it through the lens of the ebb and flow of public and private ownership and production over the decades since the mid-twentieth century.

Further Reading

Technical Follow-Up

Massimo Motta (2004), *Competition Policy: Theory and Practice*, Cambridge University Press.
Jean Tirole (2014), "Market Power and Regulation," scientific background to the Nobel Prize announcement, http://idei.fr/sites/default/files/medias/doc/by/tirole/scientific_background_economics_nobel_2014.pdf.

Classics

George A. Akerlof (1970), "The Market for 'Lemons': Quality Uncertainty and the Market Mechanism," *Quarterly Journal of Economics* 84, no. 3 (August): 488–500.
Robert Bork (1978), *The Antitrust Paradox*, Free Press.

On Competition Policy

Michael Grenfell (2017), "What Has Competition Ever Done for Us?," speech, http://www.regulation.org.uk/library/2017-What_has_Competition_ever_Done_for_us.pdf.
Maurice E. Stucke (2013), "Is Competition Always Good?," *Journal of Antitrust Enforcement* 1, no. 1: 162–197, doi: 10.1093/jaenfo/jns008, http://antitrust.oxfordjournals.org/content/1/1/162.full.

Digital Competition

Diane Coyle (2019), "Practical Competition Policy Tools for Digital Platforms," *Antitrust Law Journal* 82, no. 3.
Digital Competition Expert Panel (2019), "Unlocking Digital Competition," https://www.gov.uk/government/publications/unlocking-digital-competition-report-of-the-digital-competition-expert-panel.

Lina M. Khan (2017), "Amazon's Antitrust Paradox," *Yale Law Journal* 126, no. 3.

Joshua D. Wright, Elyse Dorsey, Jan Rybnicek, and Jonathan Klick (2018), "Requiem for a Paradox: The Dubious Rise and Inevitable Fall of Hipster Antitrust," George Mason Law & Economics Research Paper No. 18–29, http://dx.doi.org/10.2139/ssrn.3249524.

On Regulatory Policy

Andrei Shleifer (2010), "Efficient Regulation," NBER Working Paper No. 15651 (January), http://www.nber.org/papers/w15651.pdf.

Jean Tirole (2014), "Market Failures and Public Policy," Nobel Prize lecture, https://www.nobelprize.org/nobel_prizes/economic-sciences/laureates/2014/tirole-lecture.pdf.

On Specific Markets and Markets in General

Richard Green (2005), "Electricity and Markets," *Oxford Review of Economic Policy* 21, no. 1.

John McMillan (2002), *Reinventing the Bazaar*, W. W. Norton & Co.

Al Roth (2015), *Who Gets What and Why?*, William Collins.

Jean Tirole (2018), *Economics for the Common Good*, Princeton University Press, chapters 13, 14, and 16.

CHAPTER 3

The Government's Role in Production

As chapters 1 and 2 described, the modern state plays a significant role in the economy, in setting the framework of laws and regulations, including competition policy, and in terms of government expenditure on various forms of social security and welfare (covered in chapter 6). This chapter considers two forms of government intervention in producing economic output: public sector ownership and management of companies or whole sectors of activity; and industrial policies supporting certain kinds of private sector production. In the former case, the broad trend, although with differences between countries, has been for the nationalization of industries in the postwar period to give way to privatization of these state-owned industries from the 1980s, a practice pioneered in the UK. In the case of industrial policies, some countries have long implemented support for industry through a wide range of approaches. This has included promoting national champions in technology-based industries, such as computers or aerospace. In others, and in economics itself, industrial policy has been neglected since the deregulatory years of the 1980s but may now be reviving.

This chapter describes the history of nationalization and privatization, including the rationales for both, and the verdict on whether or not privatization—still continuing in many parts of the world—has succeeded in achieving its aims. The fact that a case can be made both ways underlines the existence of unavoidable dilemmas in some circumstances, namely, the existence of a natural monopoly due to characteristics such as high fixed costs (of investing in a rail or electricity network, for instance). Competition is hard to sustain in such sectors, which are therefore heavily regu-

lated even when privately owned; but there are also dilemmas about how best to regulate them. The chapter concludes by discussing the case for industrial policy in terms of the market failures it can address, despite the pitfalls experienced in some earlier versions, such as wasting taxpayers' money on national "champions" that turned out to be failures. As in so many areas of policy, good ideas to address market failures can fall victim to failures in government implementation.

Broadly speaking, the scope of government involvement in the economy has been on the increase over time, whether measured by the share of government spending relative to total economic output or by the size of the tax code and rule book. In one particular dimension, though, the pattern has been one of ebb and flow. The boundary between state and market in terms of the government's role in production activities has varied a good deal over time and between countries.

These tides have resulted from combined shifts in the prevailing political philosophy and developments in economic theory. In the 1930s, responding to the trauma of the Great Depression, the role of government expanded (including the first attempts to measure aggregate economic output). In 1936 Keynes published *The General Theory of Employment, Interest, and Money*, arguing for macroeconomic policies to manage aggregate demand and keep the level of employment high. Other economists advocated more highly planned economies, while some—notably Hayek—pushed in the other direction. The Second World War made this literally an academic discussion as all the combatant nations were forced to adopt far more central government direction of economic output to serve their war effort.

As noted in chapter 1, after the end of the war, the needs of reconstruction in the European countries and Japan, and people's demand for economic security after the successive disasters of the 1930s, led to a larger economic role for governments. In the UK, the 1945 general election led to a sweeping victory for the Labour party, which introduced the National Health Service and welfare state and also nationalized many major industries. In countries such as France and the Netherlands, economic planning bodies were established to deploy US funds provided through the Marshall Plan and to organize economic reconstruction. Only the United States, among the leading economies, did not see a wave of nationalization—and it had arguably seen more of a move toward government intervention earlier, as FDR's New Deal responded to the Depression. The economic crises of the 1970s brought more nationalizations, this time of struggling but important companies (even the US this time, with the formation of Amtrak and Conrail).

In the 1980s, the tide turned again, led by the UK. With an explicitly ideological determination to push back the state and create more space for the market, Margaret Thatcher's government set off a wave of privatizations of previously publicly owned corporations. It was an economic experiment subsequently followed by many other countries, and still continuing in some.

A critique of producer-driven, inefficient public services lacking any market or management discipline, and a new emphasis on the benefits of market forces, formed the intellectual basis for privatization. The political context of economic mismanagement and industrial unrest in the Britain of the 1970s, made worse by international events such as the end of the Bretton Woods arrangements and the OPEC oil crisis, helped popularize these economic ideas, which were actively advocated by conservative think tanks. Thatcher and Ronald Reagan used their electoral successes and forceful leadership to translate the ideas into policies curtailing the role of the state. Privatization of productive assets, such as steel and car producers, was one form this took. Another was the introduction of hybrid arrangements, such as the contracting out of public services to private businesses (confusingly sometimes also labeled as privatization) and various types of public-private partnerships.

The tide may now be turning once again: as in the 1930s, a great financial crisis and its aftermath have cast doubt on ideas about the efficacy of markets left to their own devices. Nationalization is back on the agenda for some left-of-center politicians. (Indeed, some countries had to nationalize banks during the financial crisis.) So too is bringing back into public provision some of the services contracted to the private sector, such as running prisons or building government IT systems.

Another way the role of the state is coming to the fore again is in the shape of industrial policy, meaning policies such as government funding of research, or tax breaks for start-ups, rather than direct public ownership of productive assets and companies. Industrial policy is now coming back into favor among economists for the first time in some decades, with recent economic thinking emphasizing the important coordination role of government when there are missing markets and asymmetric information, and also an important role for the production of public (knowledge) goods via investment in the science base.

This chapter links the theory and history of the shifting boundary of state and private production to specific market failures: public goods, natural monopolies, asymmetric information, and incomplete markets (assumptions A3, A4, A5, and A6 fail—see box 1.4).

The History of Nationalization and Privatization: The UK and Beyond

The nationalization of industry came in three waves, with substantial variation between countries, the US experience being significantly different. Apart from a few very early examples of publicly owned organizations (in postal services and telecommunications, initially state owned in all countries) the first wave occurred in the 1920s and 1930s, in response to the economic crisis of those interwar decades. Indeed, this occurred then in many of the industrialized nations. The next episode took place in the 1940s and 1950s, with wartime planning and the era of postwar planning. In the postwar years, governments around Europe believed in planning and extensive public ownership, while on the left many thought the "commanding heights" of the economy should be owned by the people. This period of nationalization also witnessed a substantial expansion of the welfare state and the introduction of wider access to education and health care (including the UK's totemic National

Health Service). Finally, in the 1970s and 1980s, in some countries came state rescues of important businesses ailing due to the oil crisis and broader economic crisis. In the UK, this included auto maker British Leyland and parts of the aircraft and shipbuilding sectors. By the late 1970s, public ownership and economic production was extensive (box 3.1). In France, the socialist government of François Mitterrand introduced a sweeping nationalization program in 1980–81, including electricity, steel, glassmaking, and many other sectors. Again there was variation between countries; for example, social democrat–dominated Sweden did not undertake any significant nationalizations until a banking crisis in the 1990s.

Box 3.1. Some major UK nationalizations (and privatizations)

Post office 1869 (privatized in 2013)
National telephone company 1912 (1984)
London Transport 1933 (buses only in 1994–95)
BOAC 1940 (became part of British Airways 1974, privatized 1987)
Bank of England 1946 (remains state owned)
Cable & Wireless 1946 (1981)
Coal 1947 (1994)
Railways 1948 (1994–97; track ownership renationalized 2001)
Electricity supply 1948 (1990 on)
Road freight (including Pickford's) 1948 (1982)
Thomas Cook 1948 (1972)
Steel 1949 (1988)
Docks, canals 1962 (1983 on)
Coach travel 1970 (1986–88)
Rolls Royce 1971 (1987)
Water supply and sewage 1973 (1989)
Cars—British Leyland 1975 (1986–88)
Aircraft and shipbuilding 1977 (1981 on)
Northern Rock, RBS, Lloyds, Bradford & Bingley 2008 (ongoing)

What Is a Natural Monopoly?

Chapter 2 introduced natural monopoly as a rationale for regulating some businesses because competition cannot successfully deliver economically efficient outcomes: the lowest total cost of production occurs when there is only one producer. The reason is the failure of assumption A3 (box 1.4), as there are substantial economies of scale. (Many, even most, businesses in modern economies enjoy some economies of scale, so "substantial" is a meaningful qualifier.) This section looks in more detail at why natural monopoly (box 3.2) might justify public ownership and operation of productive assets, such as an electricity or rail network.

Fixed costs are the most important reason for economies of scale. These mean average production costs are declining over the relevant range of output, and marginal cost—the cost of serving each additional customer—is less than average cost (refer to figure 2.8). This includes any sector with a network infrastructure, such as the traditional utilities—electricity and gas, water supply and sewage, telecommunications, and rail networks. It would not be desirable, in terms of costs, to have two sets of water pipes or rail tracks serving the same potential customers. The fixed costs mean one supplier can produce at lowest average cost. However, this alone is not a sufficient explanation for why governments have opted for state ownership at certain times in the past. Some countries have never nationalized these kinds of utilities, while other sectors with an extensive network infrastructure have always been privately owned—think of Google search, for instance, arguably a key infrastructure in life today, or mobile phone networks. Others have a hybrid existence, being privately owned but heavily subsidized and regulated. Private and public models co-exist for the same industry in different countries: the US postal service is publicly owned and the UK postal service has now been privatized, and both are competing now with many private operators.

So "natural" monopoly is not a wholly natural state. In addition to the existence of high fixed costs and increasing returns to scale, the operating environment and state of technology make a dif-

Box 3.2. Characteristics of natural monopolies

High fixed costs
Other large economies of scale in production
Economies of scale in consumption—network effects
No close substitutes (demand is price inelastic)
Barriers to entry high to insurmountable
Importance of scale makes geography, density of market relevant
Shaped by technology

ference as to whether or not an industry is considered a natural monopoly.

- *The size of the market*: A natural monopoly is less likely to exist in a large country with many urban areas and high population density than in a small rural one with low population density, for the range of declining marginal costs is likely to extend over less of a large-scale market than of a smaller one.
- *Whether the network infrastructure is old or new*: Networks have high *sunk costs*—that is, costs incurred up front and unable to be recovered because they have no other uses. This makes entry into old infrastructure industries harder because they have a big scale advantage. A new would-be competitor, even if a more efficient producer, would not be able to set a lower price (figure 3.1). There is a lock-in to the existing network. Competitive entry is more likely with new infrastructures.
- *The stage of the product life cycle or innovation*: As technology improves or the network deteriorates, incumbents have to make substantial new investments. New technologies can turn what was a natural monopoly on the basis of an existing technology and infrastructure into a potentially competitive market. Mobile phones had this effect on fixed-line telephone networks, and email on the postal service; and digital technology might yet disrupt the electricity sector or public transport networks.

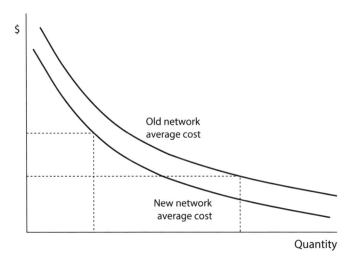

Figure 3.1. Comparison of old and new network infrastructure costs. The new producer is more efficient—its average costs are lower at every output level—but it cannot compete on price because of the scale of the incumbent.

Finally, many countries have thought it important at various times to protect "flagship" industries. These have been considered natural monopolies at some stages in their history. Flagship national airlines are a good example, now almost all privatized as the business model innovation of low-cost airlines revealed that what was considered a natural monopoly was not inevitably so after all, when the cost structure could be reconfigured. The idea that some industries are strategically important has also contributed to bailouts and nationalization of steel producers, car manufacturers, computer manufacturers, and others at various times and places.

In sum, it is not obvious how "natural" a monopoly is in an industry with high up-front fixed costs and declining average costs due to economies of scale, as contemplation of box 3.3 indicates.

National Technology Champions

By the 1960s many nationalized companies had become vehicles for an active industrial policy. They were a means of investing in

---

Box 3.3. Which of these are "natural" monopolies?

Electricity generation	Space exploration
Social media	Postal service
Car manufacturing	Roads
Broadband network	Airlines

---

new technologies in important economic sectors, and therefore seen as vehicles for delivering productivity growth, skills, jobs, and exports. In the UK, for instance, the National Economic Development Office ("Neddy") was set up in 1962 (by a Conservative government), along with the Department for Economic Affairs and the Ministry of Technology. The Labour government that succeeded it took up the intention with enthusiasm: in a famous speech a government minister, Tony Benn (later far more famous as a socialist firebrand), spoke of government's role in fanning the "white heat of technology."

One industry the UK singled out was computers, with the creation of a national champion in ICL, formed with government encouragement out of smaller predecessor companies and with the government holding a 10% stake. The UK had been a pioneer in developing programmable computers, not least because of the stellar efforts of Alan Turing, Bill Tutte, and the codebreakers at Bletchley Park during World War II, but its industry had fallen far behind the US by the 1960s. Much of the research had occurred in universities and the post office, while official secrecy prevented the Bletchley Park pioneers from even discussing their achievements, much less commercializing them. Other European countries also tried to establish national computer champions, such as Bull in France (nationalized by the Mitterrand government in 1982, re-privatized in 1994) and Olivetti in Italy (absorbed into Telecom Italia in 1999 as an office and technology services subsidiary after its initial success as a computer manufacturer in the 1960s–80s faded; now producing notebook computers). The US created its own computer industry out of its wartime efforts—particularly the mass of calculations required for the missile and atomic programs. It sustained the industry's success postwar through a more subtle industrial policy, not public ownership but rather financial support for academic and semi-academic research and for the innovations at and emerging out of RAND and Bell Labs, and a culture of enterprise.

In several countries, public ownership of electricity generators became the vehicle for new nuclear technologies. This was the case in both Britain and France, both nuclear innovators in the 1950s and 1960s. Aerospace was another industry where governments shaped the industry, including through ownership on the European side of the Atlantic (for instance, in the shape of supersonic flight via the British-French endeavor, Concorde, and later the French-German-British manufacturer Airbus), contrasting with less overt government support (through the defense budget and other government procurement) on the American side.

However, the 1970s were the high watermark of nationalization and direct government involvement in production. Privatization was on the horizon.

What Is Privatization?

The term *privatization* is used with somewhat different meanings. Most often it refers to the sale of publicly owned assets to private sector owners. Sometimes the term also encompasses the deregulation and breakup of monopoly power accompanying the asset ownership transfer. Sometimes it is a description of contracting some services previously run by public sector organizations from private sector businesses instead—this is done through various mechanisms, such as straightforward *contracting out* (awarding a service contract) or *public-private partnerships* (the public service rents the use of privately owned assets, with accompanying services). The important thing is to keep in mind three distinct issues: the ownership of assets, whether of businesses, such as a steel maker, or buildings or roads; the organization of the market, that is, whether it is competitive or not and how it is regulated; and the management responsibility for delivery of services. In this chapter privatization refers just to the sale of assets, and contracting out is used to describe the government buying services from private (or voluntary) organizations.

What Explains the Turn to Privatization?

Many of the nationalized companies failed to live up to expectations, no matter where they were. The state turned out not to be particularly good at managing large, complex companies, and these failures had become clear by the 1970s. Although in the UK a Conservative government (elected in 1970), then a Labour government (elected in 1973) intervened to support troubled heavy industries such as Rolls Royce, shipbuilding, computer firm ICL, and British Leyland to stop them temporarily from going out of business, these lame duck industries were not going to be able to waddle on for much longer. The cost to the taxpayer of supporting a failing business eventually becomes insupportable.

Even less troubled industries such as the phone company, British Telecom, had its problems. There were long waiting lists to get a phone line—it was not able to keep up with growing demand. The quality of customer service was poor and the industry highly unionized. Many nationalized firms (and public services in general—see also chapter 7) were being run more in the interest of their managers and employees than their customers, who had nowhere else to go. British Telecom also knew it needed to invest heavily in the new digital technology, but the government would not allow it to borrow to finance the investment.

By 1979 the output of the nationalized industries represented 10% of the British economy and 14% of capital investment—not out of line with many other OECD member countries. So they were significant in scale, but also characterized by poor productivity, low investment, and terrible industrial relations. Strikes were rife. The winter of 1978–79 in Britain is known as the Winter of Discontent, when many public sector workers went on strike, leading to power cuts, transport disruption, and garbage piling up in the streets. When Mrs. Thatcher won election in May 1979, conditions were ripe for a later widely imitated British policy innovation: privatization. The privatization of state-owned companies, putting the assets or shares in private hands through a means such as a stock market flotation, was not entirely new; the to-and-fro of British Steel's ownership was described earlier, and some other postwar nationalizations had been reversed, such as the travel agency Thomas Cook (brought into public ownership in 1948 and privatized in 1972). However, the Thatcher government breathed life into privatization, as well as coining the word. It was not a policy her party had been carefully planning, but the idea was timely given the sorry state of the UK economy at the start of the 1980s. The policy brought together the emerging Thatcherite economic philosophy of liberalization and free markets with the particularly dismal British experience of failed national champions.

Privatization was meant to achieve several different aims:

- Raise funds to reduce the government budget deficit.
- Make the enterprises more efficient by exposing them to competition and introducing the profit motive and the threat of takeover. The then Chancellor of the Exchequer, Nigel Lawson, summed it up: "There is no equivalent in the state sector to the discipline of the share price and the ever-present threat of bankruptcy."
- Reduce the power of unions (which the Conservative government believed had become far too powerful in general) and thus improve the quality of management and industrial relations.
- Serve customers better.
- Encourage more innovation, including by enabling the companies to borrow more or raise new capital.
- Spread individual share ownership. This was driven by political belief in the effect of asset ownership on individuals. Mrs. Thatcher said: "Through privatization—particularly the kind of privatization which leads to the widest possible share ownership by members of the public—the state's power is reduced and the power of the people enhanced."

How realistic were these aims? As discussed in chapter 2, both profit maximization and competition are required to achieve productive and allocative efficiency. Table 3.1 compares the likely out-

Table 3.1. Conditions for Productive and Allocative Efficiency

	Public monopoly	*Public competitor*	*Private monopoly*	*Private competitor*
	Network rail	*State airline*	*Cable TV in local market*	*Supermarket*
Bankruptcy possible?	X	X	√	√
Takeover possible?	X	X	?	√
Productive efficiency?	?	?	?	√
Competitive market?	X	√	X	√
Allocative efficiency?	X	√	X	√

comes for different *ownership* and *market structures*, illustrating that both are important in determining economic efficiency. Privatization in the sense of a transfer of ownership from public to private sector would not in itself be enough to deliver efficiency. It needs to be accompanied by a breakup of state monopolies to create competition in the market—and, as the electricity example in the last chapter illustrated, this is not straightforward in industries with natural monopoly characteristics. Indeed, this was part of the rationale for nationalizing some of these industries in the first place.

Regulating the Privatized Industries

The obvious problem with natural monopoly is that it is impossible to achieve both productive efficiency and allocative efficiency simultaneously. The lowest-cost production occurs when there is just one producer (although monopolies may not have an incentive to achieve the lowest possible cost, given the absence of anything disciplining the management—hence the question marks in the table). However, the competition needed to achieve allocative efficiency would make this lowest possible cost impossible to attain. So no "first best" outcome is possible. One possibility suggested by figure 3.2 as a response to this trade-off is to require the monopoly to produce at the perfectly competitive level of output but then either

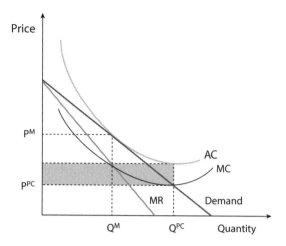

Figure 3.2. The "second best" approach to monopoly.

allow it to charge the price determined by its average cost at that level of production or subsidize the monopoly to offset the losses it would make by setting price equal to marginal cost at that level of output, the shaded amount in figure 3.2 (similar to figure 2.8). This "second best" approach is difficult to apply in practice, though, as regulators rarely have enough information about supply and demand curves to implement it.

In practice, therefore, special regulation was introduced alongside the privatization of the utilities, with essentially just two choices.

One approach to regulation is to limit the price, or the price increases, the company can charge. This price cap approach was the choice the UK's regulators initially made, and it is known as RPI-X regulation—the requirement to keep price increases X% below the general price index (the retail prices index, or RPI, in the UK at the time). For example, for the newly privatized British Telecom, X was 3%, then 4.5%, then 7.5%. If prices are allowed to rise at RPI-X, the industry will be able to maintain normal profits providing it achieves productivity growth of X%. If it does better (worse) on productivity, the formula implies supernormal (subnormal) profits. Setting X at the right level is the challenge for the regulator, embodying their best estimate of likely productivity growth.

Table 3.2. Pros and Cons of Alternative Forms of Natural Monopoly Regulation

RPI-X price cap	Cap on rate of return
Pros	*Pros*
Strong incentives for cost reduction, productivity improvement, and innovation	Prices stay in line with costs Greater assurance of high quality
Cons	*Cons*
Quality of service may suffer Prices exceed costs on average	Possible excessive investment Weak incentives for productivity improvement
Use when	*Use when*
Regulator doesn't know costs Quality can be monitored	Regulator can't monitor quality New investment is needed

The other choice is to cap the rate of return or profit earned by the company. This is used more in the United States, for example, in the regulation of electricity utilities. This reduces the firm's incentive to cut costs or increase productivity, but it is more likely to ensure that the investment needed in the network will go ahead because there is a more-or-less guaranteed return, and this in turn makes it relatively straightforward to raise capital to finance investment. The regulatory challenge is setting the permitted rate of return at the right level, which ought to be the reward the capital market needs to provide finance for investment. Set it too high, and the regulated firms will over-invest (known as *gold plating*), and vice versa.

The key arguments for the two options are set out in table 3.2. Which is better therefore depends on the context, and in particular on the nature of the information asymmetries between the regulator and the regulated firm—for the firm will always know more about its business conditions than an external regulator.

If the regulator does not know enough about the cost structure of the business, it is better to choose the method that incentivizes cost reduction, that is, price regulation. If it is hard to monitor the quality of the service, or investment in new capacity or technology is needed, rate of return regulation is better.

The conditions may change over time, especially with regard to investment need. So not only might it be necessary to vary X or the rate of return cap, it might sometimes be desirable to switch frameworks. Over time, the realization dawned on regulators that there were inherent trade-offs in the complex businesses they were responsible for overseeing while never being able to access the same information as the managers. The amount of regulatory detail and intrusion into management decision-making has increased over time, particularly in essential utilities like electricity. These sectors will always be politically sensitive even when wholly privately owned and run.

A recent attempt to escape from the horns of the regulatory dilemma involves defining the value of what is known as the *regulatory asset base* (RAB) of the business—the assets it requires to provide the essential utility in question (for example, the power stations and transmission lines for an electricity generating company). The RAB consists of the existing value of the assets, their depreciation (due to wear and tear or obsolescence), and the necessary investment to upgrade the infrastructure. This figure, it is argued, allows the RPI-X formula to be set more precisely in a way that does not discourage necessary investment in the network.

Regardless of the complexities of regulating the privatized natural monopolies, many of them unforeseen at the time, a great wave of privatization swept around the world following the British example. The US started with far fewer publicly owned organizations in the first place. Other European countries have privatized much of their industrial base, though; for example, France (table 3.3), Germany, Finland, and Italy. A range of sectors has been involved, from telecommunications and heavy industry such as steel or oil to banks and utilities. A peak in privatization sales occurred around 2000, with ups and downs over time depending partly on the stock market (and therefore the price the government was likely to get for the shares). However, the wave is continuing: in January 2018 the French government was considering plans to sell all or part of its ownership stakes in eighty-one companies, ranging from airports (Aéroports de Paris) to the state gambling company, Française des Jeux. Recently, the OECD has noted an upturn in privatization

Table 3.3. Some Major French Privatizations

Company	Sector
Saint-Gobain (1986)	Materials
Paribas (1987), merged with BNP to become BNP Paribas	Banking
Compagnie Générale d'Electricité (1987), became Alcatel	Telecoms equipment
TF1 (1987)	TV channel
Elf Aquitaine (1994), now part of Total	Oil
SEITA (1995), now Altadis	Tobacco and cigarettes
Renault (1996); 85% sold	Auto manufacture
France Telecom (1998), now Orange (state retains 27%)	Telecoms
Air France (1999); 84% sold, now merged with KLM	Airline
Electricité de France; 30% stake sold (2005)	Electricity

revenues once again, as governments seek some relief for budgets under pressure since the financial crisis; 2015 marked the high point for European privatization proceeds, with France, UK, Sweden, Greece, Germany, and Italy all making significant disposals of state-owned assets (figure 3.3).

It is not only the richest economies that have been privatizing state-owned businesses. The former communist economies of Central and Eastern Europe and the former Soviet Union privatized many companies after 1981 in a mass privatization process, undoubtedly paving the way for former state-owned enterprises to be managed more efficiently but also in some cases creating a rich new elite through a somewhat chaotic process. Following advice from bodies like the World Bank and International Monetary Fund, many low-income economies have also followed suit. In their case, there was also often little doubt about the poor quality of management in the public sector, and key utilities have long been notoriously inefficient. However, the same countries also often lack the regulatory experience to be able to ensure the markets are subsequently competitive. Even so, the process has become a standard policy

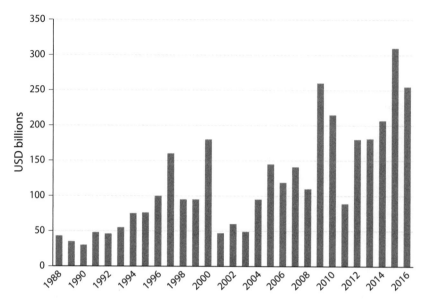

Figure 3.3. Global privatization revenues, in US dollars (billions). *Source:* OECD, Privatization Barometer, https://www.oecd.org/daf/ca/Privatisation-and-the -Broadening-of-Ownership-of-SOEs-Stocktaking-of-National-Practices.pdf.

globally, with a number of countries from Kazakhstan to Japan, Czechia to Turkey (box 3.4), explicitly doing so in order to improve the structure of the market and economic efficiency.

Has Privatization Been a Success?

The verdict on the success of the privatization wave is mixed.

Consider the experience of the pioneer, the UK. Measured productivity improved quickly in many of the privatized businesses, thanks to early workforce reductions. Since 1980 employment in the UK's steel industry has fallen by more than 75% (and is still falling), in railways by two-thirds, in electricity by half, and in water by almost as much. The asset sales made possible extensive closures of high-cost production facilities. Figure 3.4 shows that in the first decade and a half the UK's utilities narrowed much of their previous labor productivity gap as compared with the US, France, and Ger-

Events may have acted as triggers where the nationalizations (and later privatizations) occurred, but political tactics and ideology have always played an important part. Right-wing politicians largely do not think state ownership is an efficient way to organize the economy, whereas left-wing ones are more likely to support it. In some cases, these beliefs were put successively into practice in a damaging policy see-saw. In the UK, for instance, British Steel was nationalized in 1951, privatized in 1953, renationalized by Labour in 1967, and reprivatized by the Conservatives in 1988. It has remained in private hands ever since, shrunk, and some parts of the formerly giant corporation sold to other owners. But this example also shows that it can be hard for any government to keep their distance when major employers and exporters are in trouble: the most recent owner of the successor steel company has been Tata, the Indian conglomerate. When it announced its intention in 2016 to close two major UK steelworks, the Conservative government in power at the time felt compelled to intervene to try to ensure the survival of those plants and jobs. Even the US government intervenes in emergencies: in 1981, for example, it formed Resolution Trust Corporation to take over the wave of failing savings and loans. Many Western governments had to nationalize or take majority stakes in some banks in 2008–09.

Yet for all that political beliefs have played a key part in determining the state's role as a producer, there is also an economic rationale for public ownership or provision in some circumstances. The existence of natural monopolies—as chapter 2 discussed—is one justification: it may prove impossible to establish competition in the market. The private sector is also unlikely to serve important social aims, such as universal service for key utilities, as some customers cannot be served profitably. State ownership of these utilities, such that they did not have to be profit maximizing or serve shareholders, is a reasonable alternative to the complex regulatory regimes—including license conditions, such as universal service provision—that are otherwise needed. Publicly owned corporations have also often played an important role in developing new technologies in the past, when they acted as a vehicle for industrial policy—an issue the final section of this chapter picks up again.

Box 3.4. Privatization in Turkey

Turkey undertook a larger number of privatizations (fifty-four individual transactions) than any other OECD member country in the period 2010–15. The sales included electricity generation and distribution companies, the national telecoms operator, petrochemicals, a bank, and ports. The law states three aims: reducing the role of the state to improve competition in the economy, raising funds, and improving the efficiency of the capital markets. However, contributing to the government's finances has been an important motivation. Selling 55% of the shares in Türk Telekom to the Lebanese-owned Oger Telecom in 2005 was an important symbolic move. This was at the time the largest-ever foreign direct investment transaction into Turkey ($6.55 billion USD). The idea was to bring in a private partner before the company's stock market listing to enhance productivity and service quality, and therefore increase the revenues that could be raised through the subsequent IPO. This sale created close to 30,000 new domestic retail investors in Türk Telekom, while the government continues to own 31.68% of the shares.

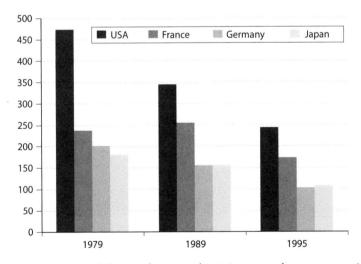

Figure 3.4. Comparative labor productivity: electricity, gas, and water sectors, 1979–95 (other countries shown relative to UK = 100). *Source*: Provided by Nick Crafts.

many (and the latter two countries also caught up somewhat on the US productivity lead).

However, large-scale job reductions can lead to compromises on safety and maintenance when the privatized firm is incentivized to cut costs. One example is in the rail industry, where the fatal Hatfield train crash of 2000 in the UK prompted the renationalization of the track operator, as reduced maintenance of the track to save money was one of the contributory causes. Similarly, Amtrak in the United States, a quasi-public company under great financial pressure, has experienced a series of accidents blamed on under-spending on maintenance. While there is little doubt many utilities were overstaffed before privatization, publicly owned utilities may be able to employ more people for maintenance and safety because of the absence of a hard budget constraint.

The job losses decimated the powerful public sector unions in the UK, achieving a key political aim of the Thatcher government. However, it is not clear that management quality improved as much as hoped. Public sector managers became private sector managers who were paid much more—often the same people in the same positions. Many were distracted by the temptation of being able to take over other companies, and they undertook a series of ill-judged acquisitions followed by write-downs and disposals. It is more glamorous to spend time closeted in boardrooms planning takeovers with investment bankers, or jumping on planes to distant cities, rather than supervising sewer replacement programs. But neither customers nor shareholders benefited. Market discipline did not improve management quality. The stock market performance of privatized businesses has fallen short of market averages by a substantial margin.

Customers have probably on balance gained from privatization. Customer service improved compared with the bad old days, although perhaps it would have improved anyway. An index of prices of privatized UK goods and services since 1980 has tracked the movement of prices generally. Labor costs in the industries have fallen, often substantially. But capital and other costs have risen. There have also been special factors in each case. For instance, technology has reduced the price of telecoms equipment, and the arrival of mobile telecommunications introduced competition in that market. Electricity and gas prices have fallen somewhat, but rail and bus fares have risen. Fears that privatization would lead to a loss of universal service or to increases in charges for poor households have proved largely unfounded—although, as discussed below, the absence of competition in utility markets has caused concern about whether customers are really getting a good deal.

In terms of their contribution to the government budget, from 1979 to 1997 privatization receipts in the UK averaged less than 2% of government revenue. It was a small contribution even at the height of the wave of sales. In addition to being small, the sale of assets that can (in principle) generate a continuing return for the sake of one-off revenue is a short-term approach to solving the government's budget challenges. The former (rather patrician) Conservative prime minister Harold Macmillan criticized his successor, Margaret Thatcher, for "selling off the family silver."

The excitement of the stock market flotations in the 1980s, accompanied by glossy advertising campaigns, did expand individual share ownership in the UK to start with. But most share certificates subsequently drifted into the hands of the insurance companies and pension funds that own shares in other British companies. There is now no big difference between the structure of share ownership of ex-nationalized companies and others. So although popular at the time—for instance, over 90% of British Telecom's eligible employees took advantage of their ability to buy its shares, to the chagrin of trade union leaders—the effect was not lasting. In the general population, the proportion of individual share ownership is just 12%, and big investment institutions continue to own most of the shares. In recent privatizations, many sales have taken the form of direct sales to other companies or to managers or private equity companies, rather than to individual shareholders.

Even those companies that seemed at first to be the clear successes of British privatization—British Steel, British Telecom, British Airways, and Cable & Wireless—were ultimately to be disappointments in various ways. British Steel—subsequently Corus, then Tata—became one of the best-managed and lowest-cost steel producers in the world, but that has not been enough for viability in a world awash with low-price steel, and it is under threat of shrinkage, sale, or closure. British Telecom (now BT) still has important market power (through its broadband subsidiary Openreach) and the mobile market has also grown increasingly concentrated, so although service quality without question improved and the technology of telecoms has been transformed, there remain concerns about competition in this sector (box 3.5). British Airways raced ahead of other European airlines at first by concentrating on cost control, marketing, and, above all, customer service, but it too is struggling (as are many former national carrier airlines) in a highly competitive environment, and has been merged into International Airlines Group. John Kay summed up the key problem: "All privatised companies start from behind. If you were setting out to establish a successful private sector business, you would not begin with a water or electricity board or a government department. You might well do better to start with nothing at all: Vodafone, which began operations at the same time as BT was privatized, is now bigger, more efficient, the quality of its management more highly regarded."

Box 3.5. The British Telecom experience

By the end of the 1970s, there were long waiting lists to get a telephone line. The state-owned post office, which provided the service, needed to invest in modernizing the system to adopt digital technology, but was not allowed to do so because in state ownership this would add to the government borrowing requirement.

The British Telecommunications Act of 1981, prior to privatization, provided for the removal of British Telecom (now BT) from the control of the post office. It also allowed other operators to run telecommunication systems, ending the monopoly that had existed since the nationalization of the industry in 1912. BT continued to have an obligation for universal provision across the UK and to retain unprofitable activities such as the 999 emergency service number.

(continued on next page)

(*continued from previous page*)

Its flotation raised £4 billion in the first stage, and £5 billion each from two subsequent stages in 1991 and 1993. Even the first tranche was six times bigger than any previous stock exchange flotation. But it was over-subscribed, and 96% of its workforce bought shares.

The six-month wait for a line quickly fell to less than two weeks. But the number of people waiting had already fallen from 122,000 in 1981 to 2,000 in 1984. Measures of the quality of service (such as time taken to repair faults) dropped sharply. The labor force fell from 238,000 to 125,000 in 1999, so measured labor productivity increased rapidly. Union influence declined, while management pay rose. Spending on investment rose by over a third; £15 billion was invested between 1984 and 1991, with the trunk network and many exchanges digitized within a few years.

The company's profits rose immensely—hence the adjustments to the RPI-X formula, with X steadily increasing. Call charges paid by customers declined—from 1984 to 1991 prices fell 20% in real terms—but they had already been falling and continued to decline in other countries where there was no change of ownership.

All in all, BT is considered to be one of the most successful privatizations—but the assessment depends on the counterfactual. Competition was slow to start in the market, and when it did it was thanks to technological change and the rapid spread of mobile telephony. In Openreach, the natural monopoly of the main trunk network, BT retains monopoly power; and it has been subject to continual complaints about abuse of its market power from its competitors. The prices BT can charge them for interconnection are regulated, but competitors claim slow and poor quality service put them at a disadvantage in the market. What's more, most of BT's profit comes from its Openreach business.

Meanwhile, the mobile telephony market in the UK, which was initially an effective source of competition for BT, has itself become increasingly concentrated through successive mergers. In fact, BT itself bought the large mobile provider EE in 2016, EE itself having acquired Orange in 2010.

To sum up the experience, within a relatively short time the British industries that were once publicly owned had split more or less completely into two groups. One group has been wholly absorbed into the private sector, operating in competitive markets, and either thriving or failing in the same way as any other business. Many of them, as just noted, failed because they found themselves in a highly competitive global environment. The other group consists of those services that are natural monopolies, central to the national economic infrastructure.

The Inescapable Dilemma of Natural Monopoly

The inventor of the RPI-X formula, economist Stephen Littlechild, saw regulation of the newly privatized businesses as a stopgap until competition could be introduced into the market, writing: "Competition is indisputably the most effective—perhaps the only effective means—of protecting consumers against monopoly power. Regulation is essentially the means of preventing the worst excesses of monopoly; it is not a substitute for competition. It is a means of 'holding the fort' until competition comes." However, regulation of the natural monopoly network industries has increased steadily in scope because competition has been impossible to create or sustain. Although owned by the private sector (or in some cases overseas publicly owned enterprises), these sectors remain completely intertwined with government and are highly, in fact increasingly, regulated.

The combination of managerial freedom and hard budget constraints—the knowledge that government was genuinely willing to allow these companies to fail—transformed the culture of businesses being prepared for privatization. However, it is not the *ownership* of the business assets alone that determines how effectively they deliver economic efficiency but also the absence or presence of competition—and the effectiveness of regulation in the context of natural monopoly when competition cannot take root.

It also became clearer over time that privatization did not necessarily mean political disengagement. Although the Conservative governments in the UK from 1979 to 1997 had an ideological commitment to take the state out of business, this was not the case with later governments. What's more, all politicians find it hard to resist interfering in businesses that are vital to consumers and where the necessity of regulation gives them an obvious channel for interference. All the privatized utilities have suffered far too much political interference in operational matters—which was exactly the problem they faced when in public ownership too. Again, it is not the ownership of the assets that matters, but the governance and the relationship with elected politicians.

Natural monopolies, whether state- or privately owned, will always have public service obligations that can override economic efficiency. They will always require regulation. Politicians will always care about how these businesses are performing, the quality of the service they provide, and the prices they charge for essential services. The model of a listed corporation has not worked especially well for natural monopoly businesses, and in several cases—such as rail and water in the UK—it may be currently unwinding.

There are several reasons for this:

- The private ownership structures—whether listed companies or private equity owners—lack legitimacy. In a regulated market economy, authority in economic matters comes either from success in a competitive market or from accountability to a political process. Private companies that are monopoly providers of public services have neither.
- It is unclear what happens if private utility provision fails. Obligations to shareholders and rules of administration do not sit well with urgent public interest, such as clean water or keeping the lights on.
- The cost of capital for a private sector corporation is often too high for a regulated utility. Some privatized companies are ring-fencing their regulated businesses because they cannot be operated under the same financial business model as competitive businesses. Governments can borrow more cheaply than corporations, so the financial case for public ownership of utilities is fairly compelling.
- Negotiations between managers, who are responsible to shareholders or investors, and regulators, who are accountable to

---

Box 3.6. New natural monopolies?

There is an active debate about the extent to which some large digital platforms are in effect natural monopolies requiring tougher regulation. The platforms concerned are sometimes referred to as GAFAM: Google, Amazon, Facebook, Apple, and Microsoft. Those arguing that they should face the same kind of regulation of prices and service quality as an electricity or water utility point out how concentrated these digital markets have become. For instance, more than two-thirds of online advertising revenue globally goes to Google and Facebook. A combination of conventional increasing returns to scale and also, importantly, network effects explain how digital markets can become so concentrated. For instance, a social media network is far more useful to me the more other members it already has. However, the claim that regulation of the digital platforms is needed is vigorously contested. Others point out that the current dominant platforms could be dethroned, just as they took over the top slot from an earlier generation of companies—Google from Yahoo, Facebook from MySpace.

---

politicians and voters, often go badly. Governance matters, and in the case of some utilities voters evidently feel the balance has tilted too far toward financial returns and away from the public interest.

There is debate now as to whether some new businesses ought to be regulated as if they were utilities, so important have the services become to modern economies (box 3.6). The same old dilemmas have taken on a new form.

The Future of Public Ownership

John Kay observes: "Nationalisation of utilities, although not a successful policy, was not adopted through sheer perversity. The issues which led to it have not gone away."

Similar issues recur when it comes to contracting out government services, as discussed in chapter 7. Yet the policy of privatizing the productive assets of state-owned companies is coming increasingly under question in the UK, which pioneered the post-1980 wave.

Opinion polls reveal majorities in favor of renationalizing key network industries, such as rail and water. There have been scathing news stories about the financial extraction of wealth from the utilities and failure to invest in the future of the networks. Regulated natural monopoly sectors, such as electricity and parts of the telecoms industry, are seeing increasing political interest in the prices they set and the detail of how they are regulated, due to concerns about prices or service.

This reappraisal in the public debate comes at a time when the tide in economic ideas has decisively turned away from "free" markets and the withdrawal of the state to an appreciation of the importance of the government's role not only in ensuring markets work well but also in engaging more actively in economic production.

Industrial Strategy Redux

One area of policy where this shift is clear is in a new appreciation of the role of industrial policy or strategy. Earlier, this chapter noted that many of the UK's national high-tech champions of the 1960s and 1970s ultimately failed. That experience scarred British politicians and officials, leaving a lasting dislike for "picking winners," given how much they had ended up "backing losers" instead. This was a contrast to some other European countries where there has been a consistent consensus about the need for a strategic role for the state in economic production. It was also a contrast to East Asia, where several countries adopted explicit export-oriented industrial policies, often aiming to reach the technological frontier or gain a lead in important new technologies. It was even a contrast to the US, where "industrial policy" is never discussed but—as described below—where most administrations have been extremely strategic about the government's role in promoting key industries.

The balance of opinion in economics about industrial policy has been shifting, despite the plentiful evidence of government mistakes in the past in supporting doomed national champions or white elephant investments. While few think the state should own and operate as much of the economy as in the past, there is increasing recognition that private businesses alone cannot invest in all complex and uncertain new technologies, or coordinate around new products. Sometimes the private sector can do so, and often does. Schumpeter's creative destruction has proved its effectiveness again and again. However, many of the innovations at the technological frontier today require vast investment in basic research, and may require significant coordination over such things as technical standards, the legal and regulatory framework, the need to serve markets where the government is itself a big customer, or markets where there are significant externalities, such as the environment (box 3.7) or health care. Governments have a vital strategic and coordinating role. Many have always thought so, including the East Asian economies

---

Box 3.7. The case for green industrial policies

Most economists think technological advances in several areas will be essential if the world is to limit CO_2 emissions by enough to limit the rise in global temperatures. While economists have largely been skeptical about industrial policies due to the evidence that many interventions in the past have not been well targeted or effective, policies to encourage green technologies are now thought by many to be essential. Dani Rodrik argues that public support for these technologies is needed because there are significant externalities that private investors would not be able capture or monetize; because the risks are far greater than the private sector would take despite the high social returns; and because carbon is under-priced, further reducing the potential private return. He notes that several countries—China, Germany, India, and the US—have significant green growth programs offering different kinds of support to firms developing relevant technologies. One example is China's multi-billion-yuan program that has made it a global leader in photovoltaics (PV) (see table), bringing down the price of solar generation for every country to which it exports.

(continued on next page)

(continued from previous page)

Annual PV Production by Country, 1995–2010

Year	China	Taiwan	Japan	Ger-many	US	Others	World
2005	128	88	833	339	153	241	1,782
2006	342	170	926	469	178	374	2,459
2007	889	387	938	777	269	542	3,801
2008	2,038	813	1,268	1,399	401	1,207	7,126
2009	4,218	1,411	1,503	1,496	580	2,107	11,315
2010	10,852	3,639	2,169	2,022	1,115	4,248	24,047

Source: Deutch and Steinfeld (2013). *Note*: Values in megawatts.

Rodrik concludes that there are bound to be some failures in industrial policy as the government is not omniscient about the future, so the real challenge for policymakers is to be able to monitor progress and quickly pull the plug on failures. This was the key to success in countries such as South Korea, for instance, whose government ruthlesslessly ended subsidies to companies failing to meet their export targets. The use of professional agencies, removed from day-to-day politics, is also important, and here the US's DARPA is the poster child for a professional, competent funder of research.

Dani Rodrik (2014), "Green Industrial Policy," *Oxford Review of Economic Policy* 30, no. 3 (October): 469–491.

and China. Some, including many European countries and the US, have always had industrial policies even if they did not describe them as such. Now the bastions of "free market" economics—the UK and some of the international agencies—are also beginning to recognize the merit of industrial policies; the UK's Conservative government published an explicit industrial strategy in 2017. Here again is an example of the links between events, politics, and economic thought.

Aims of Industrial Policy

When governments adopt an industrial strategy or policy, what problem are they trying to solve that cannot be left to the market? There are several potential market failures.

- New technologies might be too uncertain for private investors to support unless they are sure the state will back them: public investment can "crowd in" private investment when there is a lot of risk (assumption A6 [see box 1.4] fails as there are missing markets for future goods and services)
- There might be other missing markets, such as lending to start-up businesses, because of information asymmetries: potential investors do not know as much as the entrepreneurs how promising a new technology or business is (assumption A4 fails).
- Growing markets to minimum efficient scale may not be feasible when there are economies of scale because of high fixed costs (assumption A3 fails)
- Provision of skills and know-how, or creation of technical standards, needs coordinating, and only government has this convening power (there are externalities in the choices businesses make about such matters; assumption A5 fails).
- The private sector will underinvest in the provision of a key public good, basic knowledge via research, because of the free riding phenomenon (assumption A8 fails).

Some of these market failures may be becoming more acute in the advanced economies. For example, there are large fixed costs and thus economies of scale in the digital sector (as the marginal cost of selling an extra piece of software or adding an extra user of a platform may be close to zero). Only the US had market-dominating digital companies initially, but China has now grown its own competitors thanks to a combination of both its large domestic market and strong encouragement from the government for national success stories. The role of know-how is also important in advanced technologies—the kind of knowledge that is not easy to write down or learn from reading, but needs face-to-face contact and an environment conducive to the exploration of ideas. Governments are key players in creating clusters of high-tech excellence, often around universities or research institutes, by funding basic and applied research. The features of the most technologically advanced economies are leading some economists to argue for a renewed emphasis on industrial policies.

Industrial policy does not, however, have a settled definition or rest on a specific economic theory. Many of the ways the government affects the economy influence business decisions to innovate or invest. The range of policy options is wide, including

- Tax breaks, subsidies, grants
- Training through funding of apprenticeships and education
- Government funded R&D, including basic research
- Purchase guarantees through government procurement policies
- Financial guarantees so start-ups can get bank loans or private investment
- Advice/support services
- Export credit guarantees
- Investment in infrastructure

Hence there are many potential tools of industrial policy short of public ownership and management. But it is not a formal industrial strategy or policy unless it is intentional, with attention paid to which industries serve an important social need (such as reducing CO_2 emissions or addressing the challenge of caring for an aging population), lead at the frontier of a new technology (such as AI or autonomous vehicles), or build on one of the country's sources of historical national comparative advantage. Conversely, when these tools are used without a purposeful strategy in mind, they are quite likely to be wasting taxpayers' money.

The UK, like many other countries, has used a mix of all these types of policies in an ad hoc way. Sometimes they have amounted to an industrial policy for a specific sector despite never being described as such. One example is pharmaceuticals. The government helps the sector through funding basic medical research, and is a big purchaser of its products through the National Health Service. In 2013 the UK introduced a tax break called the patent box, which sharply reduced the rate of corporation tax on income derived from patents; this policy is applied in several other European countries too. In Britain, it has almost entirely favored the pharmaceuticals sector, and was at the time aimed at stopping big pharma companies from relocating research jobs overseas. Another beneficiary of Britain's accidental industrial policy has been the finance sector, favored by deregulation and substantial investment in infrastructure (light rail and an airport) serving the City of London and Canary Wharf, London's financial districts.

Unfortunately, when the country did have an explicit industrial policy, it often went wrong. For instance, Britain pioneered commercial nuclear power. But it chose a reactor type (AGRs) no other country selected, so it could not take advantage of exporting supplies or know-how to other countries. When recommissioning reactors in 1978, the government made things worse by commissioning two more AGRs but saying it would later switch to the light water reactors in widespread use in the US and elsewhere. This created immense technological uncertainty in the industry. And this is just one example of government policy failure. Some of the errors were more embarrassing, such as the $100 million-plus investment in John DeLorean's eponymous car, a futuristic vehicle only ever used in the movie *Back to the Future*, and whose founder was eventually arrested by the FBI on charges relating to illegal drugs (he was later acquitted). The original DeLorean Company went bankrupt in 1982. Britain's main industrial policy on the face of things therefore seemed to be bailing out important but struggling companies, or backing no-hopers, doomed ultimately to fail.

By contrast, other European countries have remained committed to industrial policies, although these have changed shape over time. In France, for example, the postwar sector-based support for important industries such as auto manufacture and leading technological sectors such as nuclear power, aeronautics, and telecommunications has evolved into a more "horizontal" policy of support for innovation in general. As noted above, France was an enthusiastic privatizer of former public monopolies; the focus of government policy has switched to encouraging research and enterprise, often in specially created locations, *pôles de compétitivité*. France also created a new National Research Agency (ANR) modeled on the National Science Foundation in the US. Japan is another country noted for the role an explicit industrial policy played in its postwar success (box 3.8).

The United States also offers an example of a highly successful industrial policy, although it is hardly ever discussed in those terms. Through two mechanisms—the funding of basic research in technology and medicine and the defense research and procurement budget—the US has ensured that its businesses are world leaders in some fundamental technologies, such as genetics, digital technology,

---

Box 3.8. Industrial policy in Japan

Since the Second World War, Japan's governments have implemented an explicit industrial policy through central agencies, including the well-known Ministry of International Trade and Industry (MITI) (replaced since 2001 by the Ministry of Economy, Trade, and Industry). After Japan's wartime defeat, GDP was about half the prewar level, and under its US occupiers Japan had a planned economy. The transition to a market economy began in 1949 but with a set of policies intended to enable the country to succeed in new industries, particularly through exporting. These included loans for exporters, tax relief for investing in new equipment, and subsidies for research and development. For more than two decades the economy grew rapidly, particularly in strategic sectors such as computers and autos, and Japanese exporters were highly successful. The country had almost caught up in terms of productivity with the United States. The 1980s brought intense criticism of Japan's policies from the US, however, due to the large Japanese trade surplus. Subsequently, the 1991 collapse of a massive asset bubble was followed by a long period of slow or no growth. Industrial policy shifted in this later period to emphasizing "structural" economic reforms to liberalize finance and employment, and a focus on supporting industrial clusters to enable regional growth. Yet although the content of the poli-

---

(continued on next page)

(*continued from previous page*)

cies has changed significantly over time in response to changes in the economy, successive Japanese governments have shared a commitment to having an industrial policy.

Gheary-Khamis dollars, 1990

Per capita GDP, United States vs. Japan. *Source*: Maddison Project Database.

and robotics. For instance, US military–funded research created much of the basic structure of the internet and the global positioning system (GPS); the whole world now benefits, but after American companies got an unbeatable lead. Mariana Mazzucato has emphasized the importance of US government support for the success of big American tech companies, such as Apple (figure 3.5), alongside private enterprise. More recently, funding from the National Institutes of Health has helped lead to fundamental genetic discoveries and a thriving commercial biotech sector. The state and the market delivered these innovations together.

Just as with other types of state intervention, such as nationalization and privatization, both theory and practice of industrial policy

What Makes the iPhone so Smart?

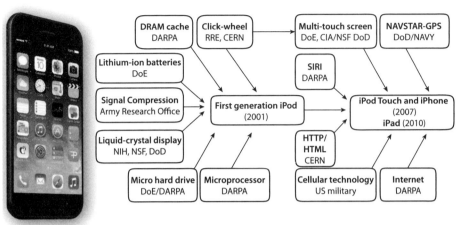

Figure 3.5. Contributions of government-funded research to flagship Apple products. *Source*: Mariana Mazzucato, *The Entrepreneurial State*.

have seen ebbs and flows. This is another of the many areas of economic policy where there is no boundary that either is right for all time or does not involve political or social judgments, as there are both pros and cons (table 3.4).

Accepting that there are significant market failures industrial policy could and should address, how can past government failures be avoided? Apart from some obvious safeguards such as bringing required skills into government (technological know-how, procurement skills), two principles are key.

One is to ensure competition law rules out state support for big businesses except in clearly defined circumstances; in Europe, the EU enforces this through its State Aid rules. Government financial support for a company should be offered on similar terms to a commercial loan, for example. This kind of policy would have prevented British governments in the 1970s from throwing taxpayers' money away on badly managed, unproductive companies operating in industries in which the country could not compete internationally. Competition policy must also ensure it is always possible for new, private firms to enter a market and grow, if they have an even better new technology, say. They need to be able to out-compete their

Table 3.4. Pros and Cons of Industrial Policy

Arguments in favor	Arguments against
The state has always been involved in significant new technologies because of the uncertainties and co-ordination needed (e.g., in setting technical standards)	Many new technologies are brought to market without government help
Governments have to fund basic research, key skills; private sector will under-provide public goods. There are significant missing markets, information gaps, and public goods	Governments will waste money on ideas that don't lead to practical innovations, or on failing businesses
The government influences the economy in many ways—why not ensure they serve strategic aims or at least are joined up?	There are too many examples of government incompetence in past industrial policies; officials don't know better than entrepreneurs

government-backed rivals if they have a better technology or more productive way of making something.

The second principle is to focus industrial policy mainly on the provision of public goods (research, education and training, infrastructure) and on the coordinating role of government. In other words, the policy should address the specific market failures of under-provision of public goods, such as basic research, information asymmetries, and incomplete markets as in the case of new products. Although sometimes a tax break or subsidy might be the right policy choice, when there is money on the table, businesses will get diverted into trying to lobby for it at the expense of other bidders; but innovation and growth in the economy is more likely to come about from the alignment of everyone's efforts, in both public and private sectors, around common aims.

Conclusion

This chapter has described the ebb and flow in the role of governments in production, either through the ownership and management of certain industries, through the regulation of key sectors—the utilities that are natural monopolies—when they are in private ownership, and through policies to encourage innovation and the growth of industries that are technology leaders or believed to be fundamental to the nation for strategic or other reasons. When theory and practice vary so much over time and across countries, it is a clear sign that there are unavoidable dilemmas or trade-offs, and no policy solutions that will be right for every time and place.

Further Reading

Technical Follow-Up

J.-J. Laffont and J. Tirole (1993), *A Theory of Incentives in Procurement and Regulation*, MIT Press.

J. Sutton, (2007), "Market Structure: Theory and Evidence," chapter 35 in *Handbook of Industrial Organization, Volume 3*, eds. M. Armstrong and R. Porter, North-Holland.

Classics

Alfred Kahn (1970), *The Economics of Regulation: Volume 1—Economic Principles*, John Wiley.

Martin L. Weitzman (1974), "Prices vs. Quantities," *Review of Economic Studies* 41, no. 4 (October): 477–491, http://www.jstor.org/stable/2296698.

Nationalization and Privatization

B. Borlotti (2011), "Privatisation in Western Europe—Trends and Issues," *Policy* 27, no. 4: 517–535, policydialogue.org/files/publications/Privatization_Bortolotti.pdf.

Dieter Helm (2011), "The Sustainable Borders of the State," *Oxford Review of Economic Policy* 27, no. 4: 517–535.

John Kay (2002), "20 Years of Privatisation," *Prospect* (June), http://www.johnkay.com/2002/06/01/twenty-years-of-privatisation.

J. Kay and D. Thompson (1986), "Privatisation: A Policy in Search of a Rationale," *Economic Journal* 96, no. 381:18–32.

W. Megginson and J. Netter (2001), "From State to Market: A Survey of Empirical Studies of Privatization," *Journal of Economic Literature* (June): 321–389.

A. Shleifer (1998), "State versus Private Ownership," *Journal of Economic Perspectives* 12, no. 4:133–150, http://scholar.harvard.edu/files/shleifer /files/state_vs_private.pdf.

Regulation of Natural Monopolies

Stephen Littlechild (2003), "Reflections on Incentive Regulation," *Review of Network Economics* 2, no. 4.

Jeff Makholm, Laura Olive, and Max Luke (2018), "Incentive Regulation in the United States: Current Trends and a Look Back," NERA, https:// www.nera.com/content/dam/nera/upload/DES_Incentive_Regulation _PBR_0818.pdf.

Industrial Policy

Mariana Mazzucato (2016), "From Market Fixing to Market-Creating: A New Framework for Innovation Policy," *Industry and Innovation* 23, no. 2.

Alberto Mingardi (2015), "A Critique of Mazzucato's Entrepreneurial State," *Cato Journal* (Fall), http://object.cato.org/sites/cato.org/files /serials/files/cato-journal/2015/9/cj-v35n3-7.pdf.

Geoffrey Owen (2012), "Industrial Policy in Europe since the Second World War: What Has Been Learnt?," LSE Occasional Paper (February), http:// eprints.lse.ac.uk/41902/.

Dani Rodrik (2004), "Industrial Policy for the Twenty-First Century," KSG Working Paper No. RWP04–047 (November).

Joe Studwell (2013), *How Asia Works: Success and Failure in the World's Most Dynamic Region*, Grove Press.

CHAPTER 4

Collective Choice

Contrary to the way they are often pitted against each other, markets and states are not mutually exclusive ways of organizing the economy. The previous chapters have discussed the need for both a competitive market and government intervention in the form of regulation, production, or coordination of activities. Nor are markets and states exhaustive categories. This chapter explores other types of economic institutions for organizing collective action and why these alternatives may be especially relevant in the presence of externalities and public goods.

These alternative forms of organizing economic activity also highlight the importance of the social dimensions of the economy. Social capital or trust is important in increasing the likelihood that any mechanism to provide public goods or manage a commons will succeed, as it reduces the extent of free riding. Social norms and influences affect people's preferences, sometimes in positive ways (as in the decline of smoking or the spread of innovations) and sometimes in negative ones (as in crime waves or status "arms races" with people signaling social status through spending on luxury goods). Finally, all allocation mechanisms—state, market, and community—need to be fair if they are to be legitimate and therefore effective; sometimes people prioritize fairness over economic efficiency.

This chapter begins with the *tragedy of the commons*—often applied specifically to environmental issues but with far wider application in the modern economy, which is characterized by what could be considered a digital commons. Garrett Hardin, the ecologist who coined the well-known phrase, believed that private ownership and state regulation are mutually exclusive solutions to this problem; but this chapter introduces Elinor Ostrom's work, showing that in fact non-state collective institutions can be a more effective way of managing common resources and externalities than either government policies or market solutions. She sets out design principles indicating when collective self-management is likely to bring about efficient outcomes. When might self-organization of this kind, neither individualized market decisions nor government intervention, work? Is there a maximum viable scale? What kinds of production technologies or economic contexts make it more or less likely to work?

The chapter also discusses the need for *social norms* and *trust* for *any* form of collective organization to function well, whether that is government, market, or people getting together to organize economic and social institutions themselves. The chapter looks at *social capital* as well as other social influences on preferences, such as Albert Hirschman's "exit, voice, and loyalty," and *positional goods*. The moral of the chapter is that getting past the false dichotomy of market versus state opens the way to a far richer range of policy options for improving social welfare.

The Tragedy of the Commons

Garrett Hardin's 1968 *Science* article on the tragedy of the commons was profoundly influential. Where Adam Smith had painted a picture of isolated, self-interested individual choices combining to give desirable social outcomes, Hardin argued the opposite: that individually rational choices involved a large social cost. The problem he diagnosed is that resources held in common will be overused because rational individual decisions impose an external cost. If one farmer grazes his cows on common land, they munch the grass at no cost to that individual, but then there is less available for other people's cows; yet no farmer has any incentive to hold back for the greater good as long as everyone else is grazing their herds on the common land. Over-grazing will be the result. The individual cost is less than the individual gain, but the social cost exceeds the sum

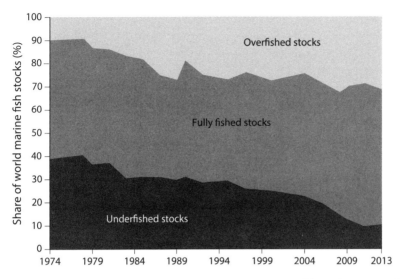

Figure 4.1. Global fish stocks, 1974–2013. *Source*: World Bank Group, "The Sunken Billions Revisited: Progress and Challenges in Global Marine Fisheries," https://openknowledge.worldbank.org/handle/10986/24056.

of those individual gains. The same phenomenon of failure to look after the commons can be observed in many contexts, from areas of common gardens in housing developments where nobody bothers to pick up the litter, to over-fishing in the oceans, to spam or circular emails that over-graze everyone's attention.

Hardin's article struck the environmental debate like a thunderbolt, leading many campaigners to conclude that natural resources could not safely be left to the mercies of the market. For it identified a phenomenon that seemed widespread. Fish stocks in many oceans were severely depleted by the late 1960s; from the 1970s more and more countries asserted their right to fish up to 200 miles from their shores (rather than the previous 3 miles), and quota systems were introduced in some parts of the world—often causing great bitterness as traditional fishing habits were halted, and yet still insufficient to prevent the depletion of stocks due to over-fishing (figure 4.1). Vast tracts of forest were being lost in regions such as the Amazon because of over-exploitation of common, as well as privately owned, lands through logging. Perhaps the most significant example is the

Earth's atmosphere, into which everyone pours greenhouse gases and pollutants, largely at no cost to themselves. Similarly, much waste is dumped into the oceans, from untreated sewage to plastic, with increasingly devastating consequences for marine life.

Hardin himself argued there were two contrasting solutions to the tragedy of the commons. One was to assign private property rights over common resources. The externality would thus be "internalized," in the way Ronald Coase had identified (see chapter 1), and the market could operate to deliver the efficient outcome (box 4.1). (Although recall that the idea this—or any—market is "free" is a misnomer, given that the state defines and assigns property rights, and enforces them through the judicial system.) Even if some external costs remain, such as cows wandering onto others' land, Coaseian transactions between individuals or via the legal system could in principle resolve conflicts of interest.

However, creating private ownership can be controversial, and moreover some countries' constitutions (such as Iceland and Ecuador) rule out private ownership of natural resources. Hardin thought that the only alternative was to have a public authority determine rules for use or regulate access to the commons. There are several potential ways of doing this:

- auction the rights of access through licenses to create temporary private ownership rights (used in many countries for the common resource of radio spectrum, for instance, where use of one part of the spectrum can interfere with neighboring bands if not controlled);
- award access rights depending on some other principle, such as merit or tradition, or being a member of a favored party (for instance, many countries used to grant traditional fishing rights);
- award access rights by lottery; or
- set up a queuing system (leases to small allotments of land are often allocated by local authorities this way, as is access to the UK's non-priced National Health Service).

One of the examples in Hardin's article suggests he found the market logic most appealing—indeed, he referred with some skepticism to

Box 4.1. The power of markets in protecting common pool resources

Among some environmental campaigners, in particular, the idea of using private property rights and markets to improve efficiency and correct externalities is controversial. Historically, the application of property rights to previously common land has involved the dispossession of the powerless, often with violence, as in the English Enclosure Movement of the eighteenth century, or the plains of the American West in the nineteenth century (greatly aided by the invention of barbed wire). Yet assigning property rights can be a powerful approach.

One example concerns a (Pigouvian) subsidy and tax break introduced in Costa Rica in 1990 to pay private landowners to keep their land as rainforest rather than using it for commercial purposes. Since then, the proportion of the country covered by rainforests has risen dramatically (from one-fifth and falling to over half) and additional tourism revenues have partly paid for the cost of the subsidy. Similar schemes of payment for ecosystem services are in place in a range of countries, including in China in a scheme to convert farmland into grassland or forest, in Vietnam by using the hydropower industry to promote clean water, in Australia to restore native plants in the bush, and in the United States to reduce pollution in the Catskills to ensure the watershed continues to provide clean water.

I. Porras, D. N. Barton, M. Miranda, and A. Chacón-Cascante (2013), "Learning from 20 Years of Payments for Ecosystem Services in Costa Rica," International Institute for Environment and Development.

attempts to manage common resources as "socialism." He criticized a local authority for making car parking a free "commons" at Christmas rather than charging for the scarce resource. This well-meaning act was the exact opposite of what should have been done, he argued, as it would make congestion worse—there would be more congestion and excessive use of the commons of parking spaces in the town center. Instead, the car parking charges should

Table 4.1. Classification of Goods

		Easy to exclude free riders?	
		Easy	Hard
Rivalrous in consumption?	A lot	Private good (e.g., clothes, cars)	Common pool resource (e.g., fish from the ocean)
	Not much	Club or toll good (e.g., subscription TV)	Public good (e.g., national defense)

have been increased. Failing that, some other rationing device should be used, such as the rules many cities introduce when pollution is severe. For example, cities from Paris to New Delhi have used schemes allowing people to drive only every other day, depending on their car number or license plate.

If goods are considered along two dimensions—are they rival in consumption or not (assumption 8, box 1.4) and is it then easy or hard to exclude free riding (which depends on physical or technological characteristics)—they can be classified as in table 4.1. Earlier chapters considered the top left and bottom right quadrants, pure private and public goods. The tragedy of the commons introduces the common pool goods in the top right quadrant, whose consumption is rival (if my cow eats all the grass, yours can't), but excluding free riding is hard. The difficulty might be legal rather than technical or physical: small areas of common land can have walls or fences built around them easily, but traditional legal rights preserve them for common use. It was harder to fence large areas of common land until barbed wire was invented in the 1860s. The bottom left quadrant of the table shows what are often called *club goods* or *toll goods*—public (non-rival) goods where free riders can be excluded. This too might depend on tradition or on technology. Chapter 1 discussed whether or not lighthouses are true public goods, given that boats can be kept out of the harbor if they do not pay fees; television broadcasts used to be non-rival and also non-excludable until digital encryption technology was invented.

Managed, Not Tragic, Commons

Hardin seemed to have identified and analyzed a pervasive problem of the over-use of natural resources. However, for all that fish stocks get depleted and land gets over-grazed, there are also many examples of people cooperating to stop the over-use of resources. Gathering examples of management of the commons, and analyzing the conditions needed for them to succeed, was the work of the only female winner (so far) of the Nobel Prize in Economics, Elinor Ostrom. Hardin had focused on non-rival goods and the existence of externalities. But he had assumed that people aim to maximize their individual self-interest (so he assumed A1, box 1.4, held although only in the short term). Hence his conclusion that "the government"—assumed to make the right choice as a benign social planner—would often have to introduce rules to bring about the optimal outcome. In reality, people communicate and cooperate, and can create and enforce a wide range of rules without invoking formal government regulation at all. Ostrom documented many examples of this kind of community regulation through cooperation.

Lobster fishermen in Maine were one of her examples of this kind of social organization. Over-fishing seems to be one of the clearest examples of the tragedy of the commons, and even by the 1920s it had led to a serious depletion in the number of lobsters off the Maine coast. Yet Ostrom found that this community of fishermen had devised a way to divide up access to the available lobsters by allocating individuals areas where they could locate their lobster pots. They implemented an escalating series of social sanctions against individuals who were observed to be fishing more than their designated share by going out of area. The first step was to tie a bow on the pots of someone fishing outside their assigned area, followed by warning visits, social pressure, and ultimately the rest of the fishermen destroying the offender's lobster pots.

Water rights from California to Spain and Nepal were another particular focus for her research (with Vincent Ostrom). She found a "polycentric" system of water management in California in the 1960s, with a patchwork of public, private, and collective bodies managing access; the system survived until destabilized by the combination of rapidly rising demand and severe droughts in 1987–91. Areas of Spain have a complex set of socially created and enforced rules that vary between drought and normal years, and have been in place for five hundred years. In Nepal, farmer-managed systems operate more successfully than government-managed ones, on certain types of land. Ostrom's explorations of the different kinds of arrangements in different terrains and climates, and accounting for the changing balance of supply and demand, informed the concept of polycentric arrangements where different kinds of organizations—families, networks, associations, civic bodies, traditional councils—combine in sometimes complicated but always clearly specified ways to make and enforce decisions about what will happen.

Ostrom's key insight, documented in detail in her subtle and important work, was that there are lots of types of institutions, not just ("free" or not) markets and "the" government. Her co-winner of the Nobel Prize, Oliver Williamson, looked at similar issues in the context of businesses as alternative institutional structures for producing private goods. As already noted, microeconomic theory starts with a single producer; but one of Ronald Coase's famous papers asked why firms exist at all if we think markets are so much more efficient than the planned or administered use of resources. What's more, Ostrom observed that the details of the context matter, the history and the geography, meaning there is no one-size-fits-all approach. In a way, it should not have been surprising to find examples of non-market, non-governmental institutions allocating resources efficiently. After all, chapter 1 described some historical examples of the provision of public goods by groups, such as the turnpike trusts and harbor authorities. Medieval English cities were governed by corporations (and the City of London still is). Many other cities around the world—in Canada and the United States, for instance—have municipal corporations of various legal forms governing them. Up until the early twentieth century, religious bodies (such as parish councils in England) had an important economic role, and continue to do so in many parts of the world today. A nation has one government but many types of institutions, all of which involve some governance.

Ostrom put the point this way in her book *Governing the Commons*:

> Both the centralizers and the privatizers frequently advocate over-simplified, idealized institutions—paradoxically, almost "institution-free" institutions. An assertion that central regulation is necessary tells us nothing about the way a central agency should be constituted, what authority it should have, how the limits on its authority should be maintained, how it will obtain information, or how its agents should be selected, motivated to do their work, and have their performances monitored and rewarded or sanctioned. An assertion that the imposition of private property rights is necessary tells us nothing about how that bundle of rights is to be defined, how the various attributes of the goods involved will be measured, who will pay for the costs of excluding non-owners from access, how conflicts over rights will be adjudicated, or how the residual interests of the right-holders in the resource system itself will be organized.

Rather than all-or-nothing property rights (you own the land or you don't), she argued that there were "bundles" of property rights associated with resources, including rights of access, for instance. Hence, although it might take some effort, uncooperative individuals can be excluded from using certain common pool resources.

This approach to managing the resources is more complicated than the private ownership/government regulation poles, but it can be successful. Based on game theory (of repeated non-cooperative games), Ostrom established the principles listed in box 4.2 for the successful design of a collective (non-state, non-market) institution.

A common thread to these principles concerns legitimacy, a dimension that does not feature in the pure economic analysis of incentives. Institutions must be shaped and enforced by their users. One reason they might succeed when government interventions fail is that often government officials are outsiders whose decisions lack legitimacy in the local community. Another reason, validated by much experimental laboratory work, is that people can be willing to suffer a loss themselves to sanction those who breach the rules. Interestingly, some of the design principles in box 4.2 rule out the likelihood of successful community management in the context of

Box 4.2. Ostrom's eight design principles

Group boundaries must be clear and set out who is entitled to what

Individual responsibilities must be *proportional* to individual benefits

Monitoring must be feasible and straightforward

Mechanisms for resolving conflicts must be in place

Users are responsible for setting rules, monitoring, and enforcement

Sanctions should start mild and *get progressively tougher*

Decisions need to be *legitimate*—users participate in making them

The community's *right to organize* needs to be recognized by the authorities

some market failures, particularly asymmetries of information, as monitoring is important. There is also a kind of property right involved—not the right to own the commons but rights of use or access. Such access rights are often established in law, so managed commons operate in the context of a nation-state or other broader political and jurisdictional framework. This emphasizes a point made in chapter 1, which is that certain contexts are inherently problematic: markets and governments tend to fail in the same situation, and so too might other types of collective institutions.

While the design of the collective institutions is important, the wider context is key in determining the success or failure of a collective arrangement. It is not only a question of the legal context and acceptance or at least tolerance by state authorities of the community's right to self-govern. The external physical context and the technology of production are crucial for the success or failure of self-management. For example, arrangements for managing water often break down during a drought, and differ for landscapes where upstream users can extract large amounts of water. Is the crop being grown a thirsty one or not, or do new seed varieties change the water needs? Do lobsters or sea urchins move much between assigned fishing areas? Does pollution from elsewhere affect parts of the fishery?

Another set of external factors concerns the people involved and their community. In some places, social tradition determines behavior to a substantial degree, and in others people make choices much more as rational, self-interested individuals. The degree of balance required between costs and benefits is thus partly shaped by how individuals behave. Above all, though, whether or not there is high social capital or trust (discussed below) affects the chances of success. Managed commons require a high degree of trust in the community and strong social norms of behavior, because the context is inherently one in which there is a temptation to free ride, ignoring the externality one's behavior imposes on others.

Sometimes collective institutions succeed and sometimes not—Ostrom found many examples of both types. It is rare to find examples that function well on a large scale. Much of her research concerned small communities in the developing world in which it was not too hard for the main decision makers to know each other, or for monitoring of compliance (or free riding) to be feasible. Garrett Hardin believed that any community of over 150 people would find it hard to manage a commons. He selected this number because the Hutterite communities in the Northwest of the United States split into smaller groups once they pass this number in size: "As the size of a colony approaches 150, individual Hutterites begin to under-contribute from their abilities and over-demand for their needs. The experience of Hutterite communities indicates that below 150 people, the distribution system can be managed by shame; above that approximate number, shame loses its effectiveness," he wrote.

Starting with the enclosure movement in the Industrial Revolution, and the fencing of the American West, private property rights now exist over much previously common land in the developed world. Collective management of water resources in the rich economies is relatively rare compared to private or government management. Formal, modern economies have steadily encroached on traditional common pool resources, such as land and water, although the tragedy of the commons certainly seems to be playing out over the oceans and the Earth's climate. In these contexts, property rights are hard or impossible to establish, and the scale of both the resource and the challenge is such that collective agreement to manage their use is extremely difficult. Negotiations that are intergovernmental (for example, over climate change) have largely failed. However, in some contexts, such as fisheries, the tide (forgive the pun) may be turning (box 4.3). Perhaps a return to local and collective management would, in some circumstances, prove a more environmentally sustainable and institutionally viable way of managing resources than the standard economic policy approach of government intervention.

Box 4.3. Successfully managed commons

Natural resources are the focus of research into community management of the commons. In the developed economies, formal government agencies have tended over time to replace community-run schemes, as the size of communities has grown, making monitoring and enforcement more challenging. However, there are many examples in developed countries of self-managed commons. One is Japan's system of irrigation management.* Japanese farming communities have had responsibility for arranging water use for centuries; although ownership of the paddy fields is private, appropriation of water for their irrigation is done in common. The arrangement was formalized in the postwar era; although the government invests in major infrastructure, the responsibility for access rights to the water is entrusted to land improvement districts, legal community bodies comprising water users. These institutions set out and enforce the rules for their own community. Indeed, the role of these water users' associations, governed by elected farmers, in managing irrigation has increased over time.

Another example in the developed world is San Diego's sea urchin fishery. Between the 1970s and 1990s, the stock of sea urchins had

---

(continued on next page)

(continued from previous page)

declined by about three-quarters due to over-exploitation. A state licensing scheme failed to halt the decline. Now sea urchin divers have agreed to a limit with the state of California, and the divers themselves monitor the catches and handle enforcement. The organization, the San Diego Watermen's Association, also started its own dockside market to improve the divers' incomes. A recent study found that the number of community-managed fisheries around the world has in fact been increasing in recent decades, in response to the evidence of the depletion of stocks.** When the fishers are made partners, the efforts from community management of fisheries are likely to be more fruitful for fish stocks and fishers alike, where greater benefits incentivize further cooperation. In the alternative scenario, imposed rules and limitations can lead to circumventing regulation in the search for maximizing private gains.***

* Ashutosh Sarker and Tadao Itoh (2001), "Design Principles in Long-Enduring Institutions of Japanese Irrigation Common-Pool Resources," *Agricultural Water Management* 48, no. 2: 89–102.

** Nicolás Gutiérrez, Ray Hilborn, and Omar Defeo (2011), "Leadership, Social Capital, and Incentives Promote Successful Fisheries," *Nature* 470 (February): 386–389.

*** Jonathan Wood (2018), "Is the Era of Overfishing Coming to a Close in the U.S.?," Property and Environment Research Center, https://www.perc.org/2018/06/11/is-the-era-of-overfishing-coming-to-a-close-in-the-u-s/.

Intellectual Property and the Digital Commons

There is a new terrain in which property rights are unclear and highly contested, with a sort of land grab taking place until laws and norms are established. This is the terrain often referred to as the *digital commons*. Digital output is a public good in the sense that it is non-rival, so in terms of the classification in table 4.1, the use of the term *commons* is a misnomer. But it provides a striking example of the importance of both clear property rights and social norms in the economy.

Intellectual property is highly contested territory (box 4.4). The legal framework for the allocation of property rights over these non-rival goods is still being tested. The law—especially the Digital Millennium Copyright Act in the US—is considered by many academics and campaigners to be too heavily weighted toward big corporations. The social welfare benefits of wider access to digital public goods probably outweighs the benefits of the (unnecessarily)

Box 4.4. Digital property rights disputes

When Amazon introduced its Kindle e-reader, purchasers of George Orwell's *1984* were surprised to find, one day in July 2009, that their book had disappeared. Amazon had concluded that the publisher who had uploaded the book to the Kindle store did not hold the copyright, and so it deleted remotely the item consumers thought they had bought and was their property. The uproar—and lawsuits—led Amazon to state it would never repeat the move, but the example illustrates the novel issues concerning digital property. A retailer could never break into your home and take back a physical book, even if copyright had been breached. More relevant here, there were conflicting property rights over this intangible product.

Many farmers buy John Deere tractors, and a top-of-the-line model fitted with sophisticated software costs a six-figure sum. In 2015 the company used the US Digital Millennium Copyright Act—designed to protect copyright in music and films—to prevent farmers who buy the tractors from accessing the software. For the first time, farmers were legally prohibited from mending their own tractors. John Deere has submitted to the US Copyright Office that they continue to own the tractors they sell. Farmers are buying, the

(continued on next page)

(continued from previous page)

company stated, "An implied license for the life of the vehicle to operate the vehicle." The company has been challenged in the copyright court, and some limited rights for purchasers to look into the tractor software have been restored. But some farmers are now turning to Ukrainian hackers to fix their tractors. General Motors is making the same case: consumers mistakenly "conflate ownership of a vehicle with ownership of the underlying computer software in a vehicle," they state. Legal action continues in this case too. Some states, including Massachussetts and California, have passed "right to repair" legislation; but the legal tussle is continuing.* The same kind of copyright legislation made unlocking a phone illegal in many places, although the law is often breached. The US Copyright Office decided unlocking phones to repair them was allowed under the DMCA only in October 2018—and at the same time allowed people with medical implants the right to access data generated about their health.**

The digital world has also spawned what are popularly known as patent trolls, or more formally, non-practicing entities or NPEs. These individuals or businesses take out or buy broad patents and threaten to sue other, genuine, technology businesses for patent infringement. NPEs have thrived in the American legal landscape. The number of these extortionate lawsuits has increased more than tenfold since 2000, to the detriment of economic growth and employment in US states that had not outlawed the NPEs' excesses.***

* http://www.wired.com/2015/02/new-high-tech-farm-equipment-nightmare -farmers/; http://www.npr.org/sections/alltechconsidered/2015/08/17 /432601480/diy-tractor-repair-runs-afoul-of-copyright-law; https://www .technologyreview.com/s/602026/how-copyright-law-stifles-your-right-to -tinker-with-tech/.
** https://www.govinfo.gov/content/pkg/FR-2018-10-26/pdf/2018 -23241.pdf.
*** Ian Appel, Joan Farre-Mensa, and Elena Simintzi (2017), "Patent Trolls and Startup Employment, HBS Working Paper No. 17-072 (February).

strong incentives to the creators of digital content. Digital goods fit into the bottom left quadrant of table 4.1: they are non-rival, but their use is excludable through a combination of technology (encryption, digital rights management technology) and the law (copyright and its enforcement).

The framework of social norms in the digital domain is contested and still being shaped. The role of assumptions about norms or conventional patterns of behavior in defining property rights is often overlooked. For example, hotels leave out signs saying the bathrobes can be purchased, in case some guests think it's OK to take them home, like the spare shampoo. If my neighbor's fruit tree drops apples into my garden, we will both assume I can keep them, and she won't call the police if I turn them into a pie. In the digital world, the early norm was that content was free, but over time businesses have made a land grab—a bit like the enclosure of the physical commons.

Social Norms

The role of social norms in determining economic as well as social outcomes is fundamental in the offline as well as the online world. One of Elinor Ostrom's principles for the success, or otherwise, of collective management arrangements is whether the social norms or conventions would limit free riding and make enforcement feasible. Changes in social norms can bring about changes in behavior far greater than financial or economic incentives alone can explain. For example, the prevalence of smoking has declined substantially in many countries since the 1970s. Although the price of cigarettes has increased, in large part due to tax increases, and this has certainly affected the prevalence of smoking (see figure 4.2 for France), assuming the whole decline in smoking to be due to higher prices would imply an implausibly high price elasticity of demand: as tobacco is an addictive drug, a low price elasticity can be expected. A combination of official restrictions, such as higher taxes, bans on smoking in ever more places, health warnings, advertising bans, and the declining social acceptability or coolness of smoking together

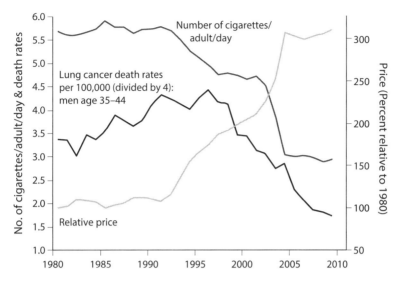

Figure 4.2. Smoking, lung cancer rates, and cigarette prices in France. *Source:* VoxEU, https://voxeu.org/article/why-india-should-increase-taxes-cigarettes.

explain the decline. Indeed, tougher regulation may have followed the changing norm as much as it contributed to it. In old movies, the hero is often seen through a haze of cigarette smoke; that portrayal would characterize the villain now.

Social norms can change quickly, as figure 4.3 illustrates. Consider attitudes to same-sex marriage in the US: in 1990 three-quarters of Americans saw homosexual sex as immoral. In 2006 only one US senator openly supported same-sex marriage. Yet the number of Fortune 500 companies offering health care benefits for same-sex partners rose from zero in 1990 to 263 in 2006. According to the Pew Research Center, public opinion swung from 57% against same-sex marriage and 35% in favor in 2001 to 62% in favor and just 32% against by 2017; and the US Supreme Court has since ruled that individual states can no longer ban it.

Rapid changes in social norms may often be part of the explanation for large-scale changes in behavior, even in contexts where economic factors also play a large part. Economists have considered changes in crime waves, for instance, where street prices (such as prices for stolen goods) and factors such as minimum wages and

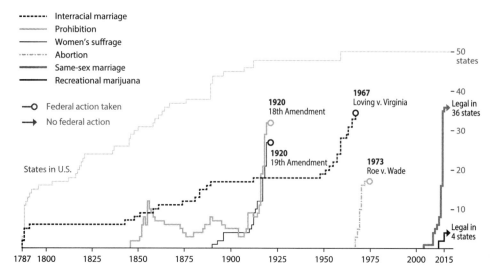

Figure 4.3. Number of US states removing bans. *Source*: https://www.bloomberg
.com/graphics/2015-pace-of-social-change/.

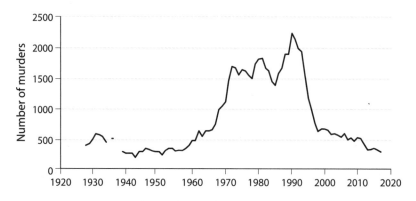

Figure 4.4. New York City homicide rate. *Source*: NYPD statistics.

unemployment strongly affect the crime rate—but so do social
influences. Figure 4.4 shows one example—a steep decline in the
homicide rate in New York City during the 1990s. Policy and policing certainly played a key part, but it is hard to account for the
scale of the decline (or correspondingly the increase in the 1970s)
using only obvious policy levers, such as the number of police or

sentencing policies, or economic variables, such as unemployment or income.

Social Capital

Somewhat distinct from the idea of norms or conventions is the concept of social capital, sometimes described using the shorthand *trust*. All economic exchanges other than simple face-to-face transactions require trust—trust that the goods will be delivered, that they will be safe and work as described. In the modern, globalized economy, people are often transacting with strangers they have never met on the other side of the world. When it comes to services, which now make up 70%–80% of the advanced economies, the level of trust required for exchange is all the greater, as it may be hard to know the quality of the service provided—certainly before the transaction and not always afterward. And it is not just markets; as Ostrom noted, a high level of trust is essential for collective institutions to function as well. One of the key scholars of social capital, political scientist Robert Putnam, saw it as the source of the distinction between northern and southern Italian towns. He took it to be a measure of the strength of civil society, in other words, precisely those institutions that are neither individual market transactions nor formal actions of the state. For one important way social capital contributes to the success of collective or community institutions is that it helps ensure there is less free riding in the context of all public goods (not just commons). Free riding is easier to monitor and discourage in contexts where there is strong social capital.

The concept of social capital, like many abstract concepts in social science, is hard to define precisely (and therefore measure). Often it is measured using survey questions. The most frequently used is included in the World Values Survey: "Generally speaking, would you say that most people can be trusted, or that you can't be too careful in dealing with people?" Despite the definitional issue, there is ample evidence that social capital makes an important contribution to economic outcomes. Figure 4.5 illustrates this in a general sense, in that trust as measured by survey questions and GDP per

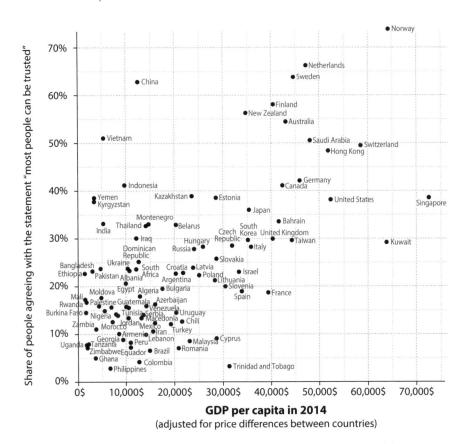

Figure 4.5. Trust and GDP are positively correlated. *Source*: Our World in Data, https://ourworldindata.org/trust-and-gdp.

capita are positively related to each other. There is also regression evidence that social capital (measured by the trust survey question) is correlated with good economic performance. However, there are different channels or mechanisms through which social capital seems to affect economic outcomes.

One well-known study by sociologist Eric Klinenberg explored the difference in death rates between different communities during a severe 1995 heat wave in Chicago. Controlling for obvious contributory factors, such as income levels, unemployment, and housing quality, a key difference explaining the "excess death rates" (that is, the extent to which the death rate was higher than usual) was the strength of family and community ties in the different wards. In some, people would check on vulnerable elderly neighbors or relatives, and in others these social obligations did not exist. The study found higher community ties and therefore a lower excess death rate in wards of the city that were otherwise extremely similar in terms of standard socio-economic indicators, such as unemployment or drug use.

Another well-known study by Mark Granovetter identified the importance of what he named *weak ties* in helping people find jobs. Strong ties are those to close family and friends; but it was more distant social connections that helped people find employment. The more extensive their weak ties, the better people's chances of finding employment. (The literature sometimes refers to *bonding* and *bridging* social capital instead.)

Social ties must also help explain why some areas or parts of cities develop clusters of business specialization, especially in high-value and knowledge-intensive businesses. There are many examples, such as Silicon Valley in California and Silicon Fen in Cambridge, England, or advanced manufacturing clusters in cities ranging from Toulouse in France (aerospace) to Shenzhen in China (electronics). The role of clusters was apparent right from the start of the Industrial Revolution, with Manchester, England, at the heart of the cotton industry. Alfred Marshall, one of the founding fathers of modern economics, thought part of the explanation for clustered industrial districts was the ease with which people could get together face-to-face to share know-how, saying that this *tacit* knowledge (as opposed to *codifiable* knowledge, which can be written down and shared) was "in the air." The increasing importance of tacit knowledge in what are described as "knowledge-based" economies seems to be driving ever-greater clustering of high-valued businesses in certain locations.

Social capital also helps make government action more effective. For example, policing is far easier if the community as a whole keeps an eye on what is going on and people generally trust the local representatives of state power. This is why simply sending in more police, or more heavily armed police, into communities like Ferguson, Missouri, during the 2014 clashes, for example, is damaging.

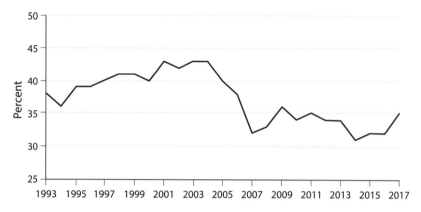

Figure 4.6. Trust in institutions, United States. The average percentage of Americans who have "a great deal" or "quite a lot" of confidence across fourteen institutions. *Source*: Gallup.

Similarly, in any emergency the real first responders are always people in the immediate community.

Given all this, signs that trust is in decline in many societies and communities are concerning. Some survey-based measures indicate declining trust to varying degrees, depending on the institution—politicians and government have fared particularly badly, as has big business, while academics and professionals such as doctors retain higher trust. Looking at these various institutions as a whole, in the US as in other countries, there has been a trend toward decline (see figure 4.6) at a time when trust is ever more essential for the health of the economy. Consider that the majority of the value of companies listed on the stock exchange consists of what accountants term *goodwill*, and could be described as the reputation of the business. When something happens to undermine that confidence, the value can evaporate in moments, as it does whenever corporations collapse—think of the value of Enron when its frauds were revealed, or the big banks as the Great Financial Crisis occurred.

There is a lot still to understand about social capital or trust, including how best to measure it. One of the paradoxes is that strong social capital can also have adverse effects. Criminal gangs are bound to each other by powerful mutual trust. So are isolated villages or societies, which therefore do not engage in the contact and trade with the outside world that would enable them to prosper. There seems to be a Goldilocks mix of social capital that is strong where it would naturally be weak and somewhat weak where it would naturally be strong. Thinking about the economic effects of social capital, three types seem worth considering for the development of definitions and measurements:

- *Network structures in the economy*: the links between individuals enabling the flow of information (of various kinds)
- *Reputation*: the extent to which economic exchange is underpinned by a reputation for honesty, reliability, quality, and so on —(in the corporate context, *goodwill*)
- *Institutions and communities*: the ability to provide public goods, manage commons, run institutions, or in general act collectively in the common interest

Exit, Voice, and Loyalty

A high level of trust or social capital is one of the factors helping to explain the success, or otherwise, of the market economy and also of the kind of institutional arrangements that are neither state nor market—the alternative ways people have found to manage common resources when there are market failures. Another factor contributing to the success or failure of both markets and other collective institutions is the mixture of what Albert Hirschman called "exit, voice, and loyalty."

Consumer choice in a market is about walking away when you're not happy. It is a yes/no vote on a product or service. The criteria are features such as price and quality. The market will sort out which firms deliver the goods consumers want at the best price and quality combination. This is *exit*. But Hirschman argued that this is often not what happens and the alternative of *voice* is more important: people complain instead, because they would rather not switch to another provider—they have enough *loyalty* to keep them from switching (although this might also involve inertia, as switching involves transaction costs).

The combination of voice and loyalty can therefore often deliver economic efficiency just as well as exit, he argued. The ideal in efficiency terms might be a mix: exit is a powerful incentive, but if it happens too fast or too much, the firm will go under, when it might have been able to improve with voice, in effect, feedback. The credible threat of exit—without it actually happening—is in fact a particularly effective kind of voice; for example, if you threaten to switch to another mobile phone company or insurer, you will often be offered a better deal. Exit, voice, and loyalty therefore interact. Loyalty raises the price of exit and makes it less likely; but as the threat of exit is a powerful part of voice, loyalty can also make voice less effective. So loyalty can be a perversely damaging thing if it weakens both the feedback mechanisms. There needs to be just enough but not too much.

In some contexts, though, the absence of the possibility of exit will do the opposite: in other words, if voice is the only option, it will be exercised more. This has been applied to understanding political parties. Parties wanting to win elections need to appeal to the middle ground to get enough votes, so will sometimes tailor centrist policies. But as their loyalists are not going to quit the party, even though they would prefer less moderate policies, their voice becomes louder. Parties need to try to appeal to the middle of the road and the activists simultaneously.

Hirschman also thought many firms with market power would prefer it if their most complaining customers just went somewhere else. Near-monopolies can produce less efficient outcomes for consumers than complete monopolies whose customers cannot exit and only have voice. Rajiv Sethi points out that this is profoundly important for the way natural monopoly industries are organized. He gives the following examples:

- A state-owned railway company can continue to underperform if its most dissatisfied customers drive instead.
- Public schools will get worse results if some parents exit and opt for private schools.
- Neighborhoods can go downhill quickly if unhappy tenants move elsewhere, but if they have no choice (for instance, they

are allocated public housing), they will campaign for a better management service.

- Shareholders will not vote in annual general meetings to improve management decisions; they'll just sell their shares.

This approach suggests that the key to the success or failure of a firm or institution is the price of exit. Where a competitive market can operate, the price of exit is low. Where there are market failures, such as natural monopolies or common pool resources, the price of exit is high, so voice and loyalty become more effective in allocating resources efficiently.

Social Influence on Preferences

The tragedy of the commons and the management of the commons refer to situations where there are external spillovers in *production*. The presence or absence of social capital is one of the important determinants of how feasible it is to manage those externalities, or to limit the scope for free riding in the presence of a public good. The remainder of this chapter discusses some significant external effects in *consumption*, or to put it another way, social influences on individuals' preferences (assumption A2 fails—see box 1.4).

One of the earliest and best-known examples of social influence is the concept of *conspicuous consumption*, a term coined by Thorstein Veblen. Veblen saw consumption as a signal of status, rather than its conventional interpretation in economics as the satisfaction of wants or preferences enabled by high income. The idle rich would spend on increasingly lavish signs of their social status and wealth, Veblen said.

A similar concept, due to Fred Hirsch, is the idea of *positional goods*. In his book *Social Limits to Growth*, he identified these as goods with true scarcity value. This can be absolute, when there is more or less a fixed supply of a specific item; or relative, when it is in short supply in relation to the supply of other items. For instance, large estates in the Highlands of Scotland and paintings by Caravaggio are scarce in absolute terms, while Chanel suits and PhDs are relatively scarce. Another way of putting it is that sometimes the scarcity that gives a positional good its value is inherent, and sometimes constructed. There are some whose supply is fixed. This may be inherent as with land, or paintings by Rubens, but equally not everyone can fly on private planes as the airspace would get congested. However, the categories blur. For instance, the art business is founded on the creation of artificial scarcity (box 4.5).

There is strong evidence from other social sciences about the importance of status in our societies, including income and consumption levels relative to those of other people to whom we compare ourselves. Individuals' preferences are therefore not independent of the consumption choices of other people, and their utility is negatively affected by the consumption of others. This phenom-

---

Box 4.5. Artificial scarcity in art

The fondness rich people have for Old Master paintings to demonstrate their wealth was deliberately engineered at the turn of the twentieth century by a prominent art dealer, Joseph Duveen.* While the supply of fifteenth-century Renaissance masterpieces cannot be increased, the demand for them as a positional good certainly can be, and that was Duveen's skill. He persuaded the wealthy of his time, the Vanderbilts and Morgans, that buying Old Masters was a signal of their taste and class. Andy Warhol's Factory, an assembly line for his famous silk screen images, was intended as a provocation to underline the mass production of expensive art. Damien Hirst's studio producing multiple spot paintings is a more recent example.**

* S. N. Behrman (2014), *Duveen: The Story of the Most Spectacular Art Dealer of All Time*, Daunt Books.
** Andrew Rice (2010), "Damien Hirst: Jumping the Shark," *Business Week*, https://www.bloomberg.com/news/articles/2012-11-21/damien-hirst-jumping-the-shark.

enon can lead to "arms races" in consumption, as people continually try to leapfrog each other by purchasing the next relatively scarce, "must-have" item to maintain superior status.

This certainly seems to be the case for some luxury goods. Expensive cars, houses, and jewelry are out of reach for most people. Wealthy people can easily deploy their money in ways that signal their status. However, even for the less wealthy, the choice of the right kind of purchases can be used as a status signal. Many luxury brands play on the fact that quite a lot of people might buy one item to establish their position in the status race, and this is why so many companies plaster their logos visibly on these goods: the signal is the point. These luxury brand producers do, though, walk a tightrope between conveying scarcity through a high enough price and expanding their market, which limits what they can charge.

There are many other examples of positional goods whose scarcity is more obviously socially constructed. These include

- degrees from elite universities;
- early adoption of new gadgets;
- membership in fashionable clubs;
- must-have designer fashion items; and
- homes in desirable areas.

Indeed, the whole fashion industry is built on a rapid succession of socially influenced preferences; if exclusivity cannot be sustained because of the ease of copying a fashion idea, it needs to be updated frequently. Signaling is important in the job market too. How do employers distinguish between different job market candidates, whose inherent ability is impossible to monitor, at least before employing them and maybe even afterward? One way has always been to select graduates of universities with elite reputations, such as Oxbridge or Ivy League schools, on the assumption that only students who are smart and work hard are admitted (although recent scandals involving rich parents paying to get their children into these institutions suggest that assumption may not be entirely correct). Another is to use further qualifications, such as advanced degrees, as a signal (box 4.6).

Box 4.6. Signaling and the education arms race

Education is in part about increasing knowledge and understanding (as well as learning to work and live independently and gain broader horizons). It is also in part a signal to potential future employers, who need some way to distinguish between candidates for a job, as Nobel economist Michael Spence observed in a classic 1973 article. A degree, along with the identity of the institution awarding it, acts as a signal.* Signaling theory is another area of economics where asymmetric information plays a big part in explaining less than fully efficient behavior and outcomes.

Increasingly, many employers now look for candidates with a master's degree, as the proportion of people with an undergraduate degree has risen substantially over time. There is a kind of arms race in educational signaling. Where once a first degree would have signaled distinct intellect or knowledge, now an additional degree may be needed. The proportion of people with a postgraduate degree in the UK, for instance, rose from 4% in 1996 to 11% by 2013.

In his book *The Case against Education*, economist Bryan Caplan argues that only a small portion of the merit of education lies in increasing students' knowledge and skills. For the most part, he reckons its function is to signal hard work and conformism. What's more, this makes it a zero or even negative sum game: my getting a further degree disadvantages others who do not have one, forcing some to undertake the expense of a further degree themselves in order to compete in the jobs market—and even in the marriage market, given that many people meet their partner while a student or marry someone similarly qualified. Arms races are hard to end, but Caplan argues that at a minimum there should be no taxpayer subsidy to master's degrees, given the high wage premium to a further degree.

* Surveyed in Andrew Weiss (1995), "Human Capital vs. Signalling Explanations of Wages," *Journal of Economic Perspectives* 9, no. 4: 133–154.

When income and consumption matter for positional reasons, and consumption arms races occur, people work and consume more than is socially optimal because of the negative consumption externality. This is reminiscent of the tragedy of the commons: rational individual choices have adverse social outcomes.

Garrett Hardin suggested private ownership rights as a solution to the tragedy of the commons. If people have property rights over sections of the river, they internalize the externality and consume only as many fish as will sustain the stock. Elinor Ostrom's examples of successfully managed commons also involve rules to allocate access to scarce resources, albeit not in the form of private ownership rights but agreed access rights instead. However, this approach makes matters worse in the case of positional goods with negative consumption externalities. People can and do own an exclusive property right to a large estate with a mansion on it, and that is exactly the problem.

An alternative solution is the application of what is essentially a Pigouvian tax on the externality, a tax on luxury goods. If people are over-consuming expensive sports cars and designer handbags, discouraging the consumption through a high enough rate of tax seems attractive. But it is not all that straightforward. The UK's Chancellor of the Exchequer, Norman Lamont, in 1991 imposed a luxury tax on what was then seen as the ultimate yuppie status symbol: the mobile phone. This is of course something that almost everyone in the advanced economies owns now. New goods almost always start out being expensive and adopted by just a few people, but it is impossible at that stage to predict which will become mass-market items. The UK's mobile phone tax was abolished in 1999. The challenge of identifying which goods to subject to a luxury tax is even harder when it comes to everyday luxuries, such as designer clothing or diamond rings. Would it really be a good idea to have government officials drawing up lists of which brands count as luxuries—Louis Vuitton but not Tula? This would just distort market choices between almost identical goods. And what about positional goods, such as choice of school? Should the government really tax attendance at an elite institution just because part of its consumer appeal is status?

In cases where the supply constraint is absolute, not just socially constructed, one possible solution is public ownership of the resource and an access or licensing scheme. The argument here is that the only way to avoid positional arms races is to prevent them from occurring at all, through the creation of a commons. This is a live debate when it comes to land in countries where there is an extremely inequitable pattern of ownership, including some developing countries (and others—box 4.7) where large landowners have great economic and political power.

Land reform programs underline the point made earlier: that property rights are socially constructed too. Rather than dealing with externalities by using the market process of exchange *given* property rights, both the reallocation of property rights and the allocation mechanism can be useful policy tools. Recall that Garrett Hardin thought the local authority was foolish to offer free parking at Christmas as it would increase demand for a fixed supply of space; it should have been using higher prices instead, to ration demand, in his view. The local authority was thinking instead about

---

Box 4.7. Land reform in Scotland

Land in Scotland arouses strong political emotions. There are large estates in the Highlands as a result of the Clearances—the departure or eviction of Scots from the land in the late eighteenth and early nineteenth centuries. Large landowners replaced community farming. The claim is that 432 people now own half the country's land area, much of it taking the form of large sporting estates. In 2012 the Scottish government launched a program to map the ownership of all land in Scotland, as an independent Land Reform Review Group (in 2014) called for an upper limit on the amount of land any individual could own. There is now a community right-to-buy scheme in the Highlands and Islands of Scotland. For now, the sellers have to be willing, but it is not impossible that the political impetus will grow for compulsory purchase. The Scottish government's Land Commission has also been consulting on a land value tax.

parking as a collective resource and choosing rationing by queuing, or getting up early. There are other examples of circumstances in which many people prefer alternative rationing mechanisms rather than the price set by the market to match supply and demand. The UK's National Health Service is an obvious one. The vast majority of UK voters think not having to pay at the point of need is essential, regardless of the economic efficiency arguments for the use of the price mechanism in light of rising demand for health services. Britons would rather queue, or have medical professionals prioritize their needs. Wartime rationing is another example. Supplies of food are limited in those circumstances. Rationing is economically inefficient and inevitably leads to a so-called black market where prices are allowed to rise to reflect supply conditions. However, many people (even many economists) consider rationing schemes to be essential at certain times, such as wartime: fairness trumps efficiency in such circumstances.

A less somber example is the outcry that greeted Coca-Cola when it experimented (in 1999) with raising the price of its drinks in vending machines in hot weather. The backlash was such that the company had to backtrack, even though failing to raise the price and thus choke off some demand made it more likely machines would run out of supplies. Yet consumers seem comfortable with the way airlines, for example, vary the price of seats according to demand. The sense of fairness in different contexts—how much people are in control of the circumstances affecting demand—seems to account for the difference.

These examples are contexts in which economic efficiency is not the most important aim of policy. Fairness matters more, or perhaps the need for all citizens to feel a sense of civic engagement, and for high trust or social capital.

Network Effects

Positional goods are those featuring negative spillovers in consumption. There are also goods with strongly *positive* spillovers in consumption. These demand side externalities are the *network effects* already discussed in the context of digital platforms in chapter 2. Telephones provide one example: my phone is more useful to me the more other people are already on the network. Likewise, I value a social media site more the more other people already use it. Many digital markets have *indirect* network effects. For instance, the more restaurants that list on a platform like OpenTable, the more useful it is to diners, and the more diners that use the platform, the more valuable it is to the restaurant to be listed. Other examples include Airbnb and other accommodation platforms, Craigslist, TaskRabbit, and many other familiar services and apps from everyday life. In all these cases, one person's decision to consume affects the preferences and choices of other people. Assumption A2 (box 1.4) fails here too.

Conclusion

This chapter has discussed failures of the assumptions that there are no external costs or spillovers in production; and that people's preferences and consumption choices are independent of each other. Sometimes defining private property rights over a commons so a market can operate may be an appropriate way to address the externalities. However, other methods can also increase the efficiency of the outcome, including restricting private property rights over a commons so the market cannot operate; enabling community management of common resources; using government allocation of access rights in other forms, such as licenses or franchises; and using non-market allocation of consumption rights via rationing.

As this summary list makes clear, there are circumstances in which it is not easy to find policy solutions to address market failures and increase economic efficiency. In these circumstances—of external costs in production and consumption—social factors not always considered by economists play an important part in how easy or difficult it is to improve economic efficiency. These include social norms, the prevalence of social capital or trust, the exercise of voice and loyalty in interaction with the threat or reality of exit (or consumer choice), and the sense of fairness. Social capital

Table 4.2. Categorization of Goods, Extended

Marginal cost of production declines				Easy to exclude free riders?	
				Easy	Hard
	Rivalrous in consumption?	Super-rivalrous	Negative consumption externality	Positional	N/A
		Yes		Private	Common pool
		No		Club/toll	Public
		Super-non-rivalrous	Positive consumption externality	Network	Network

or social norms can alleviate to some extent the likelihood of free riding or imposition of externalities on others. Considerations of fairness also play a large part in the likely success of any policies to address the externalities involved in commons goods or positional goods.

Finally, the categorization of goods introduced in table 4.1 can be extended to incorporate the phenomena discussed here. The introduction of positional goods as well as the concept of common pool resources is shown in table 4.2.

Further Reading

Classics

Garrett Hardin (1968), "The Tragedy of the Commons," *Science* 162, no. 3859 (December): 1243–1248, doi: 10.1126/science.162.3859.1243, http://www.sciencemag.org/content/162/3859/1243.full.

Fred Hirsch (1976), *Social Limits to Growth*, Harvard University Press.

Albert Hirschman (1970), *Exit, Voice, and Loyalty*, Harvard University Press.

Elinor Ostrom (1990), *Governing the Commons*, Cambridge University Press.

Payment for Common Resources

UK Department for Environment, Food & Rural Affairs (2013), *Payment for Ecosystem Services: A Best Practice Guide*, https://www.cbd.int/financial/pes/unitedkingdom-bestpractice.pdf.

United Nations Development Programme, "Payment for Ecosystem Services," http://www.undp.org/content/sdfinance/en/home/solutions/payments-for-ecosystem-services.html.

Community Management of the Commons

Edward Glaeser and Jose Scheinkman (2000), "Non-market Interactions," NBER Working Paper No. 8053 (December).

Elinor Ostrom (2009), "Beyond Markets and States," Nobel Prize lecture, http://www.nobelprize.org/nobel_prizes/economic-sciences/laureates/2009/ostrom_lecture.pdf.

Social Capital and Norms

Partha Dasgupta (2005), "The Economics of Social Capital," *Economic Record* 81, no. s1 (August): S2–S21.

J. Elster (1989), "Social Norms," *Journal of Economic Perspectives* 3, no. 4: 99–117, http://www.aeaweb.org/articles.php?doi=10.1257/jep.3.4.99.

Edward Glaeser, David Laibson, and Bruce Sacerdote (2002), "An Economic Approach to Social Capital," *Economic Journal* 112 (November): F437–F458.

Geoffrey Hodgson (2006), "What Are Institutions?," *Journal of Economic Issues* 40, no. 1: 1–25.

Geoffrey Hodgson (2013), editorial introduction to the Elinor Ostrom memorial issue, *Journal of Institutional Economics* 9, no. 4: 381–385.

Eric Klinenberg (2002), *Heat Wave: A Social Autopsy of Disaster in Chicago*, University of Chicago Press.

Elinor Ostrom (2000), "Collective Action and the Evolution of Social Norms," *Journal of Economic Perspectives* 14, no. 3: 137–158.

Positional Goods

Robert Frank (2005), "Positional Externalities Cause Large and Preventable Welfare Losses," *American Economic Review* 95, no. 2 (May).

Fred Hirsch (1976), *Social Limits to Growth*, Harvard University Press.

Rajiv Sethi (2010), "The Astonishing Voice of Albert Hirschman," http://rajivsethi.blogspot.co.uk/2010/04/astonishing-voice-of-albert-hirschman.html.

CHAPTER 5

Behavioral Policies

The previous chapter introduced the social influence of individual choices. This chapter turns to a different potential reason the choices made by individuals may lead to economic outcomes that diverge from the classic efficiency framework: human psychology. Policies based on behavioral economics have become much more widespread in recent years. The most usual approach is "nudging," built on a body of work that portrays people's choices as a series of "biases" diverging from rational, self-interested preferences. Although quite widely adopted among policymakers and economists, there are alternative approaches and some criticisms of nudging.

One alternative considers people's choices as rules of thumb that are in fact perfectly rational given the constraints on brain energy and attention. Another disputes the idea that the policy challenge is to help people satisfy their preferences better than they know how to do it themselves, arguing that—as the last chapter began to explore—preferences are partly socially determined, not just a matter of individual psychology. A final critique is related to this, pointing out that policymakers may have their own biases or preferences, so there is an unavoidable paternalism in behavioral policies that makes it hard to draw firm conclusions for social welfare.

As this range of views indicates, this is an active area of research with many unresolved questions. These include the robustness of some of the "behavioral" results in the literature. However, behavioral policies seem likely to be a permanent tool in the policymaker's kit; in areas ranging from pensions to competition policy and regulation, the psychology of individual choice is at the heart of the policy debate.

This chapter looks at a rapidly growing category of policies shaped by the fact that people do not always act like self-interested, rational maximizers. This includes the increasingly popular "nudge" policies based on behavioral economics and so called after the best-selling book *Nudge* by Cass Sunstein and Richard Thaler. A number of countries (the UK, US, Japan, and Australia, for example) have set up policy units specializing in this approach. Regulators such as competition authorities are also keenly interested in better understanding consumer choice. In this framework for organizing thinking about policies, behavioral policies can be seen as a response to a particular type of market failure (assumption A1, box 1.4, fails). Behavioral economics classifies decision-making according to some well-known *heuristics*, such as over-confidence, loss aversion, and the importance of anchors and framing (in other words, how choices are presented to people). Its approach follows from the work of two psychologists, Daniel Kahneman and Amos Tversky, and is associated with economists Cass Sunstein and Richard Thaler, among others; the literature is now vast. This chapter discusses these characteristics of decision-making—what kinds of behavioral policies have been adopted and which seem to have been effective.

This is a thriving area of research. The Nobel Prize committee has honored several behavioral economists, and there is a large popular literature on this work. The popularity of behavioral economics has grown alongside a crisis of confidence in conventional economics and the assumption of rationality, which is clearly empirically false in certain circumstances (although not all). The surge of behavioral policy-making raises some questions, however.

One is that the appropriate assumptions to make about choice seem to depend on circumstances; sometimes people (and other creatures, too, for that matter) do act like the conventional, rational, calculating *homo economicus*, maximizing some outcome of interest subject to constraints. Another question is who is evaluating the "best" outcome and according to what criteria—and how rationally, or otherwise, do they make decisions? There is in addition the danger of giving rein to the social engineering instincts—or, to put it more generously, benign paternalism—of economists and policy experts. After all, this area of psychology has its origins in the now unappealing 1950s behaviorism of psychologist B. F. Skinner, and many behavioral policies were first honed in the advertising industry. Although the policy approach is popular with governments, there is something uncomfortable about officials acting like advertising executives in trying to influence people's choices by manipulating them psychologically.

There are, in addition, some conceptual questions. The *nudge* approach—using knowledge about how people make choices in reality to construct policies that deliver a "better" outcome—faces two kinds of challenges. One is more a difference of emphasis, pointing to the evolutionary rationality of heuristics rather than presenting them as irrational quirks. It is spearheaded by Gerd Gigerenzer. The other, from economists such as Robert Sugden, challenges the idea that people have beneath their irrational choices some "true" preferences to be satisfied by the authorities as if they were making rational choices. This strand of work argues that there is no inner rational economic agent and people make their choices in particular contexts and shaped by what is going on around them.

Finally, there are many unanswered questions about the effectiveness of behavioral policies. Experiments and trials indicate highly variable results as to which particular behavioral approach works and how policies interact. There has been a crisis of methodology in the psychological research literature that inspired behavioral economics, for example, in the inability to replicate some results. And outcomes seem to depend a great deal on the particular circumstances. So there is still much to learn.

How Do Humans Make Choices?

The aim of public policy is to bring about an efficient allocation and use of resources in society. Often the decentralized decisions of individuals in the market can achieve this. Sometimes public policy interventions are needed—when there are public goods or externalities whereby social and private benefits and costs differ, or where there are information asymmetries or monopoly power. The interventions discussed so far in this book have all been based on the assumption that people make rational choices in their own self-interest. It is possible to define *self-interest* very broadly, including incorporating the well-being of other people or an altruistic motive. But all the discussion so far has relied on the rationality assumption.

Economics is all about how people make choices, so this assumption is a rather important one. Typically, economics assumes that we are like Mr. Spock in *Star Trek*: we take a logical view of the information available to us and calculate the outcomes of different choices. So on walking past a shop window and seeing a jacket, we look at the price and consult our preferences, and calculate—given our budget constraints—whether the utility from buying it is greater than our other possible uses for the money. In the case of many purchases, this is a reasonable enough decision, empirically speaking. But as we all appreciate, humans are emotional as well as logical. Sometimes we make impulse purchases. Or eat cake now knowing we'll regret it next time we step on the scales. Or choose a certain jacket just because our best friend has one like it, or we liked a picture we saw in an advertisement.

Given that everyone is aware of the role of impulse and emotion, why do economists still assume that everyone behaves like an ultra-rational Vulcan? Well, often the standard assumption does a perfectly good job of predicting how people behave. Many experiments have demonstrated that people's behavior in various contexts generates the same market outcomes as standard economic theory predicts—Vernon Smith even shared a Nobel Prize for exactly this kind of experimental work with Daniel Kahneman, one of the pioneers of the behavioral approach. For that matter other creatures, such as pigeons, rats, and monkeys in laboratory experiments, also make what appear to be rational self-interested choices in response to price incentives; this field of research is known as *biological market theory*. It would be odd to assume that humans are less capable than pigeons of making choices that achieve "rational" outcomes. This suggests that the *context* in which people (or pigeons) are making choices decisively affects how they go about it; people are particularly bad at thinking about uncertainty and calculating probabilities, so "non-rational" choices are more likely under conditions of uncertainty. What's more, substantial minorities of people do behave like the agents assumed in standard economic theory, in many or most contexts; both the conventional and nudge approaches need to avoid assuming everyone is the same.

Moreover, what appear to be non-rational choices conforming to one or the other of the behavioral biases could in fact be the outcome of a wholly rational habit of using rules of thumb (often referred to as heuristics) because this costs less brain energy. This is in line with what Herbert Simon in an older economic literature referred to as *satisficing*—in other words, making a choice that brings about a good enough outcome rather than incurring the effort needed to get the very best possible, maximum outcome. Simon's argument was that people have bounded rationality; they only spend a certain amount of time and mental energy figuring out the best course of action. Thinking through performing a calculation (which Kahneman labeled "slow thinking," as opposed to spur-of-the-moment "fast thinking," or impulsive decisions) involves a cost that a rational being will only incur when the benefits are likely to make it worthwhile.

Behavioral versus Rational Choices

The two approaches to economic decisions—rational choice and behavioral preferences—can be presented as reliant on contrasting sets of assumptions about human behavior, set out (in somewhat simplified form) in table 5.1.

Needless to say, these two sets of assumptions give rise to different predictions about economic choice. The behavioral literature has produced a long list of cognitive biases or patterns, some of which are set out in table 5.2. The length of the list is one of the issues with behavioral economics, in fact, as it means that—in contrast to the conventional assumptions—there is a need to select which behavioral assumptions to apply in analyzing any given problem. In the absence of a comprehensive theory, the selection needs to be done on empirical grounds—which can be fine if done with care, but not theoretically elegant. In this the behavioral approach contrasts with the elegant simplicity of the conventional economic assumption about choice.

Table 5.1. Contrasting Choice Assumptions

Standard	*Behavioral*
People are maximizers, given their information set and constraints	People are satisficers and follow rules of thumb
People calculate outcomes and utilities	People have cognitive "biases" and are especially bad at calculations about the future, or probabilities
Preferences are consistent	Preferences may be inconsistent, especially over time
People's choices are made independently of other people's choices	People's preferences are affected by other people's

Table 5.2. Behavioral "Biases"

Kinked utility function	People assess gains and losses, not levels—losses hurt more than gains please
Loss aversion/endowment effect and risk aversion	People demonstrate loss aversion as well as risk aversion
Anchoring and reference points	People evaluate gains and losses relative to a reference point or anchor (not in absolute terms)
Frames/choice architecture	People's choices vary depending on how a decision is framed or described
Fast and slow thinking	Many decisions are made without calculating specific expected outcomes—they are impulsive or follow heuristics
Status quo bias/inertia	People avoid the effort of calculation and choice and often take the easy option of not deciding
Hindsight/memory biases	People are bad at remembering and in particular remember best the most recent part of an experience
Over-confidence	People are over-confident; a majority claim to be above average. The role of luck is underestimated when outcomes are good, overestimated when they are bad
Social influence	People's choices are often swayed by others
Present bias/hyperbolic discounting	People care more about the near term than further into the future; but as they also put weight now on the more distant future, their choices are often inconsistent over time. Choices differ depending on when they are made.

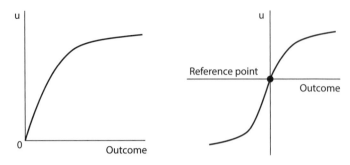

Figure 5.1. Standard utility maximization (left) versus prospect theory (right).

The first three items in table 5.2 are sometimes combined into what is known as *prospect theory*. Figure 5.1 contrasts standard utility maximization on the left with prospect theory, looking at the utility from different outcomes. On the left is a smooth utility function with positive but diminishing marginal utility (and risk aversion in versions with uncertainty), measured from the origin. It is the level of the outcome that determines utility. The standard theory also has normative weight: the aim is maximizing individual utility.

On the right is a kinked function showing the individual measuring gains and losses from a reference point—this is usually taken as the status quo or some other anchoring point, not zero. Below the reference point, people are loss averse. People evaluate not the absolute level of expected utility but expected gains and losses relative to their reference point. Often, empirically, there is also a steeper function for losses than for gains: losses weigh more heavily on us than gains cheer us. Prospect theory is descriptive, trying to capture how people evaluate their utility; to its critics, it is ad hoc, with no rigorous account of what determines the reference point.

One challenge for behavioral economics is that many of these cognitive "biases" have been identified from rather small-scale and non-replicated psychological experiments. The many popular books about behavioral economics tell lots of stories illustrating non-rational choices, but there is no over-arching general framework for reading from the assumptions in the table to predictions about people's choices. This is one reason the standard economic model remains so central: not only is it often empirically valid, it is also a consistent theoretical framework. An alternative research approach to behavioral economics aims to introduce rigor with experiments, confronting people with actual incentives in realistic economic contexts where they interact with other people.

Despite the various questions and critiques, the idea of nudge policies has a firm foothold. Many descriptions of behavioral "biases" can be found in the burgeoning popular and technical literature. Here are some of the key ones.

Thinking about Risk

People are not very good at calculating probabilities. For instance, given this list of choices and asked to select quickly,

A. 80% chance of winning $1,000
B. Win $700 for sure

A. 80% chance of losing $1,000
B. Lose $700 for sure

A. Bet $10 on a 0.1% chance to win $9,000
B. Do nothing

A. Take a 1% chance of losing $100,000
B. Pay $1,100 for insurance against this risk

most people choose B, A, A, B. If calculating expected values given the probabilities correctly, and choosing rationally, they should select A, B, B, A, as these have the greater expected value in each pair.

This pattern is observed fairly systematically in probability calculations of this kind. According to Kahneman's distinction between slow and fast thinking, calculating probabilities (slow thinking), an activity of the prefrontal cortex, uses lots of energy; the brain often jumps to the intuitive answer (fast thinking). Typical answers to choices such as those set out above demonstrate the pattern shown in table 5.3.

Table 5.3. A Fourfold Risk Attitudes Matrix

	Significant expected gains	*Significant expected losses*
High probability	Risk averse—under-estimate potential (e.g., the return to a student loan)	Risk seeking—try to avoid or recoup losses, loss aversion (e.g., financial traders "gambling for resurrection")
Low probability	Risk seeking—over-estimate potential wins (e.g., buying a lottery ticket)	Risk averse—over-estimate potential loss (e.g., insurance policies such as extended warranties for domestic appliances)

Framing and Anchoring

How choices are presented, or "framed," changes decisions because it changes what people perceive to be gains or losses; this matters because of the asymmetry described above in how people tend to value gains and losses. To see how framing affects choice, imagine you are looking at treatments for the Ebola virus in a village with 600 people at risk. The choice of treatments can be presented in four ways:

- A—will save 200 lives out of 600
- B—1/3 probability 600 people will live, 2/3 probability all will die
- C—400 people will die
- D—1/3 probability nobody will die, 2/3 probability 600 will die

All the expected outcomes are the same: 200 survivors. A and C are presented deterministically, B and D as expected outcomes. A and B have positive framing, C and D negative framing. Which presentation will make people most likely to consent to treatment? In the positive framing (A and B) they are risk averse, and choose A. In the negative framing (C and D), they are risk seeking and choose D.

Framing affects all opinion surveys too; the results depend on how the survey question is posed. Figure 5.2 shows an opinion poll

Figure 5.2. Effect of framing opinion survey questions.

example of how framing can change people's responses, flipping the majority opinion in this case.

Opinion polls and referendum outcomes cannot be interpreted without reference to exactly how the question was phrased and the choice framed. Marketers and advertisers have long known about this phenomenon, as their whole industry is based on it (and the economist Nicholas Kaldor was a critic of the advertising industry precisely because he saw it as exploiting a market failure and therefore reducing economic welfare). There are now many behavioral marketing blogs and websites (also covering *neuromarketing*, which uses findings from fMRI scans to make ads more effective). Behavioral advertising blogs and courses are full of advice about how to exploit framing, anchoring, reference points, and risk or loss aversion. For example, they advise the following:

- Say "nine out of ten customers are satisfied with our service," not "90% of customers are satisfied with our service."
- But say "only 1% of our products have a defect," not "only one out of every one hundred products has a defect."
- Compare a $400 espresso machine to $800 a year on lattes at the coffee shop—don't anchor expectations to the $2.50 daily cappuccino.

- Frame the choice by giving consumers some much less attractive options alongside the one you want them to take—often done with subscription packages, for instance.

Inertia

As people economize on the need to calculate or cogitate, there is a lot of inertia in choice. Marketers make use of this with the common tactic of automatic renewal of subscriptions, as it takes an effort to stop them after the introductory special offer has come to an end. One kind of behavioral economic policy (or marketing tool) involves simplifying choices as much as possible, so people can economize on their mental effort. Another is setting the default option so the easiest course of action, the do-nothing choice, is the one that achieves the desired outcome. Having no default option—forcing people to make a choice—can be preferable, of course. If things are too complicated, however, people stop thinking all that intensively. They are more likely to make decisions closer to their rational self-interest if the problem and choices are simplified.

Overconfidence

A frequently observed phenomenon is over-confidence, also known as the *Lake Wobegon effect* (after the Garrison Keillor radio series set in the fictional community of Lake Wobegon, "where the all the women are strong, all the men are good-looking, and all the children are above average"). Almost everyone believes they are a better-than-average driver, or that their children are especially talented. All financial traders are prone to believe they are better than average. They ascribe a run of good luck to skill, but when surprised by mean reversion in their subsequent results blame that on bad luck. As men are more prone to over-confidence than women, and most traders are men, perhaps this should hold implications for financial market regulation.

Present Bias

Another economically important example is *present bias*, or *hyperbolic discounting*.

Money now is worth more to us than money later, so it is not surprising that people discount future benefits. Suppose you are offered $100 now and $110 in a year; if you are indifferent between the two options, the discount factor (rate of time preference) is 10%. Standard *exponential discounting* in economics assumes that the rate stays constant. You should equally be indifferent between $110 in a year and $121 in two years' time. The formula is standard in economics, for example, for calculating the net present value of investment returns; and the discount factor applied to a benefit or return t periods from now is

$$\frac{1}{(1 + \delta)^t}$$

In practice, though, people put more weight on near-term sacrifices. Consider the following two choices:

A1. One coffee now
A2. Two coffees tomorrow

B1. One coffee in one year
B2. Two coffees in one year + one day

People normally choose B2 but A1, being more patient about the future. But people are also normally inconsistent and, if offered the same choice one year from now, would revert to being impatient. Thus, typically, people's preferences are inconsistent over time. The discount formula is

$$\frac{1}{(1 + \delta t)^\beta}$$

where β is positive (sometimes simply 1). Simpler versions known as *quasi-hyperbolic* are sometimes used—the parameters and form of the equation are adjusted to be able to model the kinds of choices

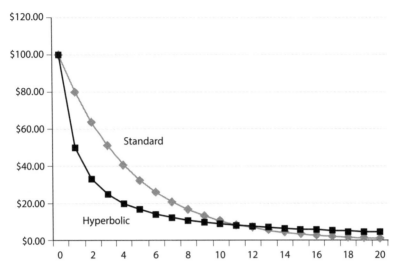

Figure 5.3. Standard and hyperbolic discounting compared.

just described, near-term impatience and long-term patience. Applying these formulas with appropriate parameter values to calculate a net present value shows that the conventional approach values the near term more highly but gives less weight to the more distant future (figure 5.3; and see "Choice of Discounting Formula" in chapter 8 for more on discounting).

There are many examples of this behavior in everyday life. Most people act impulsively in the present and also under-rate the intensity of their future preferences, thinking they will act more "rationally" than they actually will when the time comes. Today, I think I will pick the healthy option for a snack next weekend. In an experiment, 74% of people predicted they would choose an apple, 26% chocolate. Come the weekend, only 30% chose the apple, and 70% picked chocolate. Such examples often combine with *projection bias*, or expecting to feel the same in the future as I do now. One tool for tackling time-inconsistent preferences is a commitment device. Airlines do this, for example, in asking passengers to pre-order their meal—they want the information to help them order the right quantities of the various choices—but passengers can use it to commit themselves to the healthy meal option and avoid the temptation of the tasty but unhealthier choice when mealtime comes.

Behavioral Policies in Practice

There has been an explosion of interest in using nudges, by both governments and businesses. The UK was again an innovator here, the first to set up a special policy unit to develop nudge policies: the Behavioural Insights Team (BIT) in 2010 (it was partly privatized as a social-purpose company in 2014 and now provides consultancy to other governments and to businesses). Australia, Japan, and the US established similar units more recently. In Australia, New South Wales set up a Behavioural Insights Unit (BIU) in 2012. In the US, the Social and Behavioral Sciences Team (SBST) was set up in 2014 and put on ice by President Trump, but not before introducing a range of schemes and pilots in several areas of social policy. Japan set up its nudge unit in 2017, with a remit to focus on environmental, health, and education policies. Behavioral policies are now being applied around the world, including in developing countries through aid programs (box 5.1).

One of the earliest and best-known examples of a successful nudge policy was the introduction of an opt-out in place of an opt-in default in saving for retirement. One of the first studies, in 2001, documented a large increase in participation in a retirement savings plan—a 50% increase for new employees—when the employer switched to automatic enrollment. Many people save too little for their retirement. Without increasing their savings rate, they will find themselves with a much lower income than they expect or want when they retire. Saving for retirement has a tax subsidy—it is possible to earn a higher post-tax interest rate if you save into a pension plan—but this price incentive was evidently insufficient. A number of studies have now shown that changing from an opt-in to an opt-out default option does increase participation in savings plans. The switch means that rather than having to make an active effort to start or increase your savings, doing nothing means you are enrolled in the plan with automatic deductions from pay. In 2006 the US government legis-

Box 5.1. Nudges in development

The application of randomized control trials of different nudges has become widespread in developing countries, often encouraged by aid donors. For example, health care products in developing countries often require payment of a small fee. Experiments have shown that cutting the price from a few pennies to zero can have a dramatic effect on take-up, making the loss of revenue worthwhile given the impact on health outcomes. Researchers argue that a zero price conveys additional information, that the activity is socially expected, introducing a framing effect.

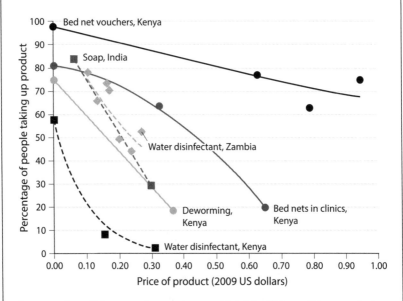

Impact of small fees on take-up. *Source*: Abdul Latif Jameel Poverty Action Lab, https://www.povertyactionlab.org/sites/default/files/publications/The%20Price%20is%20Wrong.pdf.

For people on very low incomes, there can also be an immense cognitive strain in making important decisions, particularly about complicated matters such as financial decisions. The evidence is that people compartmentalize their thinking—for example, borrowing money despite having savings—and focus on small issues rather than

(continued on next page)

(continued from previous page)

their overall financial situation. Presenting information such as loan repayments as monetary amounts rather than interest rates can help people make less costly decisions. Not surprisingly, simplified information has also been found to help people. Experiments on sending text messages as reminders in countries from Bolivia to the Philippines helped increase people's savings.

International Bank for Reconstruction and Development (2015), *World Development Report: Mind, Society, and Behavior.* Eldar Shafir and Sendhil Mullanaithan (2013), *Scarcity,* Henry Holt.

lated to encourage employers to switch to this default, New Zealand followed suit in 2007, and the United Kingdom in 2012. The effects on participation have been dramatic (figure 5.4).

Other government agencies, such as competition regulators, are increasingly interested in behavioral remedies when they find that markets are not working in the best interests of consumers (box 5.2). Recent examples in the UK include a regulation by the Finan-

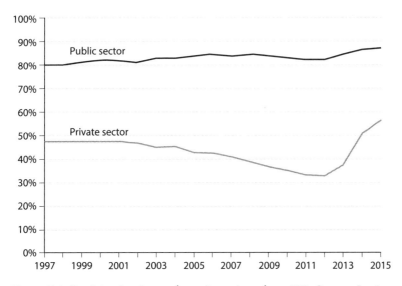

Figure 5.4. Participation in employers' pension plans, UK. *Source*: Institute for Fiscal Studies.

Box 5.2. Structuring behavioral policies

Consumer choice is particularly important in competition policy, and competition authorities are growing increasingly interested in behavioral approaches in markets such as banking and energy, where they would like to see more consumer switching to stimulate competition. It is obvious that behavioral insights could be useful in principle, but it is not always straightforward in practice. For example, in a 2005 UK competition inquiry into directory enquiry services (directory assistance in US parlance), the fear was that British Telecom (BT) would dominate this newly liberalized market as it was the incumbent monopolist, only recently privatized, and with a large market share. The regulators concluded that the solution was more choice, and also that the numbers people could dial to reach directory enquiries should be auctioned. BT bought 118 500, reasoning that people remember round numbers. A rival firm, The Number, chose 118 118 and ran a memorable ad campaign featuring twins. It turns out people are better at remembering three digits than six digits. The market also saw many smaller companies enter and bid for numbers. However, there seems to have been too much choice overall; consumers either stuck with the incumbent (inertia) or opted for the only other number they could remember. The biggest two companies ended up with a *bigger* market share after the deregulation than before.* Understanding consumer psychology seems like it would have been useful. On the other hand, the conclusion in some recent inquiries that the problem with important markets (such as energy or banking) is that consumers need to be nudged to make better choices is surely only a small part of the story in contexts of natural monopoly or highly concentrated markets.

* Rufus Pollock (2009), "Changing the Numbers: UK Directory Enquiries Deregulation and the Failure of Choice," University of Cambridge Department of Economics Working Paper No. 0916, https://ideas.repec.org/s/cam/camdae.html.

cial Conduct Authority and the Competition and Markets Authority (CMA) setting out how comparison websites for payday loans must display information so that consumers will select their cheapest option; they also required the energy companies to test different formats for information on bills to ensure consumers are more likely to switch to cheaper providers, and insurance companies to include the amount of last year's premium on renewal letters so customers could see how much they were being asked to pay had gone up. Many companies frequently try out different versions of their products on customers in what is known as A/B testing when done online, or just market research otherwise. Behavioral policies are similarly likely to need testing to see what form they have to take to deliver the outcomes the regulators wish to achieve.

Table 5.4 gives just a few other examples of implemented nudge policies, to illustrate the range of interventions in this burgeoning area. Many are in health, energy and environment, and employment, or related to the payment of taxes or fines or cost savings in government services. By now, the adoption of behavioral policies has become widespread. Usually, they involve testing exactly what kind of framing of information, or default options, or social comparisons, are most effective in bringing about the desired outcome, sometimes through the use of randomized control trials (just like testing new medical interventions or drugs), field experiments, or pilot schemes. Behavioral policies will always be subject to some trial and error, but there is a huge amount of experimentation under way. The interest in behavioral economics has done a lot to introduce these new methodologies into economics, and the applied literature is now vast and growing daily.

Issues with Behavioral Policies

Identifying the Right Choice Architecture

Structuring the choices people make in order to take advantage of insights from psychology is described as *choice architecture*. This includes setting a different default option, simplifying choices, se-

Table 5.4. Examples of Nudges in Practice

Policy type	Description
Changing the default	UK, 2012. Employers were required to enroll employees automatically in pension plans—default changed from opt-in to opt-out. Participation in pension plans rose from 61% to 83% (BIT).
Commitment device	UK, 2014. In a pilot scheme, unemployed benefit claimants were required to write down each week what they would do to look for work. This increased the number of people moving off benefits to a small (2%–5%) but significant extent (BIT).
Social norms	Australia, 2015. Fine notices were redesigned to include a message that a majority of people pay their fines on time. The new notices led to a 3.1% increase in payment, raising more than AUD$1 million (BIU).
Framing	US, 2015. Information on choice of energy plans was changed to make consumers choose between green and non-green options rather than defaulting them to a standard tariff. Pilot schemes were paused (SBST).
Framing	Australia, 2016. No-shows to hospital appointments in New South Wales were reduced by selecting—out of several options assessed—a reminder text message that told patients each missed appointment cost the hospitals AUD$125. There was a 20% reduction in no-shows, saving $67,000 a year (BIU).
Framing	Kenya, 2015. Text messages were sent to people who had taken out zero-interest microcredit loans to test which message would increase repayment rates. Messages increased repayments from men but reduced them from women (CGAP, Busara Center for Behavioral Economics).

lecting information and presenting it in particular ways, and using social comparisons. Choice architecture uses framing, anchoring, reference points, inertia, present bias, and so on, in the interest of getting people to make better decisions. A policymaker considering individuals making a sub-optimal choice because of one or more of the above cognitive habits can think about using several behavioral policies or nudges.

Consider the problem of eating too much chocolate cake. You know it is bad for you long term to eat a piece each day but cannot resist the impulse. How could you design a personal set of nudges and choice architecture to change your behavior? There are several possibilities:

- join a weight loss group (a commitment device)
- put a photo of yourself a year younger and ten pounds lighter on the fridge door (framing/reference point)
- never buy whole cakes, just one piece at a time, and have lots of apples in the house (change the default option)
- start a Facebook page with friends to record how much cake you eat (social comparison, although dangerous if all are un-reformed cake eaters)
- lobby the local café to change the counter layout so tempting-looking fruit salads and whole-grain muffins are more visible (choice architecture)

In practice, policymakers similarly opt for a mix of approaches and could even experiment to see which is most effective, either alone or in combination. It seems on the face of it hard to object to the deployment of choice architecture, because apart from anything else there is always going to be some choice architecture and surely it should nudge people to better choices rather than worse ones. If either fries or salads have to be at the front of the counter in the school cafeteria, why would you not prioritize the healthier option? Why would it be a good idea to leave the fries prominent just because that is what happens now?

The UK Behavioural Insights Team has distilled its advice into a few bullet points (box 5.3). Their recommendations sound straightforward. In fact, quite a lot of "behavioral" policy advice seems to boil down to common sense (not that common sense always prevails in policy-making). For example, keeping forms simple and making information visually attractive come into this category. But it is not always as easy as it seems to structure information and create a choice architecture in a useful way (box 5.4).

There is still a lot to understand about how information is delivered and what it should consist of, and how it interacts with conventional financial incentives. It is not always as easy as the kind of physical nudge shown in figure 5.5. There is a great deal of empirical evidence emerging from research, but it is impossible at present to generalize the conclusions for policy. The context and

Box 5.3. Advice from the Behavioural Insights Team

Make It Easy:
    Harness the power of defaults.
    Reduce the "hassle factor" of signing up for a service.
    Simplify messages.

Make It Attractive:
    Attract attention.
    Design rewards and sanctions for maximum effect.

Make It Social:
    Show that most people perform the desired behavior.
    Use the power of social networks.
    Encourage people to make a commitment to others.

Make It Timely:
    Prompt people when they are likely to be most receptive.
    Consider the immediate costs and benefits.
    Help people close the gap between intentions and actual behavior.

Box 5.4 Issues in choice architecture

Numerous field experiments have looked at how the presentation of information about their electricity use and bills affects customers' subsequent usage. In one year-long study, social influences were found to have a strong effect. Telling customers about other people's electricity consumption and bills reduced consumption of electricity by about 6%. The effect was instant and seemed to last, even though there were no sanctions for not changing behavior. However, simply presenting customers with information about *how* to reduce their consumption had an even bigger short-term impact, and a similar one over a longer period of fifteen months. However, the information had to be included with a paper bill and illustrated with a chart; it did not work when sent by email. Yet for customers signed up to

(continued on next page)

(continued from previous page)

online billing, a large financial incentive to cut their usage worked better than either of the other alternatives, reducing consumption by 10%. Confusingly, this favorable impact was greatly reduced when the customers also received the information about what other people were paying.

Paul Dolan and Robert Metcalfe (2015), "Neighbors, Knowledge, and Nuggets: Two Natural Field Experiments on the Role of Incentives on Energy Conservation," Becker Friedman Institute for Research in Economics, Working Paper No. 2589269 (April), https://ssrn.com/abstract=2589269 or http://dx.doi.org/10.2139/ssrn.2589269.

Figure 5.5. The power of choice architecture illustrated. Musical stairs in a Stockholm metro station play a note when people stand on them, encouraging people to walk rather than stand on the escalator (https://www.youtube.com/watch?v=2lXh2n0aPyw).

the details of the choice architecture seem to make a lot of difference. There is certainly no policy takeaway as straightforward as the more conventional policy approaches such as, "raise taxes to discourage consumption." Deploying nudges without the relevant nuanced understanding can be counterproductive, and it is similarly highly unlikely that behavioral policies can be transplanted easily from one country or state to another.

Finding the Right Counterfactual

There are challenges, too, in evaluating behavioral policies. For example, the opt-out default for pension savings described earlier has been successful everywhere in raising the proportion of people who save in a plan for their retirement. This seems to be an obviously good idea, but there are some questions about it. In these kinds of savings plans, people save 2%–4% of their income. This is probably too low a level for pension adequacy for most people, so more action is needed to raise the savings rate—but do people think they are saving enough because of the scheme? Nor is it clear that the increase represents new savings rather than savings diverted from other kinds of financial assets. Finally, there might be people who are in the plan by default who would be better off doing something different because of their personal circumstances—for example, if they are paying down costly credit card debt. The increase in participation in the pension savings plan by itself is not enough to evaluate the policy as a clear success. A proper evaluation needs to take into account costs as well as benefits, and to compare what happens when the default is switched with an appropriate counterfactual.

Financial and Intrinsic Motivations

One question that comes up in many behavioral policy experiments is the role of financial versus social or civic-minded incentives, referred to as *intrinsic motivation*. The importance of intrinsic motivation is not new in economics. Adam Smith's *Theory of Moral Sentiments* emphasized the importance of non-financial considerations, although modern mainstream economics has tended to ignore it and assume financial motivations are all that matters. There are some well-known stories about how the use of financial incentives backfires, including a famous and often-repeated account by Daniel Kahneman about a nursery that started fining parents for picking up their infants late. The fine made the parents feel they were buying a service and were entitled to be late, and so proved counterproductive. The financial incentive crowded out the moral imperative of guilt. Perhaps something similar happened in the energy price experiment, when cheaper bills neutralized the effect of social comparison.

There are other contexts where using social norms or intrinsic motivations is more effective as well as being cheaper (box 5.5). Experimental results suggest financial rewards are no more effective than cheap trophies in incentivizing students to get good exam results. Contests within businesses such as naming the sales associate of the month seem to be just as good as bonuses at increasing workers' efforts. The interaction between financial and social motivations is not well understood. But it clearly would be wrong to assume that financial rewards are the most effective choice or that the only way to get good performance at work is performance-related pay or bonuses.

Critiques of Nudge Policies

The impact of nudges can be immense, and there can be no doubt these policy experiments will continue. But this does not mean behavioral public policy is a no-brainer. A key question is whether government officials should be acting more like the advertising executives of *Mad Men*, "correcting" the "biases" manifested in citizens' choices, rather than economic technocrats assuming citizens are the people best able to make their own choices.

Nudge advocates argue that theirs is a benign, "libertarian paternalism." Given that there will always be a default option, or choices will always be framed one way or another, it would be foolish for the government not to select the option or framing most likely to lead people to choose the most efficient outcome. And this

Box 5.5. Blood donations

Countries have different policies about payment for blood donations. In some, including China, Germany, Russia, and the US, donors are often paid a modest fee for their blood. In others, including France and the UK, payment is banned. The World Health Organization has recommended that blood donation should be voluntary and un-paid, for two main reasons.* One is that there is a greater safety risk when payment is made, as donors are more likely to be in financial need and therefore may be ill or drug addicts. In addition, some evidence suggests people's attitudes change in a remunerated system, reducing rather than increasing their willingness to donate. One New Zealand study (based on a relatively small questionnaire sample) found more than half of donors saying they would be unlikely to continue if there was a switch to paid-for donations.** In a classic text, sociologist Richard Titmuss highlighted blood donation as an exemplar of the *gift relationship*, a link that would be damaged by the introduction of a monetary reward.*** However, the relationship between payment and altruism is still debated in academic research. Even in countries where blood donation is voluntary, payment is often made for the donation of blood plasma, necessary to treat autoimmune diseases, as there is a shortage, and the donation procedure demands far more of donors. In others, such as China and the US, prisoners donate blood plasma, but there have been scandals about infections passed on due to inadequate screening.

* https://www.who.int/bloodsafety/voluntary_donation/en/.
** https://www.bmj.com/content/312/7039/1131.
*** Richard Titmuss (1970, reprinted 1997), *The Gift Relationship*, New Press.

is clearly a valid point. People are not restricted from making the choice they prefer; it is just made a bit harder for them.

Critics worry about the legitimacy of experts and officials making such decisions, and question whose interests exactly they have at heart. Much paternalism involves getting people to do things they do not want to do. If there has to be some paternalism, or restriction, should that come from the government rather than family or community? This leads to the discussion of government failure in chapter 7, which also draws together a number of issues touched on in previous chapters. Behavioral policy does require policymakers to conclude that they know better than individual citizens, and that their evaluation of the benefits of particular choices is more correct. There is something uncomfortable about the adoption by officials of tactics long used in the advertising industry, particularly at a time when there is already a public backlash against "experts." Behavioral interventions are also increasingly used by the big online companies to encourage behaviors they deem to be desirable. Facebook, for example, has conducted a number of online behavioral experiments, such as looking at what nudges raise turnout in elections or get people to pledge to become organ donors—and perhaps others that have not become public knowledge.

In a strong critique of nudges, Gilles Saint-Paul asks why it should be considered the job of government to reduce the incidence of obesity by introducing behavioral policies to alter what people eat or drink. Such policies damage individual responsibility, he argues, and they may reduce the utility of people who are not obese, perhaps by more than it reduces the waistline and increases the utility of people who are. Critics also argue that freedom is a value that should override economic efficiency. Even benign paternalism is coercive: Why not just require people to finance their own retirement and leave it at that, rather than semi-forcing them to save in a specific pension scheme? Much public policy economics discusses the trade-off between efficiency and equity. In the context of this debate about behavioral policies, there is perhaps a trade-off between efficiency and freedom. The counter-argument might be that in an economy where companies selling products are using behavioral science to persuade people to buy products that might not be good for their well-being in some objective sense, such as diverting money away from necessities like the rent, or being unhealthy, why should governments *not* try countermarketing (box 5.6)?

These are not reasons for abandoning or condemning behavioral policies; but there is a case for caution. Policymakers need to be

Box 5.6. Selling unhealthy food

Rising obesity is a public health problem in many countries, both rich and poor. According to a 2017 OECD report, adult obesity rates are highest in the United States, Mexico, New Zealand, and Hungary, and lowest in Japan and Korea, ranging from a high of more than 30% in the former to less than 6% in the latter.*

Researchers have tried to identify the causes, out of many possible contributory factors, including people getting less exercise than they used to, rising consumption of soft drinks, and changing eating habits. Governments have tried a range of policies, such as a tax on the use of too much sugar in drinks in the UK and extra coupons to buy fresh fruit and vegetables for families in California receiving food stamps.** Although it is far from clear what the causes of the obesity epidemic are, it is hard to argue that governments should not be trying behavioral policies to change consumers' preferences between different types of food; for the food industry has for decades been employing behavioral scientists to work out how to make people buy food products, regardless of the health impacts, in a process of "food optimization" that makes food tasty by adding ingredients such as sugar or sodium.*** Equally, the fact that food manufacturers may be contributing to obesity through their formulations points to the need for regulatory and tax policies too.

* OCED (2017), Obesity Update, https://www.oecd.org/els/health-systems /Obesity-Update-2017.pdf.
** Linda Fulpone (2009), "Policy Initiatives Concerning Diet, Health and Nutrition," OECD, https://www.oecd.org/tad/44999628.pdf; Nick Triggle (2018), "Soft Drink Sugar Tax Starts but Will It Work?," https://www .bbc.co.uk/news/health-43659124; OECD (2011), Double Value Coupon Program Diet and Shopping Behavior Study, https://www.oecd.org/site /agrfcn/Double-Value-Coupon-Program-Diet-Shopping-Behavior-Study -.pdf.
*** Michael Moss (2013), "The Extraordinary Science of Addictive Junk Food," https://www.nytimes.com/2013/02/24/magazine/the-extraordinary -science-of-junk-food.html.

just as clear about the economic welfare rationale for these behavioral approaches as for more conventional policies, such as taxes or regulations, and just as modest when it comes to the limitations of their knowledge about what might be effective. But behavioral policies have joined the policy tool kit and form an exciting area of current economic research.

Conclusion

People do not always make choices in the rational, calculating manner typically assumed in economic models and policy analysis, so it is hardly surprising that interest in applying behavioral science to policy has grown so significantly. Although there is no elegant and simple model of how people choose to behave in practice, as opposed to in economic theory, there are some well-established regularities, such as the inertia, loss aversion, framing effects, and over-confidence described in this chapter. There are good reasons for taking these behavioral characteristics into account when designing economic policies. Why, indeed, should a policy analyst make unrealistic assumptions that will likely result in an intervention not working, or even backfiring? However, there is still a lot to learn about what types of behavior occur in specific contexts. Sometimes people act exactly like the abstract rational agents in standard economic models; sometimes different behavioral interventions have unexpected effects. There are not yet many systematic results in the literature. There is a danger in embracing too enthusiastically the "nudge" policies if this is not done with due attention to the specific context, and the limits of what policymakers know.

Further Reading

Technical Follow-Up

Raj Chetty (2015), "Behavioural Economics and Public Policy: A Pragmatic Perspective," *American Economic Review* 105, no. 5 (May): 1–33,

doi: 10.1257/aer.p20151108, http://www.rajchetty.com/chettyfiles
/behavioral_ely.pdf.

Fabrizio Ghisellini and Beryl Y. Chang (2018), *Behavioural Economics: Moving Forward*, Palgrave Macmillan.

Ted O'Donoghue and Matthew Rabin (1999), "Doing It Now or Later," *American Economic Review* 89, no. 1: 103–124.

Matthew Rabin (2002), "A Perspective on Psychology and Economics," UC Berkeley Department of Economics Working Paper No. E02-313, http://digitalassets.lib.berkeley.edu/main/b22239650_C075622681.pdf.

Classic Articles

Daniel Kahneman and Amos Tversky (1979), "Prospect Theory: An Analysis of Decision under Risk," *Econometrica* 47, no. 2: 263–292.

David Laibson (1997), "Golden Eggs and Hyperbolic Discounting," *Quarterly Journal of Economics* 112, no. 2: 443–477.

Herbert A. Simon (1955), "A Behavioral Model of Rational Choice," *Quarterly Journal of Economics* 69, no. 1: 99–118.

Amos Tversky and Daniel Kahneman (1974), "Judgment under Uncertainty: Heuristics and Biases," *Science* 185, no. 4157 (September): 1124–1131.

Behavioral Policies

Abhijit Banerjee and Esther Duflo (2011), *Poor Economics*, PublicAffairs.

Marianne Bertrand, Sendhil Mullainathan, and Eldar Shafir (2006), "Behavioral Economics and Marketing in Aid of Decision-Making among the Poor," *Journal of Public Policy and Marketing* 25, no. 1: 8–23.

Uri Gneezy, Stephan Meier, and Pedro Rey-Biel (2011), "When and Why Incentives (Don't) Work to Modify Behavior," *Journal of Economic Perspectives* 25, no. 4 (Fall): 191–210.

David Halpern (2015), *Inside the Nudge Unit: How Small Changes Can Make a Big Difference*, WH Allen.

Brigitte Madrian (2014), "Applying Insights from Behavioral Economics to Policy Design" (July), http://papers.ssrn.com/sol3/papers.cfm?abstract_id=2471211&download=yes.

J. Mehta, ed. (2013), *Behavioral Economics in Competition and Consumer Policy*, University of East Anglia, http://competitionpolicy.ac.uk

/documents/8158338/8193541/CCP+economics+book+Final+digital+
version+-+colour.pdf/30214557-cace-4b0b-8aac-a801bbde87bc.

OECD (2017), "Behavioral Insights and Public Policy: Lessons from
around the World," http://www.keepeek.com/Digital-Asset-Management
/oecd/governance/behavioural-insights-and-public-policy_978926427
0480-en#.WgMB30dpFDg#page1.

Cass Sunstein (2016), "Nudges That Fail," SSRN Working Paper, http://
papers.ssrn.com/sol3/papers.cfm?abstract_id=2809658.

Richard H. Thaler (2016), "Behavioral Economics, Past, Present and Future," *American Economic Review* 106, no. 7: 1577–1600, http://dx.doi
.org/10.1257/aer.106.7.1577.

Richard Thaler (2017), Nobel Prize lecture (December), https://www
.nobelprize.org/prizes/economic-sciences/2017/thaler/speech/.

Critiques

G. Harrison and D. Ross (2017), "The Empirical Adequacy of Cumulative
Prospect Theory and Its Implications for Normative Assessment," *Journal of Economic Methodology* 25:150–165.

Gilles Saint-Paul (2003), "Liberty and the Post-Utilitarian Society," http://
ideas.repec.org/p/iza/izadps/dp6911.html, and reply by Cass Sunstein
and Richard Thaler (2003), "Libertarian Paternalism," *American Economic Review Papers & Proceedings* 93, no. 2 (May): 175–179.

Robert Sugden (2018), *The Community of Advantage*, OUP.

Popular Books

Dan Ariely (2008), *Predictably Irrational*, HarperCollins.

Dan Ariely and Jeff Kreisler (2017), *Dollars and Sense: How We Misthink
Money and How to Spend Smarter*, HarperCollins.

Daniel Kahneman (2011), *Thinking Fast and Slow*, Farrar, Straus and
Giroux.

Cass Sunstein and Richard Thaler (2008), *Nudge*, Yale University Press.

Richard Thaler (2015), *Misbehaving*, W. W. Norton.

CHAPTER 6

Poverty, Inequality, and the Role of the State

One of the most obvious ways the state affects individuals' economic well-being is by providing a safety net in the shape of what Europeans would call the welfare state. This chapter looks at the government's role in determining individual citizens' levels of income, and the distribution of income among them, and also the provision of essential services such as health and education. Although the general trend for government spending on categories such as social security, pensions, health, and education has been upward, there are immense differences in the choices countries make in terms of policies such as unemployment insurance, social security, and the public provision of health and education. There are equally large differences in the ways governments (and their voters) choose to raise taxes to finance these expenditures. These are vast topics and cannot be covered in any depth in this book. In particular, the literature on optimal taxation is cited but not covered here; but it should be kept in mind that the nation's economic welfare depends on the tax side of the government's activities as well as the spending side. There is a trade-off between raising tax revenues (and the manner in which this is done) and economic growth; or between equity and efficiency.

Here the focus is on the underlying economic efficiency rationale for state intervention in incomes and the provision of services at all. Why do governments consider there is a need for reducing poverty, or providing a minimum level of income or health and education for everyone? Why should so many consider redistribution appropriate on economic efficiency grounds rather than for ethical reasons alone? Some of the different policy options for income redistribution and service provision are discussed. The size of government in relation to the economy as a whole varies significantly between countries, even among the rich OECD member countries. Broadly speaking, the European nations have bigger government sectors than the US and Japan. The chapter also explores the reasons for differences between national choices, which are determined both by history and by different national preferences.

After sketching the trends in the developed economies, the chapter considers the rationales in terms of economic efficiency for the government to take actions that affect people's income and expenditure through tax and benefits, and the provision of public services. It describes the policy challenges governments set themselves: reducing poverty and limiting inequality. It then turns to the policy tools available, a wide range from different forms of taxation to expenditure on services.

Expansion of the Welfare State

Most of the countries that are now members of the OECD have provided some poverty relief for centuries, but it was not until the franchise started to expand in the nineteenth century that governments began to consider a more extensive safety net for citizens during hard times. The first social insurance systems appeared in Continental Europe in the nineteenth century. In the UK at that time, workers were able to save for life insurance and funeral policies through (non-governmental) mutual societies. These lingered in working-class areas of the UK into the 1970s; an insurance company representative visited households and collected small sums, say, a penny per week per policy. One of the earliest nascent welfare states took shape in Germany when Chancellor Otto von Bismarck introduced a social insurance system in the 1870s. Other nations started to extend their systems during the last decades of the nineteenth century. In the US, the forerunner of the present Social Security system was established in 1935. Unemployment and health insurance were rare in these early capitalist times, however; for reasons explained below, it is rare for private markets to provide these kinds of insurance. In the first decade of the twentieth century, the UK introduced unemployment insurance and state pension provision, but coverage was limited. Ill health in particular was a terrible economic blow from which families never recovered. In the United States, there was no social security at all as the economy went into the Great Depression.

It was the experience of the Depression, paving the way for the Second World War, which led to the introduction of the modern welfare state on both sides of the Atlantic (box 6.1). Given the scale of the economic catastrophe and the wider franchise by that time, voters held governments increasingly responsible for providing more economic security. President Roosevelt's New Deal introduced the first social security scheme in the United States in 1935. From the early part of the twentieth century, national differences of approach were apparent. But government social spending on benefit payments and services such as health has increased everywhere over time, and in most cases continues to increase (figure 6.1).

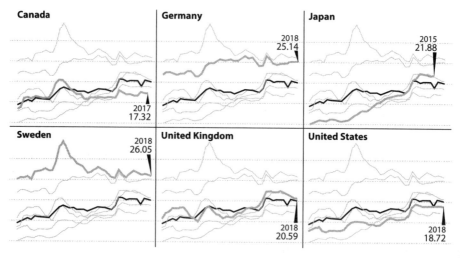

Figure 6.1. Social spending as a share of GDP, selected OECD countries, 1980–2018. Black lines show OECD average. (Social expenditure comprises cash benefits, direct in-kind provision of goods and services, and tax breaks with social purposes. To be considered "social," programs have to involve either redistribution of resources across households or compulsory participation.) *Source*: OECD, updated at https://data.oecd.org/socialexp/social-spending.htm.

Box 6.1. The Five Giants

A significant intellectual turning point came with the publication in Britain in 1942 of William Beveridge's *Social Insurance and Allied Services*, referred to as the Beveridge report. Beveridge aimed to slay what he termed the "Five Giants": want, disease, squalor, ignorance, and idleness. He wrote: "Social security must be achieved by co-operation between the State and the individual." The book was a spectacular best seller with a huge and lasting impact. People had queued the night before its publication on December 1, 1942, to buy it, and the first edition of 60,000 copies sold out quickly. It had sold 100,000 copies within a month, while a shorter, low-priced version sold nearly half a million copies. The BBC broadcast details on its World Service, and copies were sent to all British troops. A copy was even found in Hitler's bunker, with the note, "A consistent system of remarkable simplicity superior to current German social insurance on almost all points." Unemployment had vanished because of the war, but people were determined there would be no going back to the misery of the 1930s. When the British Labour party swept to a remarkable election victory in 1945, defeating Winston Churchill despite his heroic wartime leadership, the public mood was clearly ready for the introduction of Beveridge's social welfare system.

There were three parts to Beveridge's recommendations: management of the economy to achieve full employment (which he equated to an 8% unemployment rate); a National Health Service, free to users at the point of need; and a social insurance scheme people would pay into while working, and draw out from if ill or unemployed, and when they retired. It was intended as a safety net to assist people only for as long as they needed to get back on their feet financially. The mutual insurance motive was fundamental to his scheme. "Contributions in return for benefits," insisted Beveridge. This contributory framework lingers to some extent in the UK's tax and benefit system. Other Western European countries such as France adopted the principles of Beveridge's framework in their own post-war social security systems.

Although the experience of the Great Depression and then war influenced the provision of welfare in all the countries affected, the divergent histories and current structures indicate that governments have been responding to different cultures, perceived needs, and voter demands. There is clearly no "correct" degree of intervention for all times and places. The debates about social security, redistribution, and public services are often politically polarized too, so this is not territory where there is a technocratic right answer. In the early postwar years, the Western European welfare state was largely insurance-based, with a person's contributions determining what they might receive in benefits when unemployed, ill, or retired. Gradually, however, since the creation of the modern welfare state in the mid-twentieth century, as the total amount of government spending involved has increased, means testing has expanded at the expense of the contributory approach. In general, citizens' engagement with the welfare state has become more extensive. By contrast, the US, East Asian economies like Korea, and some smaller, poorer OECD member countries have had less extensive provision and have seen somewhat less growth in expenditure. Benefits in these countries are not as generous as in most EU countries, either in amount or duration or both (figure 6.2). However, in all the developed economies there is significant state provision of income to individuals when they are not earning.

Countries also make divergent choices concerning income distribution and redistribution. Governments affect the distribution of income through the tax system and welfare payments, of course. They also influence it through regulations such as minimum wages, collective bargaining agreements, or corporate governance rules, affecting the distribution of wages and salaries; and through the provision of redistribution in kind through public services such as health, education, and housing. There are therefore different historical trajectories reflecting different political choices about economic institutions, tax burdens, and the form and generosity of the welfare safety nets. What explains these choices, and does this mean welfare is really a political rather than an economic issue?

These issues are enormous in scope. This chapter explores the distinction between poverty relief and income redistribution. It also

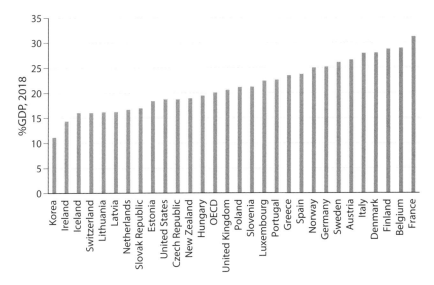

Figure 6.2. Government social spending across OECD economies as a percentage of GDP, 2018. (OECD definition of social spending: cash benefits, direct in-kind provision of goods and services, and tax breaks with social purposes.) *Source*: OECD, updated at https://data.oecd.org/socialexp/social-spending.htm.

looks at the policy tools available for governments to affect income levels and income distribution. These are newly important questions, for several reasons. For people with low and middling incomes in some OECD member countries, there has been little increase in their real standard of living since the Great Financial Crisis, and for longer in some cases. Inequality rose in many of the rich economies for the twenty or so years after 1980 (and has continued to rise in the US), reversing the previous, long postwar trend toward increasing equality. There is some debate as to whether stagnant incomes and/or high levels of inequality are affecting voting trends and contributing to the voter anger manifested in many countries, so these developments are worth understanding. There has also been much debate about the role of immigration and globalization in affecting the livelihoods of many people in the rich economies, looking back, and about the potential for accelerating automation to exacerbate inequality, looking forward. The concerns about the potential impact of automation on jobs have also led to the recent revival of interest in an old idea—universal basic income. First, though, is the question of why as a matter of economic efficiency (rather than ethical or political calculation) a government should concern itself with incomes, poverty, and distribution.

Economic Efficiency Rationales for Intervention

The terminology of welfare, the welfare state, or social security (which differs from country to country) often makes people think only about a narrow range of policies, such as unemployment benefits or government payments to people who are in special need. Governments in practice do a lot of other things that affect people's living standards, including providing public services and setting the legal and institutional framework of the labor market. What responsibility do governments have to citizens in this regard? Should they be concerned about income distribution at all, and if so, when and with what aim in mind? Should they focus simply on keeping people out of poverty, and if so, how? Historically, all Western states have provided some relief from poverty, and increasingly over time some income support during unemployment, illness, and retirement. All governments have funded these services through a progressive (i.e., redistributive) tax system, although to different degrees. They have also provided public services such as education, health care, and housing that make an important contribution to people's standard of living, are tax funded, and are also redistributive because people with lower incomes rely more heavily on public services.

Given that governments intervene in these various ways in practice, what about the theory? Is there a strong rationale? One reason might be because governments aim to create fair societies, which requires some minimum living standard or perhaps a maximum degree of inequality. The equity arguments are strong. Citizenship in a democracy brings some claim to at least a minimum ability to participate fully in the country's or community's economic and social life. What's more, extreme inequality at the upper end of the income scale can lead to an erosion of democracy, as rich people are likely to have growing influence on policies and so minority interests or the protection of monopoly rents may increasingly prevail in legislation and regulation. What, though, is the economic efficiency rationale in terms of market failures? There are in fact several. They concern asymmetric information (assumption A4 fails), incomplete markets (A6 fails), and externalities (A5 fails) (see box 1.4).

When it comes to providing an income in times of need, the most important rationale concerns the inability of individuals to insure themselves privately against some kinds of risk, because of asymmetric information and missing markets (assumptions A4 and A6 fail). The welfare state is in essence society's mutual insurance. There are some risks it is impossible for individuals to insure themselves against either because the scale is so large or because the adverse events affect everyone simultaneously such that private insurers could not diversify the risks. For example, a recession will cause a big increase in unemployment, and many people will lose their earnings through no fault of their own. Thus when it comes to unemployment insurance, the likelihood of mass unemployment in a recession is a risk no private insurer could ever cover. Insurance markets are viable for differentiated individual risks, when these can be pooled across as varied a group as possible; but not for major aggregate risks. Hence the state always has to step in to compensate people for large-scale disasters, such as floods and terrorism. Events such as these are explicitly excluded from standard insurance policies. It is similar with the downturns of the business cycle. Recall from chapter 2 the market for lemons model: if there is a big enough risk of the bad outcome (a dodgy car, a recession), and individuals do not know what situation they will be in (are they buying a lemon or not—or in the present context, whether or not they will be unemployed or seriously ill), the market may not exist. It is possible to buy some private income insurance as an individual, but generally for individuals for whom the risk of making a claim is quite low; and anyway such policies are costly.

These kinds of market failures due to asymmetric information and adverse selection are pervasive in insurance, including health insurance. People know more than the insurance company about their own health, and it is hard for others to monitor their health (although private insurers do often require people to have check-ups with doctors employed by the insurer, or, increasingly, provide data from smartphone or watch apps). Those more likely to fall ill will want to buy more coverage. There's also a potential *moral hazard problem*: if you have health insurance, you will be more likely to take risks. Or if you fall ill, you will have no incentive to economize on treatments and will take every test going. This may be good for health outcomes, but society ends up with an economically inefficient, high level of treatment (like the US, which spends more as a share of GDP on health care than other OECD nations but has worse average health outcomes). Most governments provide health care, provide insurance, or mandate regulated health insurance. The United States does so through the Medicare and Medicaid programs; more recently, its Affordable Care Act represents an extension of the principle of addressing the market failures in this domain—although it is of course a divisive partisan issue.

There are also health events that are not really insurable at all because they are, on the contrary, so likely to happen—such as the minor illnesses of old age and indeed death. The need here is for a savings vehicle, not an insurance policy. But given the well-known behavioral aspects of long-term savings decisions, described in the previous chapter, the state is likely to have to either provide care or mandate such savings. Finally, there is the scale of the need in health care. Treatment for flu or a broken leg is one thing, but some health problems have a catastrophic impact on people's lives and earning power—pricing private insurance coverage for low probability but catastrophic risks is always difficult. When it comes to health care—revisited below—the range of policy approaches is enormous, with Britain's much-loved NHS providing health care as a tax-funded public service, free at the point of need, at one end of the spectrum and the US emphasis on the private insurance market at the other.

There is another asymmetric information rationale for direct public provision, which is that professionals such as doctors and teachers know far more than their "customers" about the service being provided. Untrained people have little ability to evaluate the quality of care or teaching. And as these are experience goods, there is no real possibility of shopping around. It's possible that patients or pupils might never know what the quality of the service was, in other words, what difference it made to the outcome: Would their health have been better with another doctor or their grade with another teacher? The provision of information such as league tables based on test results or death rates can help, but they are complicated to evaluate because there are many dimensions to a complex service, and it is not possible to know the counterfactual. So having impartial experts set criteria for treatment, regulate fees or salaries, and set quality standards is desirable—although still fraught with difficulty. Ultimately, relationships of trust with individual doctors and teachers really matter, because of the information problem as well as the importance of these services. A related issue is the motivation of health and education professionals—a subject picked up in detail in chapter 7. Many people argue that a market relationship in health or education undermines the quality of the service provided. Obviously, doctors, nurses, and teachers need to get paid. But there is some evidence that a monetary relationship can undermine the quality of care, that it has some adverse effect on the intrinsic motivation of some professions.

Another rationale for government provision or subsidy of public services is that the social benefits exceed the private benefits of both health and education expenditure—there are large externalities. This applies to infectious diseases, for instance. More generally, a healthy and vigorous workforce will have wider productivity spillovers. It is also true of education: modern growth theory explains why there is a social benefit to increasing investment in education, as well as the private benefit of a higher subsequent income, as knowledge spills over between people, so one person's improved education benefits others. Poor countries are often trapped in a vicious circle whereby the private return to education is low because the jobs available are low skill, and jobs are low skill because only uneducated workers are available. This kind of externality justifies some degree of (Pigouvian) subsidy to education, in addition to private spending.

Poverty: Definitions and Trends

These arguments mean that there is a theoretical justification for what governments do in practice in providing different kinds of income support and public services. It is broadly accepted that the reduction of poverty is a priority, particularly to tide people through bad times, such as unemployment or serious illness, although in many countries social security systems have broader aims. Poverty obviously means not having enough money, but for the purposes of practical policies it needs to be defined precisely enough to measure it. One important distinction is between absolute and relative poverty:

> *Absolute poverty* is set at a fixed level, such as the $2 a day definition used by international aid agencies. In general, it is not completely absolute, but rather set with reference to the prevailing level of income in society in a selected base year. The $2 in poor countries used to be $1 a day. The absolute poverty level in rich countries would be much higher.
>
> *Relative poverty* is defined as a proportion of other incomes in society, often 50% or 60%, of median income (where median income is the mid-point of the income distribution). The definition uses the median income as the benchmark because average income is always higher, as income distributions are skewed by some very high incomes at the top end.

Poverty is usually measured by looking at household rather than individual incomes, and the measures are usually *equivalized* to take into account the composition of different kinds of households: how many children or adult dependents there are, for instance, as well as how many adults. The amount of money a household needs differs greatly depending on whether there are children or other dependents, how many people live in the household, whether any of the members are retired, or disabled, and so on. Equivalized incomes are calculated by weighting individuals on a scale: for example, in one commonly used version the first adult gets a weight of 1, other adults 0.5, children under 15 0.3, and so on. The weights decline because there are assumed to be economies of scale in running a household—for instance, the same domestic appliances can be used by several people, or several people can live in a home for the same rent.

Incomes can also be considered either before or after taking into account the taxes paid and benefits received by the household; the difference between these two is an indicator of how redistributive the tax and benefits or social security system is. Sometimes income measures after housing costs are used, as these costs are taken to be so essential they must be accounted for to calculate available income.

With these definitions in mind, absolute poverty has been in decline in the OECD economies (figure 6.3) for most of the past seven decades, with some temporary increases during recessions. However, using a relative poverty threshold in considering government policy is more reasonable, as poverty now is not the same kind of experience as in the 1930s, or even the 1990s. Indoor bathrooms, central heating, and mobile phones are now considered necessities; people do not have access to the minimum living standard enabling them to play a part in society if they cannot afford these things. And, after all, one reason to care about poverty is not only because of altruism or a sense of social justice but also because in democracies we want everybody to have the potential for civic participation. Extensive relative poverty in the sense of large numbers of people who cannot participate in everyday activities, and who experience the anxieties of not being able to afford staples, disfigures rich societies.

However, while absolute poverty trends down as long as economies are growing, in many countries relative poverty has trended upward, especially in the 1980s and 1990s. For as median income rises, the relative poverty line will move too, and some people who were above it because their income was above 60% of the old median may drop below it if their incomes do not increase as much as those of other people, and they find themselves further below the new median. The difference between the poverty line (say, 50% of median income) and the mean income of people in that category is called the *poverty gap*. The experience of different demographic

(a)

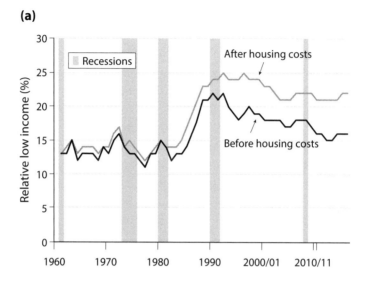

(b)

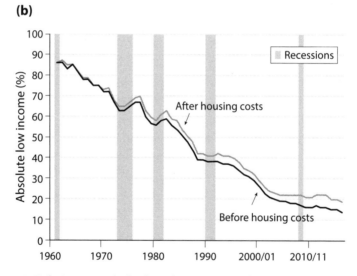

Figure 6.3. Relative (a) and absolute (b) poverty in the UK, 1960 to 2016–17. *Source*: Institute for Fiscal Studies, "Households on Below Average Income," https://assets.publishing.service.gov.uk/government/uploads/system/uploads /attachment_data/file/691917/households-below-average-income-1994-1995 -2016-2017.pdf; https://www.ifs.org.uk/uploads/publications/bns/bn19figs_2016 .xlsx.

groups can also change significantly over time. For example, in the UK pensioners used to be one of the age cohorts most likely to be living in poverty, but over time they have become the least likely to be in the lower-income deciles, whereas children are now the age group most vulnerable to poverty.

The policy options for tackling poverty are discussed a little later, after looking at trends in inequality; there is an obvious overlap in policies, as any actions raising low incomes are likely to reduce income inequality.

Inequality: Definitions and Trends

Inequality too can be defined and measured in several ways. For example, it is important to be precise about whether income or wealth inequality is being referred to. The distinction matters because some people with high wealth can have low incomes and yet still enjoy the privileges and power of the rich. It is also important to be clear whether income is being measured before or after taxes, or what other of the adjustments noted above are being made.

One common approach is to rank a population by income and look at shares of different groups—say, the share of the top 1% or 5% of the income distribution in the total; or at ratios, such as the 10:90 ratio of the total income of the top 10% of the distribution to the bottom 90%.

A more complicated measure, requiring more data but also revealing far more about the whole of the distribution rather than just the extremes, is the *Gini coefficient*. In figure 6.4, the curve showing the cumulative income of the population ranked according to the size of their incomes is known as the *Lorenz curve*. The deeper its curvature is, compared to the 45-degree line (i.e., the bigger area A is in the figure), the more unequal is the income distribution. The Gini coefficient measures this curvature, so a number closer to 1 is more unequal (see table 6.1 for a comparison of some countries' Gini coefficients).

The availability of data on income inequality for different countries has improved enormously in recent years thanks largely to the

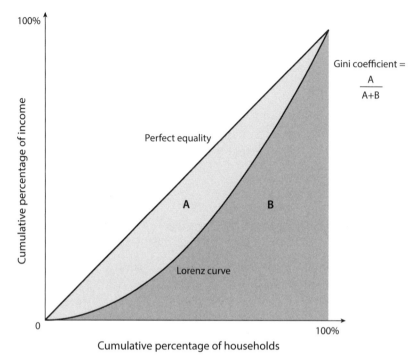

Figure 6.4. Calculating the Gini coefficient.

efforts of a group of economists in establishing the World Wealth and Income Database (WID; http://wid.world/). The statistics need to be treated with some caution. It is harder to measure very high incomes than low and even normally high incomes, as those with low incomes are more likely to be claiming benefits and therefore reporting their finances to the government, or just paying their taxes, while people with very high incomes have accountants who help them hold money offshore away from the eyes of the tax authorities. Data on wealth inequality is particularly sparse, as very rich people are good at keeping their wealth private. Yet the sustained influence that comes with great wealth probably has more important political consequences than a high income that could come to an end. In what follows, though, this chapter is referring to the income inequality figures unless otherwise stated.

Thanks in part to the enormous success of Thomas Piketty's 2014 book, *Capital in the 21st Century*, drawing on the new data, many

Table 6.1. Gini Coefficients

	2008	2009	2010	2011	2012	2013	2014	2015	2016
China	42.8				42.2				
France	33	32.7	33.7	33.3	33.1	32.5	32.3	32.7	
Germany			30.2	30.5		31.1		31.7	
India				35.1					
Sweden	28.1	27.3	27.7	27.6	27.6	28.8	28.4	29.2	
US			40.4			41			41.5

Source: World Bank estimates.

people are now aware of these trends in income inequality. Globally, people on low incomes have enjoyed big gains thanks to rapid economic growth in countries like China and India, and the very well-off have also seen their incomes rise further. The group that has not fared so well is the OECD middle class (box 6.2). There are some common trends across different Western countries—and some important differences. The message from the data is a clear one. In the rich OECD economies, the common pattern is a steady and substantial decrease in inequality over the postwar decades until around 1980. From 1980 to the mid-2000s, this went into reverse and in some countries the increase was large. This includes the US, UK, Canada, and Australia, but also some previously egalitarian countries, such as Sweden (and former communist countries too). In some other European countries, however, the rise in the highest incomes (the top 1%) has been relatively muted. Figure 6.5 shows both the similarities and differences between the US and France. Since the 2008 financial crisis, the increase in inequality has halted or even reversed a little in most countries, although the US is a striking exception. The United States is also exceptional in the extent of its inequality. Members of the top 1% in the US are back where they were in the Gilded Age of *The Great Gatsby*, as figure 6.5 shows.

The fact that the broad trend of declining, then increasing, inequality over the twentieth century is common to all these developed economies means any explanation needs to be sufficiently general. The main candidates to explain this pattern are globalization and

Box 6.2. The global middle

It should not be forgotten that there has been a substantial decrease in income inequality *globally* since 1980, in large part due to rapid economic and income growth in two important and large low-income countries, China and India. Millions of people previously living in poverty in these and other low-income countries have experienced large and rapid increases in income. At the same time as this global middle class has emerged, the middle classes within the OECD member countries have seen little increase at all in their incomes, while the very rich in the rich countries have experienced large gains. While low-income countries remain very unequal, high-income countries have become more unequal over this time period. Economist Branko Milanovic has charted the changes by global income group, labeling the result an "elephant graph" for obvious reasons.

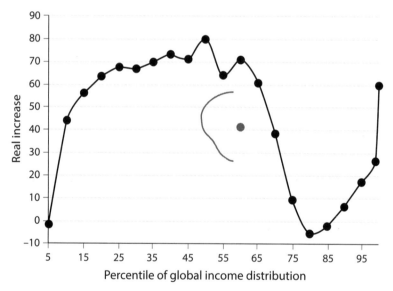

Change in real income between 1988 and 2008 at various percentiles of global income distribution (calculated in 2005 international dollars).

Branko Milanovic (2016), *Global Inequality: A New Approach for the Age of Globalization*, Harvard University Press.

(a)

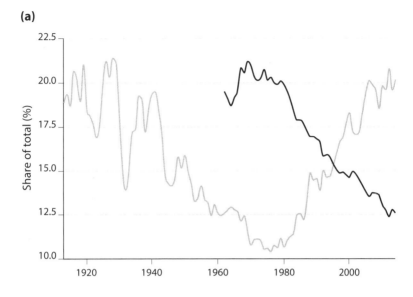

(b)

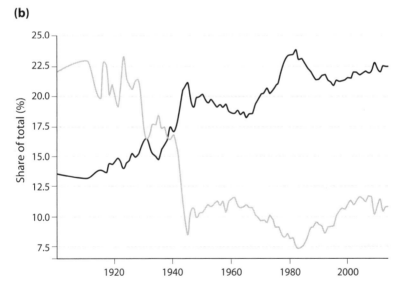

Figure 6.5. Income inequality: (a) United States and (b) France. Top 1% (gray) and bottom 50% (black) share of total national income. *Source*: World Inequality Database (WID) (pre-tax incomes), https://wid.world/.

technology. Both have contributed to increasing the wage premium earned by skilled workers while at the same time limiting increases in the earnings of medium- and low-skilled workers. The research literature by and large finds technological change to be the main driver of income inequality. It has increased demand for workers with the advanced cognitive skills that complement new technologies. Demand has also increased for workers with skills that cannot be automated (at least yet), often traditionally low-paid personal services, such as cleaning, caregiving, hairdressing, retail sales, and so on. However, the supply of highly qualified workers has not increased in line with demand, while supply at the low-skilled end of the earnings distribution has increased because workers displaced from routine work (such as manufacturing or secretarial work) have had to look to these less-well-paid jobs. There is a common pattern across the OECD member countries of a "hollowed-out middle" or polarization in employment, with increases in numbers employed at low and high skill levels and a drop in the middle. Figure 6.6 illustrates the hollowed-out middle for the UK and the US.

More recently, there has been evidence that globalization has been playing a bigger part than technology in the polarization phenomenon (although globalization through international supply chains is itself a technologically enabled phenomenon). The impact of trade with low- and middle-income countries, such as China, in manufacturing communities in OECD member countries has, again, reduced the demand for workers with routine kinds of skills (box 6.3).

Given the general global trade and technology effects, the scale of the increase in inequality, like the level of inequality, differs greatly between countries, and these differences require explanation too. Institutional and political differences must play a part in explaining these distributional outcomes. These differences include the presence and power of trade unions, the level of minimum wages, social norms concerning the acceptability of high pay, the importance of very highly paid sectors such as finance or technology in different economies, and differences in the systems of education and training affecting the supply of skills.

Each of these factors has probably played some part. Strong unions obviously help maintain their members' earnings, albeit

(a)

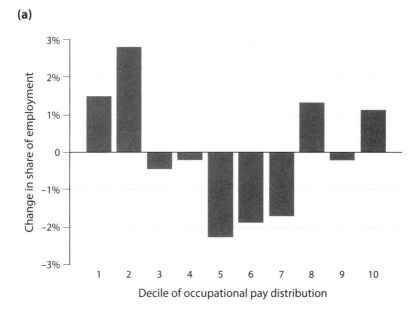

(b)

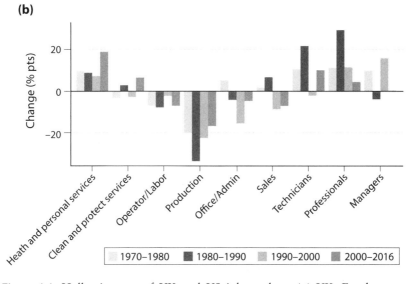

Figure 6.6. Hollowing out of UK and US job markets. (a) UK: Employment shares of deciles of occupational wage distribution, 2002–2010. *Source*: Alan Manning, http://blogs.lse.ac.uk/politicsandpolicy/lovely-and-lousy-jobs/. (b) US: Changes in occupational employment shares, working-age adults (percentage change by decade). *Source*: David H. Autor (2019), "Work of the Past, Work of the Future," Richard T. Ely lecture, AEA Annual Meeting (January), https://economics.mit.edu/files/16560.

Box 6.3. The China shock

Economists David Autor, David Dorn, and Gordon Hanson use the entry of China into world trade in manufacturing at substantial scale from the mid-1990s as a natural experiment to show large, geographically concentrated effects on manufacturing employment and earnings in the United States. Their findings do not take into account other, diffuse, benefits of trade, such as lower prices paid by consumers, and have not (yet) been confirmed for other countries. On the other hand, it would be surprising if the dramatic growth in imports to the OECD member countries from low- and middle-income manufacturing nations, particularly China, had not played any part in the hollowing-out phenomenon. More recent research suggests that the trade and technology shocks are continuing to diminish the earnings prospects in many formerly well-paid jobs: the wage premium to people with college or university qualifications has increased over time. The accompanying graph shows US data; the pattern is common to all the developed economies.

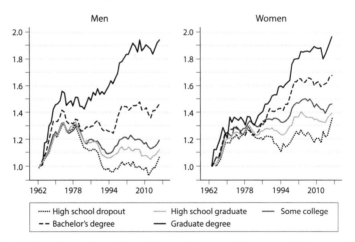

Cumulative change in real weekly earnings, working-age adults, ages 18–64. *Source:* David Autor (2019), Richard T. Ely lecture, AEA Annual Meeting (January), https://economics.mit.edu/files/16560.

David H. Autor, David Dorn, and Gordon H. Hanson (2016), "The China Shock: Learning from Labor-Market Adjustment to Large Changes in Trade," *Annual Review of Economics* 8: 205–240.

sometimes at the expense of non-members who might be more likely to be unemployed or to earn a lower rate. It was not socially acceptable in the 1960s and 1970s for executive earnings to be hundreds of times higher than median earnings, but the prioritization of "shareholder value" and the emergence of performance incentives linked to share option schemes throughout the corporate sector has helped justify soaring earnings for top executives. In some sectors of the economy, high earnings probably reflect the ability of some individuals to extract monopoly rents in markets that are insufficiently regulated or where there is significant market power; as noted in chapter 2, a number of studies have raised concerns about diminishing competition in some sectors of the economy. Finally, the supply of skills also affects income distribution, and some countries do better than others when it comes to education and training, providing people with the skills they need to work alongside the technology rather than being replaced by it.

Is Inequality Really a Problem?

All societies have in place measures to try to reduce poverty, which by definition affects the income distribution by raising low incomes. However, there are significantly different approaches in different countries, and there is also a lively debate about whether new policies (although often old ideas), such as a universal basic income, are needed. There are even greater differences in the approach to policies that can affect the distribution of income, as different electorates seem to have different tolerance levels for the substantial increase that has occurred in top incomes. As the figures above indicate, the big increase in inequality occurred in the 1980s, but the subject has only been a matter of active policy discussion far more recently. Piketty's *Capital in the 21st Century* certainly got the policy world discussing it as never before. The debate has also been most vigorous in the US, where inequality is extreme and has continued to rise, and where there has indeed been political momentum for tax cuts that would increase the share of the top 1%–10% of incomes even further. On the other hand, the US is an outlier, and

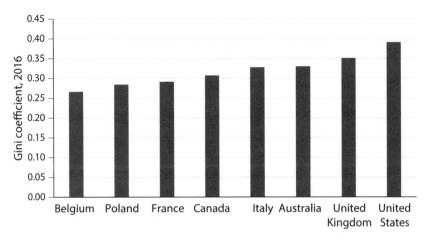

Figure 6.7. Inequality in some OECD countries in 2016, as measured by the Gini coefficient (0 = complete equality; 1 = complete inequality). *Source*: OECD.

income inequality is less extreme in other OECD member countries (figure 6.7).

So, accepting that reducing poverty is important, should governments aim in addition to affect the distribution of income?

Humans (and other animals) do have a strong fairness instinct, but there are plenty of examples of inequality that do not bother us. For example, it is not considered unfair if someone wins the lottery. Lots of other outcomes and decisions in life affecting income are also lotteries. For example, inheriting talent is a matter of pure luck. Career choices such as going to stage school or writing novels is a bit like entering a lottery as there is a high probability of being poor and a low probability of becoming a rich and famous star. This is true of professional sportspeople, opera singers, authors, and musicians too. Few people begrudge Venus and Serena Williams or J. K. Rowling or Benedict Cumberbatch their incomes, even though these are the result of luck as well as hard work. Nor do we usually begrudge the income of someone who has invested years of training and hard work. Surgeons are extremely well paid, as the return on medical training is high, but few people think this is outrageous. Entrepreneurs who succeed have usually worked immensely hard for their high earnings. They tend to be admired rather than envied. All in all, there are few calls for policies to penalize the "deserving" rich, beyond the normal *progressive* structure of income tax, which taxes at a higher rate on slices of income above certain thresholds.

On the other hand, there are people who might not seem to deserve their high incomes in the same way, or at least not as much as they are actually paid, and these cases are contentious. The pay packets of corporate executives or financial traders seem—to many people—to far exceed what can be justified. It takes some skill and effort to be a successful CEO, but surely not 400 times the median corporate employee.

Sometimes economists emphasize the theoretical trade-off between inequality and efficiency, arguing that the possibility of getting rich is an important incentive to effort, and that progressive income taxation or other taxes to enable redistribution causes inefficiencies—making the high earners work a bit less hard, discouraging some investment. However, some people would make the opposite argument: that extreme inequality can disincentivize low earners from any additional effort because they do not believe they will benefit. There is no strong correlation between the degree of income inequality and the economic growth rate across countries.

Milton Friedman in 1962 set out a list of justifications for unequal incomes, and argued strongly against government actions to redistribute through taxation and spending. His list is a helpful way of understanding the intuition set out above about deserved and undeserved high incomes. Here it is (with some commentary):

- People deserve higher pay for skilled, difficult, or dangerous work, or anything that has required years of training, such as surgery, or working on an offshore oil rig (although it must be acknowledged that many other people work in unpleasant jobs for low pay, while some highly skilled people such as ballet dancers or nurses are mostly not well paid)
- Risk-taking should be rewarded (entrepreneurs deserve to get rich)
- Inheritance is a matter of pure luck—but so is talent and we don't begrudge the earnings of, say, basketball players or writ-

ers who have innate skills—that's life, and we should not give in to the politics of envy

- High incomes enable people to accumulate wealth so they can finance innovation and investment, provide patronage for new ideas, or fund philanthropy
- Freedom is more important than coercive action to promote equality
- As it happens, the more capitalist a society, the more equal it is (this was true in the 1960s when Friedman wrote this, but not now)
- Government itself enables people to earn unfairly high incomes by creating barriers to entry to the professions or regulations that enable monopolistic rent seeking (see chapters 2 and 7)

But Friedman also states that society needs a sense of social justice to function; and that income and wealth are the result of property rights, which are determined by the state and society. There is not a difference in principle between the state allocating the right to own property and limiting that right by imposing taxes, on pain of fines or even imprisonment for non-payment. So he also makes powerful arguments against "too much" equality. Perhaps this is the point some Western democracies have reached now: that there is too much inequality, promoting a political backlash in terms of increased votes for some anti-establishment parties and politicians. And perhaps it is why Piketty's book struck such a chord.

A further angle on the question of whether or not inequality per se is a problem is what the future trends are likely to be. The balance of opinion among economists is that technology has played the biggest role in increasing inequality in the OECD member countries in the past twenty to thirty years. Many believe that more technological change should be expected, reinforcing the same kind of trends in patterns of employment by skill level, and consequently earnings. The expanding role of automation and digital technologies has been *skill biased*: greater cognitive skills are needed to work with the technology, and the return to higher education in the shape of higher relative earnings (known as the *skill premium*) has been going up. There is in addition the *superstar* phenomenon. The biggest movie stars always earn a far bigger premium over B-listers than the difference in their talent would objectively justify because, given that watching a movie is an experience good, audiences opt for what they already know. This superstar effect has spread from areas like movies and novels to many other job markets, such as professional services, consultants, non-fiction writers, game players, and so on, thanks to the reach of digital markets.

The big concern now is that the next wave of automation will be at least as large and rapid as the last one, perhaps bigger, and so may drive still greater increases in inequality as the relevant high-level skills always seem to lag behind demand. Although not at all certain, it is one of the fears accounting for the interest in mitigating income inequality: If robots will be able to do all the jobs, what will people do to earn a living? Even if the most dramatic fears are not realized, one of the lessons to take from the experience of deindustrialization in the 1980s and 1990s is that the policies deployed then failed to protect millions of people from the loss of jobs and earnings due to technological and trade shocks. It would surely be desirable to do better in the future, and avoid the scarred lives and devastated communities in the event of further economic disruption.

Policy Choices

The decision about how much policy effort to direct to reducing poverty, never mind reducing inequality, will always be a political one because it cannot avoid redistribution. All options involve in some way taking income away from some groups of people in taxes, backed by the ultimate force of the state, and giving it to others. All governments in fact do some redistribution, and some do a lot.

The standard perspective is to look at tax revenues and social security or benefit payments and analyze how these affect different deciles (that is, tenths) of the income distribution.

Taxation

Rich countries raise 35%–50% of national income from taxes, of which about three-quarters come from taxes on labor income. This proportion has shown a strong upward trend since the early twentieth century. Most countries have *progressive* income taxes, imposing a higher rate on higher slices of income, which are redistributive. But there are many other forms of taxation, and calculating who pays how much is not always straightforward. Taxes on capital income (dividends and capital gains) tend to be progressive in their effect because rich people are far more likely to have such income. Taxes on consumer expenditures, such as sales taxes or VATs or duties on alcohol and tobacco, are *regressive* because people pay a higher proportion of their incomes in such taxes when their incomes are low. They are particularly regressive when charged on some items that form a large proportion of small budgets, such as energy. All other taxes, all ultimately paid by people, also have some distributional effects, but it can be difficult to identify where the tax burden falls—for instance, higher corporate taxes could result in higher consumer prices, or lower dividends to shareholders, or lower wages to employees. They are therefore omitted from distributional analyses.

Although the OECD member countries have progressive income taxation, delivered usually through a stepped schedule of income tax rates on bands of higher income, tax systems are no longer as progressive as they used to be. The top marginal rate (the rate on the highest portion of earnings) was 98% in the UK in the 1970s (income tax plus a surcharge for the super-rich—who included the Beatles, prompting their song "The Taxman"—and 91% in the US in the 1960s (figure 6.8). The decline in top marginal tax rates has been more pronounced in the US than in other OECD member countries, but it has happened everywhere.

The key argument against an income tax that is (too) progressive is that it diminishes effort. This may be plausible when the government is taking all but a few cents in each extra dollar, assuming that earnings at the relevant level do actually involve extra work effort

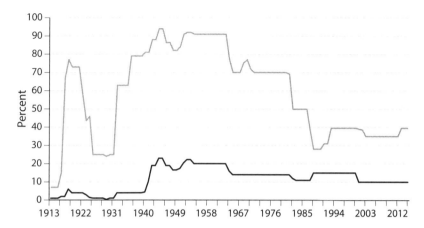

Figure 6.8. Highest (gray) and lowest (black) marginal tax rate in the US, 1913–2013. *Source*: Federal Reserve Economic Data, https://fred.stlouisfed.org/series/IITTRHB.

(as opposed to extra sales of an album that has already been made, for instance). It seems less plausible at lower levels of income tax. Too high a rate of tax may also reduce the revenue raised if it diminishes work and thus earnings and taxes paid.

Optimal Taxation

What then is the optimal rate of taxation (box 6.4)? If the government's aim is to maximize social welfare, it is looking for the rate of tax enabling it to spend on social transfers while recognizing that taxes may affect individuals' level of effort. Most social welfare functions imply that redistribution of income increases social welfare (because of the diminishing marginal utility of income, making an extra dollar worth more in terms of utility to a poor person than it costs in lost utility to a rich person), but the taxes and transfers that enable redistribution affect incentives to work and to save and invest. This is the classic equity-efficiency trade-off. There is a large economic literature on optimal taxation. Broadly speaking, it concludes that there should be high marginal income tax rates on high earners and subsidies to low earners, although there is a lively debate

Box 6.4. The Laffer curve

The relationship between rates of taxation and government revenue is sometimes known as the *Laffer curve*, after economist Arthur Laffer, who popularized it during the 1970s and 1980s in his advocacy for lower tax rates. He believed reducing income tax rates in the US from their then prevailing levels would increase tax revenue. Laffer, a conservative, is sometimes mocked, but there is logic to the curve. Tax revenues would be zero at a zero tax rate, but this would also be true at a 100% tax rate, because nobody would work if all their earnings were taxed away. However, empirical estimates put the revenue-maximizing tax rate around 70% (which is higher than the top marginal rate of income tax currently prevailing in most countries). The Laffer curve, more broadly, refers to the relationship between rates of taxation for any type of tax and the revenues raised, and depending on the tax can take other shapes rather than the hump shape in the diagram.

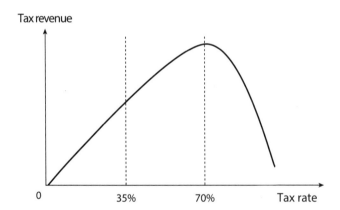

Don Fullerton (2008), "Laffer Curve," in *The New Palgrave Dictionary of Economics*, eds. Steven N. Durlauf and Lawrence E. Blume.

about the former conclusion in particular. Some economists argue for lower income tax on very high earners because of the adverse incentives for saving and investment otherwise. The empirical results from applications of the theory depend on estimates of the elasticity of top incomes with respect to the tax rate or, in other words, how much is effort discouraged by high tax rates? Thomas Piketty and his co-authors have argued the rate could be as high as 80%, but other economists, such as Greg Mankiw, argue the marginal tax rate should actually decline at high levels of income.

It is further argued by those who oppose high top rates of tax that high earners are now footloose between countries, so if one country imposes too high a rate its rich residents will move elsewhere. There are indeed examples of this phenomenon. For instance, in 2012 France's Socialist president François Hollande introduced a 75% supertax on earnings above €1 million. Some high-profile high earners, such as actor Gérard Depardieu and businessman Bernard Arnault, did move overseas, as did many entrepreneurs who thought the government did not want them to earn a reward commensurate with their risk-taking. The new supertax raised small amounts of revenue, however, €260 million in 2013 and €160 million in 2014, and it was dropped in 2015. Yet as the top decile of the income distribution provides a significant proportion of income tax revenues in many countries, the threat of top earners moving abroad to a lower tax country is not one to be taken lightly. Many economists would prefer taxes on wealth instead: for example, on expensive properties (which cannot be moved) or inheritances (as there are no adverse incentive effects on the dead); but these ideas are usually extremely unpopular with rich people, and sometimes with everyone. Inheritance tax, for example, is widely considered to be unfair (box 6.5).

Welfare Benefits

Alongside the rising share of tax in GDP, government spending on social transfers has also risen (table 6.2). Social security or welfare benefits are an important component of low incomes for people at

Box 6.5. What is a fair tax?

Economists consider inheritance tax an attractive policy because it is redistributive and does not reduce work effort, unlike progressive income taxation. However, in the US and UK majorities of voters consider inheritance tax to be unfair, and it is politically unpopular.

Tax fairness
Percentage of UK citizens who say each of the following taxes are fair or unfair

	Fair	Unfair
Tax on cigarettes and tobacco	70	17
Tax on alcohol	63	21
National insurance	56	21
Income tax	55	26
Council tax	42	38
VAT	40	39
Tax on gasoline & diesel fuel	31	51
BBC license fee	30	51
Air passenger duty	24	46
Stamp duty	21	48
Inheritance tax	22	59

Source: YouGov, yougov.com, March 17–18, 2015, https://yougov.co.uk/topics/politics/articles-reports/2015/03/19/inheritance-tax-most-unfair.

Table 6.2. Government Spending in Selected OECD Countries, % of GDP

All %GDP	US			UK			France			Japan		
	2014	2015	2016	2014	2015	2016	2014	2015	2016	2014	2015	2016
Total government spending	37.9	37.4	37.7	43.0	42.2	41.4	57.0	56.6	56.4	40.3	39.4	39.0
Education	6.1	6.1	6.1	5.0	4.8	4.6	5.5	5.4	5.4	3.6	3.4	3.4
Health	8.9	9.1	9.2	7.5	7.5	7.6	8.2	8.1	8.1	7.7	7.7	7.6
State pensions	7.0	7.1	7.2	6.3	6.2	6.2	114.0	13.9	-	9.5	9.3	9.4
Income support (working age)	0.6	0.6	0.6	3.7	3.5	3.5	3.0	3.0	2.9	1.2	1.2	1.3
Social spending	18.8	18.9	18.9	21.9	21.6	21.2	32.2	32.0	32.0	21.9	21.9	21.9

Source: OECD.

the bottom of the income distribution. These payments go to people in specific circumstances—they are unemployed, single parents of small children, those who are unable to work or with costly needs because they are disabled or have a long-term illness. Governments also run state pension systems, almost all on a "pay as you go" basis, in other words, paid for from current taxes rather than from the return on accumulated investment funds; in many countries the pension system is unsustainable because aging populations mean there are fewer workers paying taxes to support the pension obligations. Pension reform, by some mixture of cutting the level of state pensions, increasing the level of contributions, raising the retirement age, and introducing compulsory personal saving, is on the cards everywhere—and politically difficult everywhere as pensioners are the age group most likely to vote in elections.

There are some key choices in benefit systems. One is whether or not they are contributory: Is there a link between what people pay in and what they receive if in need? Many systems started this way in the twentieth century. It was one of Beveridge's principles for the postwar UK system, for example. However, this principle has tended to weaken over time. The other is universality (for the specified group) versus means testing; in other words, is the amount paid the same for everyone regardless of their situation, or is it dependent on the recipient's other income and assets? There is an unavoidable trade-off. Universal benefits ensure that everyone in society feels they have a stake in the social safety net. But they are more expensive to provide at any given level, as by definition they are not targeted at those most in need.

So means testing is better targeted on need and is therefore a less costly approach. But the drawback, apart from the risk of increasing the social divide between rich and poor, or of decreasing voter approval for social support because it is a transfer from rich to poor, is that it creates a *poverty trap* or *welfare trap*. If someone tries to move off means-tested benefits into a job to earn their own living, they lose their benefits, which usually includes things like free or cheap prescriptions, subsidized housing, food stamps, and so on. The *marginal effective tax rate*, including the rate at which benefits are withdrawn for people with low incomes moving from benefits into work, can be far higher than the posted marginal income tax rate (figure 6.9). It can be above 100%, so the person is actually worse off if they get a job. In addition, means testing is costly to administer as well as intrusive, and it quickly becomes very complex because it needs to take into account all the complications of people's living situations and employment arrangements.

What's more, most social security or welfare systems have become extremely complicated, administratively costly, and unpleasant to traumatic for recipients. As different benefits have been introduced and altered over time, the schedule of marginal effective tax rates has developed spikes and can create more than one welfare trap. It is difficult and often demeaning to apply for benefits, difficult to understand one's eligibility, and all but impossible to foresee the financial consequences of moving off benefits into work, given the loss of various benefits and often unexpected costs of working (such as travel, clothing, meals).

This is not a good state of affairs. Yet simplifying it is often politically contentious and in itself a complicated process. The UK government has been trying and failing to build a new, simpler Universal Credit for more than seven years (it was announced in 2010), writing off (so far) one major computer system costing billions. It is not clear it will ever work. Moreover, given the increase in social spending described earlier in this chapter, and the desire

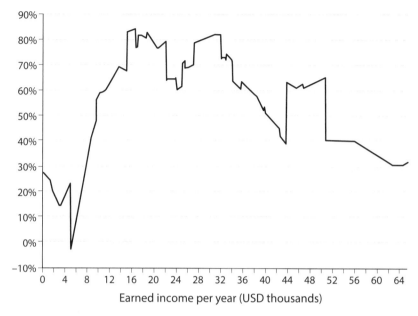

Figure 6.9. US effective marginal tax rate on single parent with one child, 2017. *Source*: US Congressional Budget Office, https://ftalphaville.ft.com/2017/08/25 /2192736/americas-benefits-system-is-backwards/.

of many governments to decrease their budget deficits, there is pressure to continue moving from universal to means-tested benefits.

Yet universal benefits give all citizens a stake in the system of welfare benefits. The more means testing is involved, so that there is redistribution from rich to poor, the less likely high earners are to support the system. But the less means testing is used, the bigger a role the state has in determining everybody's level of income. Beveridge's original conception of the welfare state as a mutual insurance system, into which all pay in and all can draw out in proportion, seemed attractive and relevant to the market failures that cause individuals to be unlikely to protect themselves against all misfortunes through private insurance. In practice, tax and benefit systems have moved away from that contributory framework over the decades, as they have become larger and more ambitious in terms of what they deliver for the lowest-income citizens. However, Beveridge saw the other elements of his report—high and stable employment, and the free health service—as delivering the necessary universality.

Tax Credits

Some countries like the US and UK have a system of tax credits for low earners, especially people with children. These are in effect benefit payments but are delivered through the pay packet as if they were negative taxes, so they increase take-home pay. The aim is to ensure people have an incentive to work, as one of the main drawbacks of conventional welfare or social security benefits is the welfare trap—the immense disincentives they create to get a job and earn an income rather than passively receiving benefits. In this respect, tax credits have been a success, removing a big jump in the marginal effective tax rate for many people on low wages. Their drawback is that they can end up subsidizing employers, who can get away with paying lower wages than they might otherwise have to. For this reason. the introduction of the Working Families Tax Credit in the UK in 1999, based on the Earned Income Tax Credit in the US, was accompanied by the introduction of a legal minimum wage. This interaction creates a different incentive, however: a government wanting to cut spending might be tempted to save on tax credits by increasing the minimum wage more than is desirable in terms of its potential effect on the level of employment.

Universal Basic Income

A currently fashionable proposal for addressing poverty and inequality is an old idea newly revived. This is the idea of a *universal basic income* (UBI), which gains new support every time there is a scare about what automation will do to jobs. The idea was popular in the 1960s and early 1990s, for example. UBI can take many forms but at its simplest is a *negative income tax*, proposed by Milton Friedman (figure 6.10). People earning below a certain threshold income would receive payments; those above would pay a proportionate or progressive income tax. Friedman's structure avoids cre-

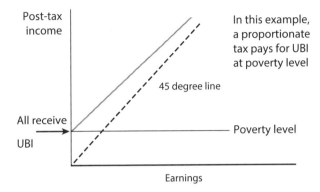

Figure 6.10. Negative income tax.

ating the disincentive effects of a high marginal effective tax rate, but other forms of UBI have been proposed. UBI has been extensively debated and advocated in the past few years—indeed, its advocates are evangelical about it—but it has not been implemented anywhere despite a few small-scale trials in cities in various parts of the world, from the US to Finland.

Like any universal payment, it would be costly, although advocates say the cost could be less than is spent now on the complex social security system it would replace. But it is not clear that the complexity would vanish—either UBI would need to be means tested, or if literally everybody got a payment regardless of need, then any livable level would be expensive. The OECD has tried to estimate the likely cost of a national UBI for some countries, including taking into account the savings from abolishing all current benefit payments. It concluded there would need to be substantial increases in tax revenues to provide everyone with an income at the current level of provision through the welfare system.

Although it has passionate advocates, it is not clear that UBI would be either easy or popular (box 6.6). In a 2017 referendum on introducing a nationwide scheme, Swiss voters rejected the idea by a three to one margin. Apart from the likely cost, the idea of everyone getting "something for nothing" may be unattractive to some voters. The effects on work incentives are not clear, because although the scheme can be structured to prevent jumps in the

Box 6.6. UBI pilots

In January 2017 Finland introduced a pilot UBI program paying a random sample of 2000 working-age unemployed people €560 a month. If any recipient gets a job, they continue to get the payment. They are under no obligation to get a job, however. The €20 million trial was launched with the aim of testing UBI as a way to reduce Finland's 8% unemployment rate by altering the incentives to stay unemployed versus finding a job—for example, removing the high effective marginal tax rate of moving from unemployment to work due to loss of benefits. It has not tested different levels of UBI payment or the effect on other groups of people. The trial ended in 2018 and the report on its effects found it had made recipients happier but no more likely to be in a job.

The start-up accelerator YCombinator launched a five-year pilot program in 2016 giving one hundred families in Oakland, California, a basic income, with a trial of payments between $1000 and $2000 a month, made to a range of people with different incomes and both employed and unemployed. YCombinator said it was important to run such a trial because of the potential impact of automation on jobs.

The non-profit organization GiveDirectly introduced a trial scheme in Kenya in 2017, involving 6,000 people for twelve years. The scheme is simple to administer because payments are made through the nearly ubiquitous mobile money scheme MPesa.

One completed large-scale pilot project, giving 6,000 individuals in Madhya Pradesh, India, unconditional cash payments for twelve to eighteen months, compared a range of social outcomes to a control group of villagers who had not received the basic income payments. In this context of very low incomes, there were improvements in areas ranging from sanitation to nutrition and school enrollment.*

It will be some time before the results of several trials under way in developed economies are known, and they are unlikely to be decisive. But in a disappointing development for advocates of UBI,

(continued on next page)

(continued from previous page)

Swiss voters in 2016 overwhelmingly rejected (77% to 23%) a plan to give every citizen a basic income of SFR 2500 for each adult and SFR 625 for each child.

* http://sewabharat.org/wp-content/uploads/2015/07/Report-on-Uncon ditional-Cash-Transfer-Pilot-Project-in-Madhya-Pradesh.pdf.

effective marginal tax rate, having a no-strings income might itself have disincentive effects.

Changing the Distribution of Market Incomes

The classic policy tools of taxes and benefits, along with newer proposals such as UBI, aim for raising low incomes and perhaps also the redistribution of incomes for a given prior distribution of income before taxes and benefits (the *market distribution*). An alternative set of policy options aims to alter the market distribution itself. One is to set a legal minimum wage employers may pay, to raise low incomes. Others include trying to reduce high incomes by reducing barriers to entry in well-paid professions or other measures to discourage rent seeking and excessive top pay; and improving the educational attainment of people with low skills to try to increase the labor market supply of more advanced skills and thus reduce high earnings, given that demand for skilled employees is high due to the character of technological change.

Minimum Wages

Employers, and especially small businesses, never like increases in the minimum wage for the obvious reason that it increases their costs and squeezes profits if they cannot pass it on to customers. Depending on the impact on employers, the obvious potential downside of the policy is that a minimum wage could reduce the level of employment. The evidence about the employment impact of minimum wages is hotly debated, but on balance suggests that if increases in the minimum wage are small enough or implemented slowly enough, big adverse employment effects do not occur. Context is all-important; increases in the minimum wage have different effects depending on the general state of the economy at the time, the size of the increase, and the characteristics of the workforce. The "safe" level to set the minimum wage, or increase it, depends on how tight (or not) the local labor market is and how much of a cushion employers have in terms of their profit margins. Some economists argue that substantially increasing the wage paid to people on low earnings is beneficial for their employers because it encourages more effort and higher productivity, and means workers have more income available to spend and thereby boost the economy, demand, and ultimately employers' profits. There is little evidence for the existence of this virtuous circle. The most recent evidence (as of 2019) is that the effects of minimum wage increases differ as between small and big increases, with big ones more likely to have adverse effects on employment and small ones likely having positive employment effects. Big 2018 pay increases to $15 an hour (compared to the US legal minimum of $7.25) in some US cities, such as Seattle, or by certain employers, such as Amazon (for its UK and US employees) provide a new opportunity to consider the evidence on the employment impact of big wage increases.

One effect that is clear is that minimum wages lead to a clustering of wage rates at the minimum level, as figure 6.11 illustrates for the UK case. All those who would otherwise have been paid less, and perhaps some who might have been paid more, are paid the legal minimum, so the distribution of earnings spikes at that point.

Tackling Rent Seeking

Since the 1980s there has been a dramatic increase in the earnings of the top 10% (or 1% or 0.1%) of the income distribution (figure 6.12 shows the US example—the most extreme among OECD member countries). The average pay of a US CEO has increased from about 40 times the workforce average to more than 340 times as

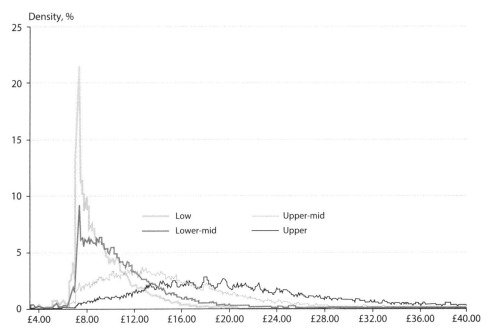

Figure 6.11. Distribution of nominal pre-tax hourly earnings of full-time workers by skill group, UK, 2016. *Source*: Office for National Statistics, https://www.ons.gov.uk/surveys/informationforbusinesses/businesssurveys/annualsurveyof hoursandearningsashe.

big. However, it is not easy to figure out how much *rent seeking* has contributed to income inequality. This is a general term for using regulations or other government policies that diminish competition to the benefit of certain incumbent groups. This might include, for example, professional licensing requirements for lawyers or financiers, limiting entry into the job market; regulations that make it hard for new competitors to enter the relevant market at all so that profits are unduly high and paid out to high earners; corporate law that makes it possible for companies' remuneration committees to be a cozy club, increasing each others' earnings and stock options. Although reducing these barriers would improve economic efficiency, as well as possibly reducing earnings at the top end of the income distribution, professional groups and big, profitable companies are often very good at the political mobilization and lobbying needed to prevent this from happening. For sure, as chapter 7

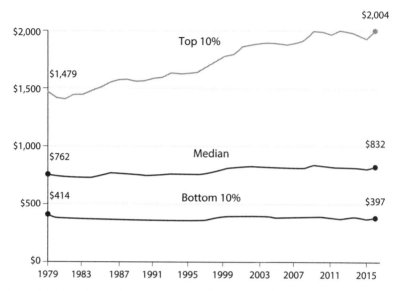

Figure 6.12. Real weekly wages across the income distribution, United States. *Source*: US Bureau of Labor Statistics.

describes, large sums of money are spent on lobbying governments to protect market power.

Education and Training

A very long-term approach, but probably the most important option given the technological drivers of inequality discussed above, is increasing the supply of workers with the skills being demanded by employers. Evidence from the nineteenth and early twentieth century suggests the spread of educational opportunity and greater equality of skills contributed to convergence in incomes, albeit slowly, after another period of great inequality. Unfortunately, although the link between education and growth in the long term is clear, the economic benefits of particular increases in government spending on education or educational reforms take at least a decade to manifest themselves, so it is often not a politically compelling option. Moreover, there is little consensus about exactly which educational approaches are most effective, or provide future generations with skills that complement new technologies rather than being automatable.

However, it is pretty clear that in many countries the education system is failing children and young people, so trying something different can only be an improvement.

Expenditure on Public Services

One important redistributive tool sometimes overlooked in discussions of how government can tackle poverty and inequality is the provision of public services. Services such as free education, health care, local libraries, public transport, sports facilities, and so on are more important in redistributing money than is often appreciated. In the UK, for instance, their value exceeds that of cash benefits (figure 6.13), and because the services are accessible to all, and used more by people with lower incomes, their provision is progressive in terms of distribution. The OECD estimates that spending on public services on average among its members is equivalent to a 29% increase in household disposable incomes. This means a larger proportionate increase for low-income households: a 76% increase for the lowest-income fifth of the population compared with 14% for the highest-income fifth (table 6.3).

Table 6.3. Income-Increasing Effect of Benefits of Public Services

	Percentage					
	Q1	Q2	Q3	Q4	Q5	Total
Education	30.6	18.5	14.2	10.4	5.6	11.8
Health care	34.9	22.2	15.8	11.8	7.2	13.9
Social housing	1.8	0.7	0.4	0.2	0.1	0.4
Early childhood education & care	4.5	3.0	2.4	1.5	0.8	1.8
Elderly care	4.0	1.9	0.7	0.4	0.2	0.9
Total	75.8	46.4	33.5	24.3	13.7	28.8

Source: OECD, http://www.keepeek.com/Digital-Asset-Management/oecd/social-issues -migration-health/the-causes-of-growing-inequalities-in-oecd-countries_9789264119536 -en.
Note: By quintile (Q1 poorest to Q5 richest) of the income distribution, average for 27 OECD countries, 2007.

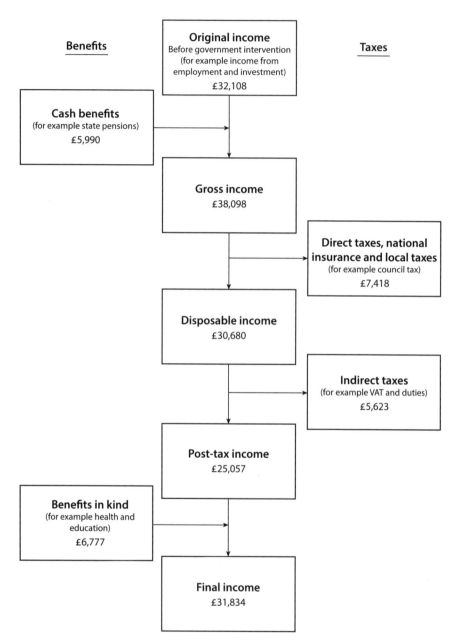

Figure 6.13. Redistribution through taxes, benefits, and services: UK, 2016. *Source*: Office for National Statistics.

The reason the collective provision of services is such an important policy tool is that public services provide individuals on low incomes with access to health care, education, and transportation, and on a reasonably comparable basis to those who are better off (although the quality of public provision is variable of course—the subject of the next chapter). Even if the market can deliver these services (bearing in mind the market failures described at the start of this chapter, which imply the private sector would under-provide these public goods), poorer people would certainly only be able to afford lesser- or worse-quality services. Amartya Sen argues persuasively that income is only one of the things people need to attain the living standard and kind of life they want; other *capabilities* are at least as important. For example, physical and mental health, education, freedom, and participation in civic life are also important. Government spending on public services, such as education, health care, public transport, or infrastructure, is an important means of providing everyone with such capabilities.

While public spending on services is redistributive in financial terms, there is also something inherently equalizing about using the same services as people from other walks of life—sending children to the same schools or sitting on the same trains. The everyday contact increases understanding of others and reduces fear of the unknown. One of the regrettable aspects of the increased income inequality of recent times is the extent to which different social groups have become isolated from each other, their paths never crossing.

Health Care

Looking at all public service provision in detail is beyond the scope of this chapter (and there is a huge academic literature on this area), but one kind of service in particular is worth some discussion, both because it is particularly resonant politically and because it is characterized by the substantial market failures set out at the beginning of this chapter. This service is health care. There is every reason to believe private insurance markets alone cannot be efficient because of the inherent adverse selection and moral hazard when it comes

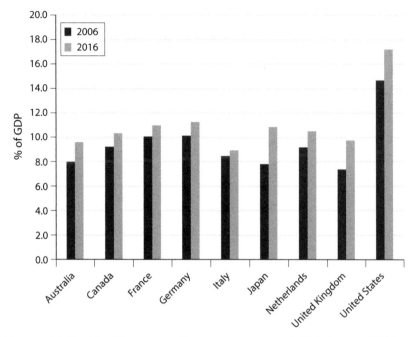

Figure 6.14. Total health care spending as a percentage of GDP. *Source*: OECD.

to people's health. Different countries make significantly different policy choices, although everywhere both political division and rising health care costs due to an aging population and rising expectations mean health policy is a contentious question as more government spending is required (figure 6.14). The two extremes are the US and the UK, one largely funded by a private insurance market and the other largely a publicly funded system with most services available for free. Other OECD member countries provide public universal health coverage through a range of forms of payment, including compulsory insurance, and models of provision, both private and public.

The UK's National Health Service

As described earlier, the UK's National Health Service (NHS) was one of the founding elements of Beveridge's vision of the contract between state and people. Although its introduction was strongly opposed by the medical profession at the time, there is now no institution in the United Kingdom more passionately supported by voters. Just over 10% of the population buys additional private insurance for certain procedures or for private rooms. Over time the share of NHS services provided by private companies has also increased (this controversial "contracting out" is discussed in the next chapter). Nevertheless, most people in the UK get most of their health treatment free, paid for through general taxation, and some relatively low user fees (compared to the cost) for prescriptions, dental, and eye care. (These fees are waived for those claiming benefits, and for children and pensioners.) There is always likely to be excess demand for something free, so general practitioners act as gatekeepers, waiting lists for treatments can grow long, and there is some rationing of certain treatments and (specifically) expensive drugs through an independent agency, which assesses their likely cost-effectiveness.

The UK system is highly redistributive. It is the only OECD member country where access to health care does much not depend on how much you earn. The method of financing through general taxation (and constant pressure to find savings) means the NHS is also highly efficient on several measures, such as length of inpatient hospital stay or prices paid for pharmaceuticals (as the NHS negotiates a bulk buy from drug companies). People in Britain spend far less out of pocket on their medical care than in other countries. The corollary is that the quality of care in some regards does not match that in other countries. For instance, the UK has fewer hospital beds per person, fewer general practitioners and hospital doctors, and fewer items of equipment (such as CT or MRI scanners) than comparable countries such as France or Germany. Every winter brings news stories about a shortage of hospital beds or people being discharged too early. Nevertheless, Britons are grumblingly and passionately attached to the sometimes shabby, crowded waiting rooms of NHS hospitals and local practitioners' surgeries. And a comparison of eleven countries (by a US foundation, the Commonwealth Fund, table 6.4) concluded that the NHS is the best health system in the world on a mixture of criteria (although next to last on health care outcomes).

Table 6.4. Health Care System Performance Rankings

	AUS	CAN	FRA	GER	NETH	NZ	NOR	SWE	SWIZ	UK	US
Overall ranking	2	9	10	8	3	4	4	6	6	1	11
Care process	2	6	9	8	4	3	10	11	7	1	5
Access	4	10	9	2	1	7	5	6	8	3	11
Administrative efficiency	1	6	11	6	9	2	4	5	8	3	10
Equity	7	9	10	6	2	8	5	3	4	1	11
Health care outcomes	1	9	5	8	6	7	3	2	4	10	11

Source: Commonwealth Fund analysis, http://www.commonwealthfund.org/~/media/files/publications/fund-report/2017/jul/schneider_mirror_mirror_2017.pdf#page=5.

This situation is not a settled one, however. Demand for health care is climbing steadily for several reasons: the aging population; general expectations about treatment as medical technology and drugs advance; the rising prices—above general inflation—of medicines and equipment; and the fact that health is a *luxury good* (a technical term meaning spending on it increases more than in proportion to incomes). The budget for the NHS has increased but not enough to keep up with demand. Conservative governments have in addition long been keen to increase the market elements of health provision, both to improve the quality of the public service through competition in supply and for philosophical reasons.

Any UK government will before long have to decide whether to meet rising demand

- through an extension of public provision of health services (paid for through general taxes);
- through a continuing erosion of the present service in terms of its availability and quality, relying on individuals to buy their own additional private insurance or to purchase services such as physiotherapy that are heavily rationed in the NHS; or
- through an open public debate about which parts of health care should be protected in a free-at-the-point-of-need NHS and which parts can and should be left to private purchases in the market.

For instance, as we all grow old, there is no uncertainty that the need will arise for some relatively straightforward treatments, such as varicose vein operations, flu shots, podiatry procedures, or cataract removal. The ailments vary from person to person, but the uncertainty is about timing (and the small possibility of early death); so this is not an insurance market fraught with adverse selection problems, but rather a savings market. Some of these treatments could be moved outside the NHS boundary, as long as people know they need to have saved enough to pay for such procedures. However, given the voters' devotion to the idea of the NHS, and politicians' aversion to making or even debating hard choices in public, many health experts in the UK regretfully believe the middle option—gradual erosion of quality—is the most likely outcome.

For all these difficult questions about the future of the NHS, most Britons and indeed other Europeans (where there is generally a mixed system of public and private provision, and some private insurance or payment) consider the US health care system scandalously unfair and inefficient. Of course the incomprehension is mutual, although—as the temperature in the recent political debate shows—some Americans are also scandalized by the US health care system.

The US Health Care System

The same report that ranked the UK health care system at the top out of eleven comparable countries ranked the US system eleventh, at the bottom for both health care outcomes and equity of the system. Yet US spending in total on health care is almost twice as much as in the UK as a proportion of GDP (16.5% versus just under 10%, figure 6.14).

US health care is mainly privately provided, by a mix of for-profit and not-for-profit provision. In terms of state funding, Medicare provides coverage for short hospital stays, doctor visits, and prescription medicines for almost all individuals over sixty-five. It is therefore almost universal, although people still need to find the money themselves for other costs, such as nursing home stays. Medicaid offers limited provision for low-income families and disabled people. But most health care for people under sixty-five is financed by private insurance, and most Americans get their coverage through tax-exempt employee and employer insurance contributions or premiums. This leaves many people without medical coverage. (Other nations such as Switzerland, France, and Germany have either private insurance funding where the insurance coverage is mandatory or a social insurance scheme.) In 2014 15% of Americans—about one in seven—were uninsured and had no access to Medicare. The 2010 Affordable Care Act ("Obamacare") was intended to tackle this problem, and by 2015 the proportion of those without coverage had fallen to 10%.

The US therefore has a costly system by comparison with other countries, as described above, spending a higher share of its GDP on health care yet with poor health outcomes by international standards and less access to care for the people at the bottom of the income scale. Part of the explanation is the administrative complexity of the system. There may also be over-provision of tests and procedures, a moral hazard problem noted earlier as one of the market failures. The system is also regressive, in contrast to Europe; people on low incomes have to pay the same price yet typically have greater need for health care (indeed, ill health is one important reason people have low incomes). The US system can trap people in jobs they might otherwise quit, because they cannot afford to be without their health insurance, so it may make the labor market operate less efficiently. Finally, like other OECD member countries (though to a lesser degree), the US has an aging population and rising demand for health care as a result. The share of GDP spent on health will continue to rise for reasons of demography as well as technical advances and increasing costs of health care services.

Nevertheless, many Americans are strongly opposed to a different approach and the Affordable Care Act was controversial. Choice in the market is seen as the most important principle, and there is a far stronger tradition of individualism than in Europe. The US Congress has reduced the initial increase in the scope of coverage through the Affordable Care Act, and the policy outcome is far from settled (as of 2019). In the context of this chapter, however, the point is that the largely privately funded US system is regressive whereas in other OECD member countries public spending on health care is progressive: like other forms of public service, such as education and transport, it involves a significant transfer of resources through the tax system to people on low incomes.

Conclusion

This discussion, written by a European, demonstrates how much history and political culture play a part in shaping the relationship between the state and the individual at the most fundamental level: What is the responsibility of the government for guaranteeing the level and stability of living standards for all of its population? In the US, the tradition of individualism and hands-off government is stronger than in Europe, even the UK. There is also a question of who is to be included in the population to which this aspect of the social contract applies. The increase in migration globally during the past generation has led some people to challenge whether immigrants should be eligible for the social security and public services provided.

This chapter has argued that although political choices are inevitable when it comes to providing a minimum standard of living or set of capabilities, and particularly to redistributing resources between different groups of people, there are some basic economic efficiency principles. Some forms of insurance can only be provided collectively, and most efficiently at scale by the government, either because the risks are aggregate (such as the risk of a recession, causing unemployment) or because adverse selection leads to under-provision of insurance by the market.

For all the complexity and dilemmas of different countries' social security nets, the post-tax and benefit income distribution is less unequal than the original market distribution. Without progressive taxation and payments such as unemployment benefits and state pensions, there would be still greater income inequality, and greater levels of poverty in our societies. The generosity of different systems varies, including the proportion of benefits expenditure going to different groups. The distributional implications vary widely. For example, the UK spends a higher share of GDP on payments to families than do many OECD member countries (through tax credits), but its total government social spending is heavily skewed toward retired people as successive governments have made state pension payments increasingly generous. This means that children in the UK are at much greater risk than pensioners of living below the poverty line.

Although the present welfare state structures do achieve some poverty reduction and redistribution, few people are satisfied with them, perhaps least of all the beneficiaries. The tax and social security systems are politically contested everywhere. The scale of the spending has been on the increase since World War II, and yet poverty has not been defeated and inequality has risen. Taxation (except in the rare case of Pigouvian adjustments for externalities) creates inefficiencies and, other things being equal, therefore tends to reduce the economic growth rate. The system is unpopular with voters too. The structure of benefits, and their scope, may have had counterproductive effects; although the causality is hard to pinpoint and the evidence hotly debated, most Western economies have deeply embedded clusters of problems linking poverty, low education, ill health, and drug dependency—despite their expensive and (to date) ever-expanding social security systems. The systems we have do not seem satisfactory. They do not keep people out of poverty or help them into work, and are often demeaning. Government officials intrude into individuals' lives and circumstances to check their eligibility and apply means tests. And yet simplifying a complicated structure is itself a complicated task, and would create winners and losers. It is no wonder the simplicity of UBI, sweeping away this mess, can seem appealing, but we are far from having evidence it would be effective.

All countries' actual tax and benefit systems and public services are far from meeting the textbook ideals of economic efficiency. There are some dilemmas, such as universality versus means testing. There is also simply an accretion of complexity, malfunctioning, and political dispute in most countries when it comes to the payment of benefits, the tax system, and public services. The next decades are likely to see significant change, for several reasons, though. Among them are demographic change and the rapid aging of the population in most Western economies; technological disruption; the sheer vulnerability of complex and malfunctioning systems; and the current volatile political context. These issues are all discussed in large research literatures and could fill several textbooks. Meanwhile, the demands of reducing poverty, limiting income inequality to tolerable levels, and enabling fair access to public services put immense pressure, in the complex economies of the developed world with their legacy of divisive social problems, on the capacity of governments to deliver. Yet, as the next chapter discusses, government failure is widespread.

Further Reading

Technical Follow-Up

Anthony Atkinson and Joseph Stiglitz (2015), *Lectures on Public Economics*, revised ed., Princeton University Press.

Nicholas Barr (2012), *Economics of the Welfare State*, 5th ed., Oxford University Press.

Thomas Piketty and Emmanuel Saez (2013), "Optimal Labor Income Taxation," chapter 7 in *Handbook of Public Economics, Volume 5*, North-Holland.

Classic Articles

Kenneth Arrow (1963), "Uncertainty and the Welfare Economics of Medical Care," *American Economic Review* 53 no. 5: 941–973.

Milton Friedman (1962), "The Distribution of Income," chapter 10 in *Capitalism and Freedom*, University of Chicago Press.

Sherwin Rosen (1981), "The Economics of Superstars," *American Economic Review* 71, no. 5: 845–858.

Poverty and Inequality

David H. Autor, David Dorn, and Gordon H. Hanson (2013), "The China Syndrome: Local Labor Market Effects of Import Competition in the United States," *American Economic Review* 103, no. 6: 2121–2168.

Congressional Budget Office (2011), "Trends in the Distribution of Household Income between 1979 and 2007," US Government Printing Office, http://www.cbo.gov/ftpdocs/124xx/doc12485/10-25-HouseholdIncome .pdf.

Michael Foster and Marco Mira D'Ercole (2012), "The OECD Approach to Measuring Income Distribution and Poverty," in *Counting the Poor*, eds. Douglas J. Besharov and Kenneth A. Couch, Oxford University Press.

Claudia Goldin and Laurence Katz (2009), *The Race between Education and Technology*, Belknap Press of Harvard University Press.

Maarten Goos and Alan Manning (2007), "Lousy and Lovely Jobs: The Rising Polarization of the Labor Market," *Review of Economic Studies* 89: 118–133.

Branko Milanovic (2016), *Global Inequality: A New Approach for the Age of Globalization*, Harvard University Press.

OECD (2011), "Divided We Stand: Why Inequality Keeps Rising," http://www.oecd.org/els/soc/dividedwestandwhyinequalitykeepsrising.htm.

Thomas Piketty (2014), *Capital in the 21st Century*, Harvard University Press.

Taxation

Peter Diamond and Emmanuel Saez (2011), "The Case for a Progressive Tax: From Basic Research to Policy Recommendations," *Journal of Economic Perspectives* 25, no. 4: 165–190.

James Mirrlees et al. (2011), *Taxation By Design*, Institute for Fiscal Studies, https://www.ifs.org.uk/publications/5353.

Social Security Systems

Lillian Liu (2001), "Foreign Social Security Developments Prior to the Social Security Act," Special Study #8, SSA Historian's Office, https://www.ssa.gov/history/pre1935.html.

Nicholas Timmins (2001), *The Five Giants: A Biography of the Welfare State*, HarperCollins.

UBI

OECD (2017), "Basic Income Policy Brief," https://www.oecd.org/social/Basic-Income-Policy-Option-2017.pdf.

Michael Tanner (2015), "The Pros and Cons of a Guaranteed National Income," Cato Institute, http://object.cato.org/sites/cato.org/files/pubs/pdf/pa773.pdf.

Minimum Wages

David Card and Alan B. Krueger (2000), "Minimum Wages and Employment: A Case Study of the Fast-Food Industry in New Jersey and Pennsylvania: Reply," *American Economic Review* 90, no. 5: 1397–1420.

J. Clemens and M. R. Strain (2018), "The Short-Run Employment Effects of Recent Minimum Wage Changes: Evidence from the American Community Survey," *Contemporary Economic Policy* 36: 711–722, doi:10.1111/coep.12279.

David Neumark (2015), "The Effects of Minimum Wages on Employment," Federal Reserve Bank of San Francisco Economic Letter (December), http://www.frbsf.org/economic-research/files/el2015-37.pdf.

OECD (2015), "Focus on Minimum Wages after the Crisis," www.oecd.org/social/Focus-on-minimum-wages-after-the-crisis-2015.pdf.

Rent Seeking and Top Pay

Marianne Bertrand and Sendhil Mullainathan (2001), "Are CEOs Rewarded for Luck? The Ones without Principles Are," *Quarterly Journal of Economics* 116, no. 3: 901–932.

Josh Bivens and Lawrence Mishel (2013), "The Pay of Corporate Executives and Financial Professionals as Evidence of Rents in Top 1 Percent Incomes," *Journal of Economic Perspectives* 27, no. 3: 57–78.

Skills

James Bessen (2015), *Learning by Doing*, Yale University Press.

Claudia Goldin and Lawrence Katz (2008), *The Race between Education and Technology*, Belknap Press for Harvard University Press.

Public Services

European Commission (2013), "The Distributional Impact of Public Services in European Countries," Statistical Working Paper, https://ec.europa.eu/eurostat/web/products-statistical-working-papers/-/KS-RA-13-009.

OECD (2017), "Health at a Glance," http://www.oecd.org/health/health-systems/health-at-a-glance-19991312.htm.

CHAPTER 7

Government Failure

The book has been exploring when markets do and do not work well, whether public policies can correct market failures of different kinds, and whether there might be non-government collective solutions to problems caused by market failures. This chapter looks at the roles of market and state in the ordering of the economy from the perspective of government failure. Touched on in passing at various points so far, government failure, many economists would argue, should get (at least) equal billing with market failure. Indeed, there have been plenty of examples already of the inadequacies and failures of government policy.

After a reminder about the way attitudes toward the role of government in economic policy change over the decades, this chapter describes the public choice revolution, which turned the lens of economics on the choices of policymakers themselves, scrutinizing their incentives. This includes issues of regulatory capture and collective action problems, resulting in policies being shaped to benefit industry lobbies or special interests rather than the public in general. Public choice theory was an intellectual and—starting with the Thatcher and Reagan governments—political response to perceived government policy failures. This was at first mainly an Anglo-American phenomenon, but the approach has gained momentum elsewhere. The chapter goes on to discuss how to respond to the questions public choice theory has raised about the motives of policymakers, and their capacity to implement policies. The questions it asks concerning the motivation of public officials have led to other approaches to public provision in many countries more recently, such as target setting and "contestability" in public services and public-private partnerships.

Despite these policy innovations and the awareness of the pitfalls prompted by public choice theory, there are plentiful examples of government failure. What's more, there is little sign that views about how much government should regulate, or how public services should be run, are converging. Countries differ greatly in the approach they take to key public services, but have in common the fact that the debate tends to be politically highly polarized. Ideology and belief, as much as evidence and expertise, determine the approaches governments take. Analyzing and implementing public policy is not a purely technocratic exercise, for all the insights economics can bring.

What Is 'the Government' and Why Might It Fail?

So far this book has used the implicit notion of a wise and benign government aiming to maximize social welfare by analyzing market failures and responding appropriately. Yes, there are difficult trade-offs in some decisions, and policies in practice always create losers as well as winners. So the scope for Pareto improvements is limited, and policy choices need to be made according to an idea of social welfare that might in practice be a bit vague but could in theory be specified. Identifying the type of market failure in a given situation is a way of considering some relevant policies to increase allocative and/or productive efficiency.

Yet as earlier chapters have illustrated, no solution to market failures is appropriate for all times and all places. If it were simply a matter of getting the economic analysis right, there would surely not have been such big swings in the scope of governments' economic interventions over time, or such differences across countries. Often these tides moving between different degrees of government activity and leaving things to the market have been responses to major economic events, such as the Great Depression, or the war. The major economic event that shaped a strong intellectual swing away from active government management of the economy toward "free markets" was the crisis of the 1970s, when Western economies experienced high inflation and slow growth, and when some publicly owned enterprises and publicly managed services were perceived to be run by their managers and unions in their own interests rather than in the interests of taxpayers and citizens. This was not the case everywhere, but it was the mood that led to the election of Margaret Thatcher in the UK and Ronald Reagan in the US, and the subsequent wave of privatization and deregulation that started in Britain before being adopted elsewhere.

The 1980s shift in both economic and political thinking is discussed further in this chapter, focusing on "the government"—what it is, and the competencies and motivations of public officials and politicians. The scale and scope of government has continued to increase, as noted in chapter 1, either in terms of government spending as a share of GDP or the quantity and scope of regulation. But the forms of government activity and intervention have changed substantially. The tide of ideas may be shifting again, in favor of more government economic intervention, given the Great Financial Crisis and the current voter backlash against globalization; it is too early to be sure. But one lesson from the past few decades of experience that will not be forgotten is the ample evidence of government failure. Government failure will ensure that debate about the scope and activities of "government" or "market" is bound to continue, abstract as these terms are.

Earlier chapters have described how disillusion with government gradually set in after the expansionary postwar period. Nationalized industries in Europe became sclerotic, and were often captured by their unions. Their inefficiency became evident. The same was true of many public services too. For instance, the NHS in Britain was widely welcomed after World War II because of the vivid memory of how financially devastating falling ill had been for so many people (and their families) in the 1930s, and of course the British still care passionately about their health service. But by the late 1970s there were long waits for treatment, hospitals were shabby, and the UK had less impressive health outcomes than comparable countries.

The prevalence of producer rather than consumer interests, and the absence of any competition in provision, was blamed for this.

The problems were not just due to union power or management incompetence, however. Although the historical context paved the way for the public choice theorists to question successfully the postwar big government consensus, there are some fundamental challenges when it comes to devising policies to address market failures.

One of the sources of the efficiency of markets is that they deliver welfare-enhancing outcomes using decentralized information. The inability to substitute for market signals is a profound reason for the ultimate failure of the centrally planned economies. To implement effective public policies, the government does need a lot of information—and often does not have it in practice. How can officials know whether Pigouvian taxes or subsidies, for example, are set at the right level? Another key virtue of markets is that they adjust constantly to new information, whereas policies do not. The context might change; perhaps a new technology bringing about competition in what had seemed a natural monopoly, or new social norms making a welfare state built around a sole breadwinner ineffective. What's more, all too often policies are based on an analysis that does not or cannot take into account how behavior will change after the policy is implemented. There are many examples of policies backfiring due simply to a failure to recognize that people will react to the policies. A related issue is sheer competence: Do officials have the skills needed to implement policies? Often they do not; the people who work on policy are often analysts with little practical experience, while the front line officials are rarely involved in policy analysis. All the focus in political discussion of proposals is on the analysis, not the practicalities. Wishful thinking features far too often, especially in areas of spending such as infrastructure projects or defense procurement, although the eternal over-optimism about cost control and timely delivery comes at a high cost to taxpayers.

The other question is motivation. In some countries, not only in the developing world, corruption is a major hindrance to effective economic policy. But even absent overt corruption, the introduction in public choice theory of the idea that politicians and officials have their own interests they will seek to further—perhaps the size of their budget or their organizational power base or their beliefs—rather than acting as best they can in the public interest has been profoundly influential. It has shaped efforts to reform public services since the 1980s, as described later in this chapter.

Government failure can therefore be understood in terms of these questions about "the government," understood to be composed of many individuals in different departments and agencies, with a range of incentives, experience, skills and duties, motivation, and competence.

Public Choice Theory

Incentives and motivation are at the heart of the public choice school, which applies economic analysis to political and bureaucratic decisions. It has provided much of the intellectual basis for turning the tide in economic policy away from the state and back toward the market since the late 1970s. Public choice theorists asked about the motivation of the officials and politicians who implement policies. James Buchanan, who later won the Nobel Prize in Economics for his work, wrote: "Economists should cease proffering policy advice as if they were employed by benevolent despots, and they should look to the structure within which political decisions are made." The public choice theorists took the standard economic model of rational individual choice to further self-interest and extended it to politics and bureaucracy. They pointed out that policymakers have private incentives and are motivated by these as well as a sense of public interest or duty. Public choice theory was therefore a powerful counterweight to the earlier "social engineering" mind-set of economic policy in the postwar decades, and, with the economic events of the 1970s, it found a ready reception both intellectually and in practical politics.

The key founding texts of the public choice school were *An Economic Theory of Democracy* (1957) by Anthony Downs and *The Calculus of Consent* (1962) by James Buchanan and Gordon

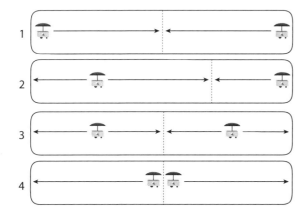

Figure 7.1. Competing ice cream sellers divide the territory.

Tullock; Downs extended a model of the spatial location of retailers (dating back originally to Harold Hotelling in 1929 and formalized in 1948 by Duncan Black) to political choices by voters. Consider how two rival ice cream sellers would choose their location on a beach (figure 7.1). Suppose the sellers start at either edge, dividing the territory between them. They will each get half the customers. But this is not a stable situation. Each has an incentive to move closer to the center and get a bit more than half the territory. Once one does so, the other has to follow suit. They both end up next to each other in the center—with half the beach each.

Downs applied this model to votes, explaining why parties that claim different ideologies seem to end up in the middle of the left-right partisan spectrum, trying to appeal to the median voter. He also argued that voters were "rationally ignorant": there was no incentive for individual voters to spend a lot of time analyzing policies, so most would make their choice according to party label. The model seemed very apt in the 1960s and for decades after (although perhaps not so much today as voting patterns fragment and the simple left-right spectrum applies less well in many countries). Buchanan and Tullock extended the basic insight that economic models apply to politics to analyze voting behavior more generally, and to explain how coalitions of self-interested groups form for certain policies.

The insight that government consists of people who have their own aims, motivations, and weaknesses was of course not brand-new to these mid-twentieth-century economists. In his *Essays: Moral, Political and Literary*, the eighteenth-century Enlightenment philosopher David Hume raised the same question, writing: "In contriving any system of government, and fixing the several checks and controls of the constitution, every man ought to be supposed a knave and to have no other end, in all his actions, than private interest. By this interest, we must govern him and, by means of it, notwithstanding his insatiable avarice and ambition, co-operate to the public good." So there are two fundamental mental models of public officials. Either they are Hume's "knaves" needing to be monitored or held accountable in some way if they are not to make passive "pawns" of the public, or they are "knights" who can largely be trusted to act in the public interest.

Regulatory Capture

One key insight from the question raised by public choice theory about the incentives faced by officials or politicians is *regulatory capture*. The term was first coined by George Stigler, who asked who benefits from regulations and what explains the shape they take. His answer: "Regulation is acquired by the industry and is designed and operated primarily for its benefit." His original 1971 paper looked at the US trucking industry and the development of regulations on carriers. The licensing regime and restrictions on the weight of trucks proved to be correlated with the power of agricultural and rail interests in each state. Over time there was huge growth in road freight traffic and a growing number of license applications—and yet fewer, bigger carriers. Where farm lobbies were weakest and shipping more dependent on road than rail, trucking companies were able to build their market power using regulation to restrict competition from new entrants. Stigler concluded that industries and occupations try to use political power and influence to restrict entry and thus earn monopoly rents; hence their efforts are often described as *rent seeking*.

Other examples—some already mentioned in chapter 2—include

- taxi license or medallion holders trying to prevent new entrants, including Uber and Lyft, operating in their cities (although taxi drivers everywhere have used city regulations to limit competition since long before the new apps appeared);
- the increasing scope of professional licensing for lawyers, doctors, and accountants, but increasingly also for professions where training, safety, or competence standards seem less pressing, such as tour guides, fitness trainers, scrap metal recyclers, barbers, and manicurists;
- import quotas or other restrictions on imports, such as health or environmental standards, restricting competition from overseas, which—although they will ultimately raise prices paid by consumers—are less visible than import tariffs.

Clearly, such regulations also have benefits such as adequate health, safety, and environmental standards. Even where there are strong reasons to regulate for consumer protection, though, the regulatory barriers limit competition and the scope for new entry into an industry. Finance and pharmaceuticals are good examples (box 7.1). They certainly need regulating, but it is equally certain that they can deploy regulatory complexity to their own advantage, by employing small armies of lobbyists and lawyers to interpret the rules to their own advantage while making it hard for newcomers to comply.

The extent of direct lobbying of governments by industry bodies and individual companies is evidence of the significance of regulatory capture: the monopoly rents earned from market power must exceed the costs of the lobbying effort (table 7.1). It is not easy to work out the total cost because registers of lobbyists do not capture the full scale of the spending—at all levels of government from the local to the US federal government or European Commission, taking in all the regulatory bodies too, and on everything from PR spending in the media and funding research by think tanks to corporate hospitality or simply buying lunch or coffee. Whatever the exact figure, it is billions of dollars, euros, or pounds, all ultimately paid

Box 7.1. Regulatory capture in Danish banking

In 2018 a whistle-blower reported that the Estonian branch of Den Danske Bank had been involved in laundering money after a staggering €200 billion of Russian and other ex-Soviet state funds flowed through the tiny office over nine years. Denmark's Financial Supervisory Authority (FSA) was accused of regulatory capture due to its lackluster response to the scandal. Although the bank's chairman and chief executive were ousted and criminal investigations started in the US, Estonia, and Denmark itself, the then-head of the FSA said rumors of large fines were exaggerated. The FSA's previous chairman had also been Danske Bank's finance director. As a result, the Danish business minister announced the regulator would be reviewed, saying that, although its officials needed to have banking experience, "How we can ensure that we don't have ties that are too close between the financial sector and the authorities?"

Richard Milne (2019), "Denmark Shakes Up Watchdog after Danske Bank Scandal," *Financial Times* (January 2), https://www.ft.com/content/ee686644 -0527-11e9-99df-6183d3002ee1.

by consumers. Industries with a small number of large companies tend to be the biggest spenders on lobbying, such as oil and gas, banking, and technology (figure 7.2).

Although generally interpreted broadly, the term *regulatory capture* is sometimes used to refer to just one specific form of the phenomenon, namely, the closeness of the links between industry or sector regulators and the companies they regulate. There is an inevitable revolving door, where people who work in the businesses, or in the specialist consultancies hired by them, subsequently get jobs as regulators, and, conversely, where former regulators or policymakers move into the private sector to work in the companies they were charged with regulating. This movement is not only inevitable but also probably healthy up to a point, in that people gain important experience of how things work on the other side of the fence. But it is only human nature that the individuals involved also

Table 7.1. Lobbying in the US

Ranked lobbying sectors, 2018	
Health	$421,531,641
Finance/Insurance/Real Estate	$400,553,808
Miscellaneous Business	$382,753,390
Communications/Electronics	$318,941,742
Energy/Natural Resources	$248,760,215
Transportation	$184,375,885
Other	$171,644,016
Ideology/Single-Issue	$107,040,342
Agribusiness	$101,155,289
Defense	$94,121,731
Top lobbying spenders, 2018	
US Chamber of Commerce	$69,125,000
National Association of Realtors	$53,778,430
Pharmaceutical Research & Manufacturers of America	$21,821,250
Open Society Policy Center	$20,590,000
Business Roundtable	$17,430,000
Blue Cross/Blue Shield	$17,170,126
American Hospital Association	$17,168,724
Alphabet Inc.	$16,760,000
American Medical Association	$15,542,000
AT&T Inc.	$14,669,000

Source: Center for Responsive Politics, opensecrets.org/lobby/.

develop shared perspectives, and indeed that sometimes their motive is personal financial gain. For this reason most jurisdictions have restrictions such as "gardening leave" periods in the UK, when someone leaving public service must stay home before starting a new private sector job. It is also why the phenomenon is a staple of media stories—an important form of accountability.

There is a trade-off between regulation and competition in using policies to achieve greater economic efficiency. Regulators rarely think less regulation is needed, and politicians like to respond to crises by being seen to do something, not undo something, and still less do nothing. There is therefore a natural upward ratchet in the

(a)

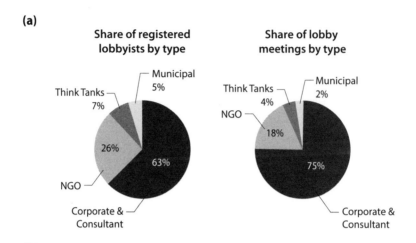

(b)

Rank	Name	Lobby Budget (€)	Meetings	Lobbyists (FTE)	EP Badges
1	Microsoft Corporation	4,500,000	17	7	4
2	Shell Companies	4,500,000	6	7	7
3	ExxonMobil Petroleum & Chemical	4,500,000	5	8	5
4	Deutsche Bank AG	3,962,000	13	8	3
5	Dow Europe GmbH	3,750,000	6	6	3
6	Google	3,500,000	29	9	8
7	General Electric (GE)	3,250,000	26	9	4
8	Siemens AG	3,230,169	4	14	10
9	Huawei Technologies	3,000,000	7	6	6
10	BP	2,500,000	13	3	4
11	Electricité de France (EDF)	2,500,000	12	14	7
12	Daimler	2,500,000	8	8	5
13	Total SA	2,500,000	1	7	5

Figure 7.2. Lobbying the European Commission and Parliament, 2017. *Source*: EU Transparency Register.

amount of regulation. When competition cannot work, for example, to counter inevitable asymmetries of information or in a natural monopoly, regulation is necessary. But often competition delivers greater economic efficiency. It is too rare for regulatory bodies to have specific duties to prioritize competition where it is possible.

Collective Action Problems

In a famous book, *The Logic of Collective Action* (1965), Mancur Olson extended the idea of regulatory capture. He pointed out that small groups always find it easier than the public at large to organize and lobby to get policies or regulations in their own interest. The *collective action problem* is that it is easy to free ride on the efforts of others. If I will benefit from a proposed new regulation on banks' ability to speculate, my potential benefit is 1/67 millionth of my society's total, whereas a bank's benefit from not having the regulation runs into the hundreds of millions of pounds. So they have every incentive to lobby and I have every incentive to be passive. Special interests usually win the policy argument over the general public interest.

Once alerted to it, it is easy to see the logic of collective action in all kinds of areas. For instance, agriculture is now a small part of most developed economies, but farm subsidies are substantial (box 7.2). The biggest beneficiaries tend to be the largest farmers. Agriculture also frequently benefits from production quotas and import restrictions in many countries. The cost is the direct taxpayer cost of the subsidies and higher food prices paid by consumers compared to prices in the absence of trade restrictions—costs spread over many millions of people and therefore hard to observe. One example is Europe's Common Agricultural Policy, which cost €58 billion in 2018 (albeit a total that has been shrinking in recent years) in direct subsidies; food prices in the EU are higher than they would otherwise be (by a disputed amount, given how hard it is to untangle the contribution of different influences) because of the policy. US farm cash subsidies amount to $25 billion a year, and the Government Accountability Office estimates that from 2008 to 2012, $10.6 million was paid to farmers to produce nothing.

Why Is Regulatory Capture So Common?

Industry lobbies therefore have a concentrated voice, while the voice of public interest is dispersed. Concentrated interests always beat diffuse ones. Part of the reason for the prevalence of regula-

Box 7.2. Regulatory capture and lobbying in the food industry

Farm lobbies have been notoriously good at ensuring governments subsidize agriculture generously; subsidies that began at a time when food security was a real issue after World War II continued to grow for many years, before shrinking from 2000 on as the schemes in the EU and US were reformed. The consequence of subsidies to farmers, as many economists have pointed out, is higher prices for food paid by consumers.

Even the US, which is not the worst culprit, has a number of surprisingly large stockpiles due to farm support. The US Department of Agriculture announced in 2018 that the cheese stockpile (due to over-production of milk at guaranteed minimum prices) had reached 1.39 billion pounds, which, according to one analysis, would make a cheddar cheese the size of the US Capitol building.* It was not until 2015 that a US Supreme Court ruling that the "strategic raisin reserve," a national stockpile of raisins, was unconstitutional that this policy intended to keep a floor under the price paid to raisin farmers was abolished. Each year between 1949 and 2015 the Raisin Administrative Committee had set a quantity farmers had to stockpile in order to prevent the price from falling too low.

Other countries have had similar schemes. Canada has a strategic maple syrup reserve to boost prices, which the *Economist* compared to OPEC, the oil cartel. The maple syrup warehouses were subject to a notorious heist in 2012, when thieves took a quarter of the stock. (The robbery was featured in the Netflix series *Dirty Money*.)

Europe's once notorious mountains and lakes of produce have shrunk after successive reforms of its Common Agricultural Policy, but at one time—probably apocryphally—the European butter mountain was said to weigh more than the population of Austria. As of 2019 just a few foods—beef, milk, and sugar—have consumer prices much above world prices.**

* https://www.vox.com/science-and-health/2018/6/28/17515188/us-cheese-surplus-billion-pounds.

** https://www.ecb.europa.eu/pub/pdf/other/mb200712_focus05.en.pdf?ecdd317c1aee2d0bb3c8e26925f8cb8c.

tory capture is the formation of unholy alliances—political or lobbying alliances between groups whose interests appear to be wholly at odds but in fact converge in the case of specific proposals (box 7.3).

Box 7.3. Unholy alliances

One example of an unholy alliance is the coalition between temperance campaigners and dealers in illegal alcohol to bring about Prohibition in the United States (it lasted from 1920 to 1933). The campaigners wanted fewer people to drink alcohol for moral reasons, while the bootleggers wanted the higher profits they could earn in an illegal market with restricted supplies. If the aim of the temperance lobby was to reduce violence—which they blamed on alcohol—they failed. The econometric evidence shows that banning alcohol and drugs in the United States, including during the Prohibition era, has caused an overall increase in violence.*

Another example is the support by both environmental groups and coal producers from the eastern United States for the Environmental Protection Agency's decision to require on all new power stations scrubbers, equipment that cleans emissions. The story is documented in the 1981 book *Clean Air, Dirty Coal* by Bruce Ackerman and William Hassler. Why did the coal producers join this apparently green coalition? The answer is that coal mined in the western states is naturally cleaner than Appalachian and Midwestern coal—it emits less SO_2 when burned—and therefore could command a higher price; requiring all new power stations to install the high tech equipment, no matter what coal they purchased, removed a competitive advantage for cleaner western coal. Requiring only new plants to invest in scrubbers resulted in a lengthening of the life of the obsolete old plants that are the big polluters. These old dirty power plants were actually protected from mandatory scrubbing by the 1970 Clean Air Act. Installation of scrubbing devices cost billions of dollars and was counterproductive for clean air. The EPA's mistake was to regulate the means by which reduced emissions were to be

---

(continued on next page)

(continued from previous page)

brought about, rather than the outcome. If the regulation had instead applied to the level of emissions regardless of the fuel and technology used, it might have been effective in reducing SO_2 emissions. Even better than mandating a certain environmental performance, in terms of economic efficiency, is ensuring all generating plants have an incentive to minimize their emissions. Incentive-based schemes also encourage technological innovation. The US EPA introduced tradable permits that successfully reduced levels of CFCs and lead in gasoline; but not in this case.**

A similar unholy alliance between environmentalists and the logging industry was the 2010 European Timber Regulation, which restricted imports of certain timber products resulting from illegal logging in areas such as the Amazon basin. The industry supported those concerned about the environmental and societal impacts of logging in order to reduce competition from imports.***

* Adam Smith and Bruce Yandle (2014), *Bootleggers & Baptists: How Economic Forces and Moral Persuasion Interact to Shape Regulatory Politics*, Cato Institute.
** Jeffrey Miron (1999), "Violence and the US Prohibition of Drugs and Alcohol," NBER Working Paper No. 6950.
*** Metodi Sotirov, Maike Stelter, and Georg Winkel (2017), "The Emergence of the European Union Timber Regulation: How Baptists, Bootleggers, Devil Shifting and Moral Legitimacy Drive Change in the Environmental Governance of Global Timber Trade," *Forest Policy and Economics* 81: 69–81.

There are other reasons for the prevalence of regulatory capture, as well as unholy alliances:

- Powerful potential losers may need to be compensated if regulations are eased or removed.
- New sectors, which could counter old lobbies (for example, fintech start-ups versus incumbent big banks), take time to organize their lobbying activity.

- Lobbyists may create work to preserve their jobs, even when what they are lobbying for would not be in the interest of their clients.
- People hold such strong beliefs that they are unwilling to be pragmatic—like the temperance campaigners or environmentalists in the examples in box 7.3.

This adds up to a strong tendency for regulation to ratchet up over time. It is one of the reasons why economists advocate more widespread use of cost-benefit analysis in deciding whether or not to introduce a regulation, as discussed in the next chapter.

Policymakers Are Human Too

The insight of public choice theory is that officials and politicians are human and respond to incentives to act in their own interest, whether that is financial or something less concrete, such as power. Yet remarkably often in designing policies, those officials and politicians forget that other people are human too and in their turn respond to the incentives altered by new policies. It is surprisingly rare to see anticipated behavior changes feature in policy analysis (box 7.4). In a commercial market, customers can quickly vote with their feet (or wallet), and businesses will then change their prices or improve their goods and services. Policy-making is a slower process involving consultation, persuasion, and even elections. Yet people do often act on a choice even when it comes to government regulations, ranging from ignoring the rules to working around them in many, often creative, ways. Any policy analysis that does not take into account the likely reaction of those it affects is bound to be less effective, and will possibly be counterproductive.

It is easy to find examples of people working around regulations and taxes in this way (box 7.5). Tax-related examples are particularly common, to the extent that it has its own phrase—tax avoidance (meaning changing behavior legally to minimize payment of tax—as opposed to tax evasion, illegal non-payment). In short, there are many policies designed to regulate people's behavior that people

Box 7.4 Unanticipated behavior changes

So-called sin taxes on harmful substances, such as alcohol or tobacco, are often justified as a means of using financial incentives to reduce consumption and at the same time raise tax revenues in a manner that is (at least sometimes) less politically unpopular than others. However, the choice of substances to tax, and tax rates, needs to be made carefully as it can backfire. Sugar is the most recent addition to the roster of harmful substances, with the aim of tackling rising obesity. The UK has introduced a tax on sugary drinks. A number of US cities and states have also done so. However, a recent study of the tax on sugar-sweetened beverages introduced by the city of Philadelphia and implemented in January 2017 found that it achieved none of the intended effects and had some undesirable results.* The tax of just over $1 on a 2-liter bottle costing just over $1.50 before tax led to a large increase (30%–40%) in soda prices and a 42% decline in purchases. However, the purchases were made outside the city border instead (where prices did not increase), so there was no overall impact on consumers' calorie and sugar intake. But people on low incomes were less likely to go outside the city to purchase and so simply ended up paying higher prices. The city did get more tax revenue ($79 million) but less than predicted ($92 million), and its impact was regressive as people on low incomes were harder hit.

Most governments considering a new tax or a tax change do use estimates of price and income elasticities for the product being taxed, and its substitutes, to try to take into account the different choices people will make after the policy is introduced. However, there are many examples of the failure to include all the possible ways people may respond to the policy change. And it may be that the past is not a good guide to the future if an intervention prompts a significant enough change in behavior.

* Stephan Seiler, Anna Tuchman, and Song Yao (2019), "The Impact of Soda Taxes: Pass-Through, Tax Avoidance, and Nutritional Effects" (January 9), https://ssrn.com/abstract=3302335 or http://dx.doi.org/10.2139/ssrn.3302335.

Box 7.5. Counterproductive regulation

In 1974 in response to the OPEC oil shock, the US government introduced a 55 mph speed limit to reduce the use of gasoline. This seemed perfectly rational. However, compared to the previous 70 mph speed limit, this added 16 minutes to a 70-mile trip. The average wage in 1974 was $4.30 an hour, so an extra 16 minutes' travel time cost $1.15. To save that much on gasoline over 70 miles, the average worker would need to save 2.17 gallons (as a gallon cost 53 cents). This would have required the slower speed to double a typical car's fuel efficiency. As this did not happen, drivers had a strong financial incentive to evade the new speed limit. By 1984 drivers in New York State were driving above the speed limit 83% of the time. The number of CB radios installed in vehicles jumped from 800,000 in 1973 to 12.25 million in 1977, as the habit grew of warning other drivers about speed traps. The police bought radar to catch speeding drivers instead. Drivers went out and bought radar detectors. Congress repealed the federal speed limit in 1995.

In the UK the Dangerous Dogs Act of 1991 was passed speedily in response to an unusual cluster of dog attacks in the early months of the year. The Act banned the breeding and ownership of four named breeds of dogs: the Pit Bull Terrier, the Japanese Tosa, the Dogo Argentino, and the Fila Brasileiro. The legislation has had no discernible impact on the number of dog attacks, and a walk around any park will reveal dogs who look as if they (and their owners) are capable of aggression. Breeders and owners simply moved on to other breeds.

In January 2018, an EU regulation to ban retailers from adding a credit card surcharge on transactions came into force. Previously, many stores added an extra 3% or so to the price to cover the fee they themselves were charged by the credit card provider (Visa or Mastercard). To the surprise of the governments implementing the surcharge ban, retailers introduced administrative charges in its place, often far higher than the now illegal surcharge. Why this was a surprise is not clear as the retailers still faced processing costs they needed to recover from somewhere, and in this case did so from unregulated charges. A supposed consumer protection measure ended up making consumers worse off.

try to get around when they are implemented. So many policies may be ineffective or even counterproductive, and yet all impose costs. An estimate by the US Office of Management and Budget put the annual cost of the regulations enacted in the previous decade at $40–$46 billion in 2006, although this was about half the estimated level of the aggregate benefits.

In principle the likelihood of a behavioral response is easy to address. The policy analysts should aim to identify likely responses and estimate their scale—if small, there is nothing much to worry about. This approach is often taken when it comes to estimating the likely effect of a tax change on government revenues. These tax revenue elasticities estimate the revenue impact, taking into account the adjustments in supply and especially demand as a result of the tax rate changes. Often the calculations are done for the immediate period, whereas ideally they need to be calculated over time; the differences between short- and long-term tax elasticities can be significant, although it also varies considerably between countries. However, practice in this regard also varies between countries, and the approach is rarely applied to regulations in terms of their non-monetary behavioral outcomes.

This kind of behavioral adjustment is evident in situations where people face risks. It is known as *risk compensation*, or the Peltzman effect. Peltzman's argument was that automobile safety regulations, such as compulsory seat belts and shatter-proof windshields, had led people to adopt riskier driving behavior. He concluded the measures had led to no decrease in injuries because people drove less carefully; although there were fewer injuries of drivers and passengers, there were more injured pedestrians. This is a version of *moral hazard*, when people do riskier things if they're insured; in this case, people act in a riskier way because they feel safer. (A wider version in psychological research is known as *risk homeostasis*.) There has subsequently been a large empirical literature with mixed results, but a recent survey concluded that risk compensation does occur, although not always. "Never assume that behavior will not change," it concluded.

One conclusion to draw from this might be that if people are made to feel less secure, they might act in a less risky way. This has

Figure 7.3. Implementing the concept of shared space in London's Exhibition Road. *Source*: Richard Keatinge, CC BY-SA 4.0 license.

informed some policy design, particularly in traffic management. Pioneered by Dutch cities, the idea—known as *shared space*—is to remove road markings and the signs and lines separating pedestrians, cyclists, and motorists. Not knowing where they are supposed to drive or who has the right of way makes motorists (and pedestrians) cautious. The idea was adopted elsewhere, including on one of London's busiest streets in the museum quarter (figure 7.3). However, it might be too soon to count this a policy success, and in fact the London experiment has been scrapped. The behavioral adjustment is not always instant either. In Sweden, following an overnight change from driving on the left to driving on the right, there was a drop in crashes and fatalities, which was linked to the increased apparent risk. The number of motor insurance claims went down by 40%—returning to normal over the next six weeks. Fatality levels declined sharply, and took two years to return to normal.

The inevitability of a behavioral reaction to policies, and the phenomenon of risk compensation, mean it is always worth thinking about the *zero option*—doing nothing—in response to a perceived problem. This is particularly so with policy ideas thought up quickly in a knee-jerk reaction to an event or accident. Unfortunately, doing nothing is rarely politically popular in precisely these circumstances, not even with the voters whose behavior will limit the effectiveness of the policies.

Official (In)Competence

Most policy officials are analysts, without professional experience of the various fields they are analyzing. They are typically economics graduates or have degrees in other social sciences and humanities, or perhaps a legal or accountancy qualification. It is rare to have civil engineers, say, or managers of local housing services, or school principals switch to administrative and policy roles.

The practical experience issue—or rather the lack of it—among officials is a particularly serious problem when it comes to big projects, such as significant new infrastructure investments. The next chapter discusses how much uncertainty is involved in the first place in making these multi-billion-dollar or -euro investment decisions. Given that a project is going ahead, the amount of money at stake if the project goes wrong or is simply late is enormous. Even so, there are many examples of eye-watering overspends on projects that are completed late and never achieve the predicted benefits.

To some extent, it is unfair to single out public sector mega-disasters. They happen in the private sector too, but rarely with the same scrutiny. There are also some exceptions. For instance, in the UK, successive governments had spent £12 billion on a central NHS computer system by the time it was scrapped in 2011; but on the other hand London Underground's Jubilee Line opened on time and on budget in 1979, and Terminal 5 at Heathrow Airport more or less so, though with glitches, in 2008. Unfortunately, cost overruns for big public sector projects are more usual (table 7.2).

What are the implications of these delivery failures? Take the Sydney Opera House, a notorious mega-disaster near the top of table 7.2. It was first expected to cost AUD$7 million and, with work starting in 1958, to be open by 1963. The final cost was AUD$102 million, and it did not open until 1973. Even then it had its flaws. The home of the Australian Ballet, the footprint is so nar-

Table 7.2. Mega-project Cost Overruns

Project	Cost overrun (%)
Suez Canal, Egypt	1,900
Scottish Parliament Building, Scotland	1,600
Sydney Opera House, Australia	1,400
Montreal Summer Olympics, Canada	1,300
Concorde supersonic airplane, UK, France	1,100
Troy and Greenfield Railroad, USA	900
Excalibur smart projectile, USA, Sweden	650
Canadian Firearms Registry, Canada	590
Lake Placid Winter Olympics, USA	560
Medicare transaction system, USA	560
Bank of Norway headquarters, Norway	440
Furka Base Tunnel, Switzerland	300
Verrazano Narrows Bridge, USA	280
Boston's Big Dig Artery/Tunnel project, USA	220
Denver International Airport, USA	200
Panama Canal, Panama	200
Minneapolis Hiawatha light rail line, USA	190
Humber Bridge, UK	180
Dublin Port Tunnel, Ireland	160
Montreal Metro Laval extension, Canada	160
Copenhagen Metro, Denmark	150
Boston–New York–Washington railway, USA	130
Great Belt Rail Tunnel, Denmark	120
London Limehouse Road Tunnel, UK	110
Brooklyn Bridge, USA	100
Shinkansen Joetsu high-speed rail line, Japan	100

Source: Bent Flyvbjerg, 2014.

row that mattresses line the walls offstage so that when dancers exit with a leap, they can bounce into a mattress and be caught before they catapult back on stage. There have also been major roof leaks and a long closure for refurbishment. Yet the building is an Australian icon, on every postcard of Sydney. Surely nobody would

---

Box 7.6. User fees

User fees or charges are increasingly seen as a means not only of creating a suitable incentive for private contractors involved in infrastructure projects to ensure they deliver a high-quality product on time and on budget, but also of bringing much needed funding for new infrastructure investment when government budgets are being squeezed. For example, in the US, federal investment in transport infrastructure was historically funded from tax revenues on gas and diesel paid into the Federal Highway Trust Fund. However, the Fund has often been in deficit and the deficit is expected to rise. Some policy analysts in the US have therefore begun to advocate an extensive road pricing system so drivers pay directly in proportion to their use of the road. Road pricing schemes are becoming common in many cities and countries, such as London and Singapore, as well as toll motorways in many places. They have the additional advantage that they can be used to manage congestion and reduce pollution. They were indeed proposed by William Vickrey in 1969 principally as a way to reduce congestion, giving people a time savings in return for the monetary payment.* In the US, Oregon has been piloting a broad road usage fee program since 2006 and is currently debating a full-scale rollout after favorably evaluating the results.**

(continued on next page)

argue it should never have been built. Similarly, countries absolutely must have infrastructure—dams, bridges, rail lines, and airports—so the fact that overspending is common cannot imply infrastructure should never be built.

The lesson is therefore about ensuring governments have the competence to draw up realistic cost estimates, manage projects, scrutinize contracts properly, and monitor construction work. Often they lack this basic project management know-how in-house, assuming everything can be contracted out to the private sector either at the construction stage or once the new infrastructure is operational. But such contractual relationships are fraught with *asym-*

(*continued from previous page*)

In other countries, road charges are becoming more common, but user fees are also being applied in other areas of infrastructure. In London, the water provider Thames Water is building a new "super-sewer," the Thames Tideway Tunnel, which water users will pay for via charges on their bills.

User fees are seen as fair because people pay for what they use, and the fees introduce a form of price signal that ought to improve allocative efficiency, for instance, in determining people's choices between taking the bus and driving their cars. They also ensure there is adequate funding for the maintenance of infrastructure as well as for the initial investment. The user fees idea is an extension of the way energy and telecoms networks are paid for, by customers through their bills.

* William Vickrey (1969), "Congestion Theory and Transport Investment," *American Economic Review* 59, no. 2: 251–260, *Papers and Proceedings of the Eighty-First Annual Meeting of the American Economic Association* (May).
** https://www.oregonlegislature.gov/lpro/Publications/Background-Brief -Mileage-Based-Road-Funding-2018.pdf.

metric information—the contractor knows more than the government customer—and therefore there are agency problems of the kind that have cropped up repeatedly through this book. These issues come up again later in this chapter, in the contracting out of public services more generally.

One way to help overcome this problem in the case of infrastructure is by paying for the financing of the project through user fees or charges (box 7.6). If the government agency simply pays a private contractor from tax dollars—even through a competitive tender— the contractor has the ability and incentive to exaggerate the true costs or to skimp on quality. Linking revenues to use through user fees creates an incentive to operate the infrastructure well, and also to maintain it properly, whereas the traditional public funding approach favors high-profile new schemes and hence photo ops rather than boring maintenance. User fees also help guard against white elephant projects as the contractor will have an incentive to respond to likely demand. Adam Smith made this point about infrastructure: "When high roads are made and supported by the commerce that is carried on by means of them, they can be made only where that commerce requires them. . . . A magnificent road cannot be made merely because it happens to lead to the country villa of the intendant of the province." (*Wealth of Nations*, Book 5, chapter 1, iii.) The obvious challenge is in forecasting demand for use with sufficient accuracy, and when forecasts prove to be overly optimistic, the private contractor might well ask to renegotiate the terms of the deal: the public sector is not necessarily able to pass all the risk to the private sector, along with the reward. It is also possible that contractors bidding for projects might over-bid to win the contract, a version of the *winner's curse* in auctions. In any case, the need for more government officials to have practical skills and commercial know-how when it comes to negotiating contracts and monitoring the work of private contractors is widely acknowledged.

Reforming Public Sector Management

In highlighting the systematic ways government policies can fail, the public choice theorists prompted substantial political and policy change. One form this took was the privatization of state-owned and -run companies, discussed in chapter 2. Alongside this sale of public assets to the private sector, there has been significant policy innovation in the provision of public services, much of it under the rubric of *new public management*. This is a 1980s label applied by political scientists to a range of reforms intended to hold to account "knavish" (i.e., self-interested) officials. The underlying idea is to make public sector managers and administrators act more like their private sector equivalents by creating appropriate incentives. The challenge is how to design those incentives to achieve accountability when the profitability bottom line, or competition in the market, are not possible or not relevant.

The approach has evolved over time since the 1980s. The initial emphasis was on target setting. This has more recently evolved into contracting out public services to the market; and most recently providing enough information to enable user choice and "quasi markets," creating *contestability* even where a private competitive market is not possible because of the existence of market failures. Each approach has had its drawbacks.

Targets

It might seem obvious that introducing targets for public services and monitoring whether or not they are reached is a way to hold officials to account. But target setting rather quickly backfired. With hindsight, it is obvious why: if people are incentivized to achieve specific targets, they will distort their activities to ensure the target is reached. Centrally planned economies always had this problem. Production targets were set in volume terms—number, weight, length. Setting targets for radio production in terms of the weight of radios produced, say, would lead to the manufacture of heavy radios; using the number of radios as the target led to a large amount of low-quality production. Quantitative targets distort outcomes just as much as regulated prices can do. As one study of the use of targets in the UK—an early and enthusiastic adopter of the public choice approach—put it: "In the 2000s, governments in the UK, particularly in England, developed a system of governance of public services that combined targets with an element of terror. This has obvious parallels with the Soviet regime, which was initially successful but then collapsed."

The effectiveness of targets depends on some important, but usually implicit, assumptions (illustrated in box 7.7):

- Measurement problems are unimportant—it is possible to measure accurately enough something that reasonably well represents the service being delivered. In practice this is often not

---

Box 7.7. Targets in UK health and education

On the face of it, targeting has achieved some remarkable successes. In the UK health care system, for instance, the country's different component nations run their health services separately. Only England introduced formal targets, whereas Scotland, Wales, and Northern Ireland did not. In this natural experiment, patients' waiting times declined dramatically in England in the early 2000s, but not in the other three cases. There were concerns that hitting the target to reduce waiting times compromised the quality of care, however.*

There are also plentiful examples of service outcomes crowding toward the target. One example is the frequency distribution of ambulance response times in the UK's NHS, before and after a maximum wait target of eight minutes was introduced. One study concluded: "For one ambulance service, more than 900 calls were recorded as having been met in seven minutes and fifty-nine seconds, with just a handful met in eight minutes. . . . Crews were split and given bikes or small cars, allowing a lone paramedic on a bike to hit a target, even if he couldn't take you to hospital."**

Targets for public services in the UK are now more carefully designed than was the case in the early years of their use. Increas-

---

(continued on next page)

the case. This problem is compounded by departments or agencies being set multiple and often vague or conflicting targets.

• The distribution of outcomes does not matter—targets rarely specify ranges of tolerance. Yet in reality overshooting might be much worse than undershooting (a seven-hour wait to see an emergency room doctor is much worse than a one-hour wait, around a four-hour target) or vice versa. Similarly, big misses might be disproportionately far worse than small misses.

• The chosen target is not vulnerable to gaming by agents—in other words, people will not change their behavior if they know the result will be used to control or reward and punish them. However, gaming frequently occurs. One variety often found

(continued from previous page)

ingly, the emphasis has been on providing information to enable people to choose their provider. For instance, school league tables give prospective parents information about school performance in terms of pupils' attainment in exams. But these have had to evolve continuously as teachers and schools figured out how to deliver each upward ratchet in outcomes. In England's schools, targets were first set as the proportion of pupils achieving five of the top three grades, A to C, in the GCSE exams taken at age sixteen. This led teachers to focus on pupils on the D/C grade boundary and on the selection of easier subjects. Subsequently, the subjects were restricted to the more academic ones, and "value-added" scores based on pupils' progress were introduced. The rankings are more informative but also more complicated to monitor.

* Health Foundation (2015), "Evidence Scan: The Impact of Performance Targets within the NHS and Internationally," https://www.health.org.uk /sites/default/files/TheImpactOfPerformanceTargetsWithinTheNHSAnd Internationally_0.pdf.
** Tim Harford (2014), "Underperforming on Performance," https://www .ft.com/content/bf238740-07bd-11e4-8e62-00144feab7de.

in practice involves never missing the target, but never exceeding it either if next year's target will be set according to this year's performance. Most targets in fact are vulnerable to *Goodhart's law*: "Any observed statistical regularity will tend to collapse once pressure is put on it for control purposes." The reason is precisely that people—including public sector officials—change their behavior when the incentives change.

Contracting Out

As a result of these challenges, in place of targeting, private sector providers are increasingly contracted to deliver certain public services, sometimes competing with public sector bodies. For instance, the US and UK have government-contracted privately run prisons, while Sweden, Finland, and the Netherlands have state-funded private schools. Many local authority services, such as waste collection and leisure services, are wholly contracted out to private providers.

Contracting out remains politically controversial in the UK, where it has been expanding rapidly thanks to budget cuts imposed by central government on local authorities, especially in England. (As noted above, the devolved nations of Wales, Scotland, and Northern Ireland have been slower than England to adopt any of these approaches, making the UK as a whole a wonderful natural experiment for assessing such policy changes.) Recent Conservative governments have tried in particular to expand the proportion of the NHS budget spent on private providers of medical services, to increase efficiency through competition and choice. The NHS spends a lot of money on private providers already—from the firms that supply stationery and office furniture, the suppliers of medicines and equipment, and the payroll service to cleaners, laboratories, and providers of some medical procedures. Most of these examples are not at all controversial. The objections concern the private provision of medical treatment, due to the special status of the NHS in Britons' hearts and minds and thus in political debate.

Yet contracting out hospital cleaning—which saves a lot of money largely because the successful private bidders pay lower wages—might have been a mistake. The number of infections in hospitals has been on the increase; the fact that cleaning staff are no longer directly supervised by senior nurses could be part of the explanation. For it is hard to tell just by looking whether a surface is clean enough for a hospital environment, and the medical staff who care about health outcomes are not involved in the cleaning process. This underlines an important point about contracting out (as true in private as in public sector contracts). This is a situation where there is a *principal* contracting work to an *agent*, and a significant asymmetry of information. There is insurmountable difficulty for the principal (the public sector agency) in monitoring the actions of the agent and the results in a timely fashion. On the other hand, there are many routine medical procedures, such as varicose vein

treatments or tests not affected by the asymmetric information problem, that could be contracted out to a private provider safe in the
knowledge that the quality of the service and its outcomes can be
monitored and enforced.

Contracting out the running of a prison to a private firm is vulnerable to the same kind of problem. Private prisons are most prevalent in the US, where their performance seems to leave much to be
desired. Academic research suggests people who have been held in
private prisons are more likely to reoffend. Prisoners sent to private
rather than public prisons are incarcerated for longer even with the
same-length sentences, and are more likely to experience violence
in prison. The profit motive gives private providers incentives to
have more people imprisoned for longer (some contracts even guarantee a minimum number of inmates), and to cut costs by having
fewer staff, providing less training for prisoners, and so on. The US
is due to start phasing out private prisons.

There is an inherent problem because the state agency—the principal—is not able to monitor the quality of service being provided
by the prison company—the agent (box 7.8). The contract between
state and private provider is incomplete, because it is difficult to set
out in legal detail the actions the private provider needs to take to
achieve the desired outcomes (good training, low reoffending rates,
etc.). And there is an unavoidable asymmetry of information, as no
inspection regime can ever know whether the quality of service
being provided is consistently good, when there are very strong
incentives for the private company to cut costs and increase profits.
Just as a hospital floor that looks clean might actually be awash
with bacteria, a prison might not be helping inmates with training
and support for their rehabilitation.

There are several reasons contracting out may fail to deliver efficient results, in addition to the principal-agent and asymmetric
information problems. One is that contracts are *incomplete*, meaning it is not possible to write down in sufficient detail all the possible
contingencies, particularly in complicated public services with many
stakeholders. In addition, a real-world factor is that public officials
responsible for procurement often have little relevant business experience, tend to be junior with little autonomy to use their judg-

---

Box 7.8. Principal-agent problems

Principal-agent problems are widespread in the economy—after all, economic growth is a matter of exchanges whereby somebody else performs a service or produces a good you need. There is a large academic literature on the subject.* One example is the management of a company acting as an agent for the owners (shareholders, the principals). Taxpayers are principals with public officials acting as their agents, and in turn public bodies are principals when they contract out services to other providers. Some of the most egregious problems arise in the areas where it is hardest to monitor the quality of the service being delivered, such as defense contracting and software systems. The quality is unknowable until they are actually used. For this reason, the Packard Commission in the US recommended the military should always contract to two producers for equipment, but the costs of doing this can be high, and it may have adverse effects on the incentives of the producers if it affects their expectations about future work from the government.

* David E. M. Sappington (1991), "Incentives in Principal-Agent Relationships," *Journal of Economic Perspectives* 5, no. 2: 45–66.

---

ment, and are generally required to go for the lowest-cost bid. Contracting out can deliver improved public service outcomes, but is most likely to succeed where it is possible to have reasonably complete contracts and where outcomes can be monitored in a straightforward and timely way.

Contestability

The latest evolution in public service reform has been to enable user choice, to improve efficiency, by trying to introduce a form of competition. In this public service context, the term used is not competition but *contestability*.

The hope is that citizens should be well informed and empowered, able to shop around for public services just as they would for private goods and services. Public services should experience competition; and although not profit-making, their budgets should be tied to people's selections, in quasi markets.

One form this takes is an evolution of early target setting into more detailed and sophisticated targets and league tables or ranking. In the example given in box 7.7, this involved publishing schools' "valued-added" information on how much progress their pupils had made, in theory therefore adjusting for the fact that pupils at different schools come from contrasting backgrounds and their degree of social and economic advantage. Parents can in principle look at detailed information about how pupils at various alternative schools perform in terms of a range of measures—although, given how tricky it can be to interpret the detail, it is probably only highly motivated parents who do so. Similarly, hospitals can be required to publish information like the success rates of various procedures, even down to the level of individual surgeons, although critics argue that surgeons may be unwilling to take on difficult or risky cases for fear it will put off other patients in the future.

There are different models for implementing contestability, from permitting some choice about which public service provider to select, to offering tax credits for private expenditure on a tax-funded service, such as education or health, to trying to replicate a market by giving the users of a service vouchers they can spend as they choose with any provider. Vouchers may be universal, or restricted to children from disadvantaged families (as in many US states).

The idea of trying to replicate in public services the effects of consumer choice in private markets, in order to improve performance, is, like all the other types of reform, controversial. Opponents argue that private schools select the most able and the better-off pupils, and that the schemes take funding away from the public sector, which is left with the most disadvantaged pupils. School vouchers were first proposed by the prominent free market advocate Milton Friedman in 1955, who founded what ultimately became EdChoice, which campaigns to extend school choice programs, such as voucher schemes; fifteen US states now offer voucher schemes. The idea remains associated with conservative political views.

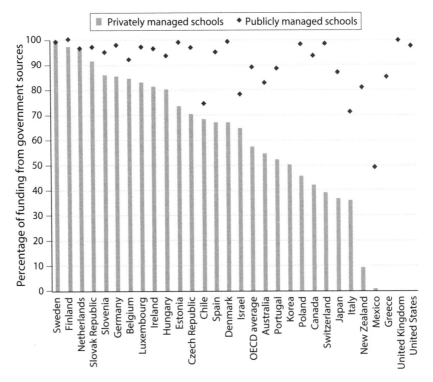

Figure 7.4. Sources of school funding, OECD countries, 2009. Countries are ranked in descending order of the percentage of private school funding from government sources. *Source*: OECD, "Public and Private Schools: How Management and Funding Relate to Their Socio-economic Profile," 2012.

Education offers an illustration of the wide variety of models of public service provision in different countries. Across the rich countries making up the OECD, on average 84% of students are in publicly run state schools, 12% attend schools that are privately run but government funded, and 4% are in independently funded and run private schools. However, there is tremendous variation between countries (figure 7.4).

The OECD, looking across all its member countries, concluded that school choice is becoming more common, although with a great variety of approaches and also outcomes in terms of both average pupil attainment and the inequality of outcomes. Design of the schemes and governance—how much of their funding comes from the government, what do private providers have to deliver, and how are they held accountable if they get public funding—are key issues. In particular, pupil outcomes are less unequal when there is a higher proportion of government funding of private schools and the private providers are correspondingly accountable. The market alone does not deliver good outcomes for all pupils, the study concluded; it has to be managed appropriately. If it is, choice, and hence competition between schools, can be effective.

How Well Have Reforms Worked?

The debate about how to organize public services, triggered initially by the public choice revolution, is far from over. The asymmetric information and incentive problems in the principal-agent relationship described above are not trivial.

One of the key points made by the public choice theorists is that the personal motivations of government employees, officials, or politicians must be taken into account, just as much as the profit motive in the case of the private sector. This is surely valid. Even in countries like most of the OECD where outright corruption is relatively rare, regulatory capture is readily observed.

Yet the progression from producer-run public services in the 1970s to target setting and contestability has been and remains controversial. The fear is that if you assume people are knaves, you drive them to knavery. Does the assumption of self-interested motives among public sector employees drive out what is known as *intrinsic motivation* or sense of public service? Can the two kinds of motivation co-exist? Public-spiritedness clearly exists, but it would be naive to think every public sector worker has an inner vocation to serve. However, the public choice approach leaves no room for the existence of public service or intrinsic motivations. Many people who work in public sector jobs might like the idea of job security and a decent pension, but are also motivated to help other people. It is sometimes argued that the procession of reforms from targets to quasi markets has in fact crowded out intrinsic motivation, and brought about the dominant role of private motives it claimed merely to be describing. If your professional status and career depend on targets and league tables, the argument goes, why bother to put effort into genuinely improving outcomes if they happen not to be well measured?

The UK has been one of the countries at the forefront of the various public service reforms described in this chapter, just as it was with privatization. And as noted earlier, the natural experiment of devolution in the UK to the separate component nations—England, Wales, Scotland, and Northern Ireland—has been a good test of different public service delivery models in similar contexts. England has implemented far more of these kinds of reform than have the other nations. British economists have done a substantial amount of empirical research to evaluate the results. The answer, not surprisingly, is that they are mixed. But on balance, the English approach of targets and tables, choice and contestability, has delivered better outcomes—at least in terms of what can be measured. English schools perform better than Welsh schools in the OECD's authoritative PISA rankings of results. English hospitals outperform hospitals elsewhere in the UK as long as they are competing on patient outcomes and not just cutting costs. However, the evidence is mixed as the organizational details make a big difference. The debate is inevitably a political one. The next chapter therefore poses an important question for economic policymakers: Can decisions about policy ever be technocratic, or will they always end up being a question of political choice? What is the role of evidence and economic expertise?

An Alternative Perspective

In an ideal world, policy choices would be objective and impartial. The policymaker, taking due account of democratic preferences and of minority rights, should be able to evaluate the relevant evidence and select the course of action that maximizes social welfare. However, as this chapter has emphasized, this is a far more difficult task than the "market failure" perspective of the earlier chapters made it seem. Perhaps the fundamental problem is the question of what is the right perspective for assessing policy choices. Whose social welfare is included? Who is calculating it? What do they know and what are their incentives? How will other people respond to their decisions?

Maybe, then, the top-down perspective on the social welfare question is inherently flawed. For markets and governments fail for similar reasons. Externalities mean prices give a misleading signal of social benefits and costs. The market does not internalize them in prices. But governments do not have the information needed to calculate them either. Information asymmetries mean private insurance is problematic. But government insurance does not remove the problems of moral hazard and adverse selection. Perhaps it just means people cheating on benefits rather than lying to insurance companies.

Chapter 4 discussed other institutions, neither markets nor state, as examples of different approaches societies have taken to making choices in the general interest. Communities have organized these institutions themselves, in a bottom-up manner.

Friedrich Hayek saw the market itself as a form of social self-organization. Markets are social institutions, just as much as the lobster-fishing arrangements in Maine outlined in chapter 4. The differences lie in the assignment of property rights and the process for conveying information and monitoring people's behavior. There is in fact a rich tapestry of economic institutions, not just the market and the state. There is nobody designing society. Nor is there a benign social planner figuring out how to achieve maximum allocative and productive efficiency.

The bottom-up perspective is gaining ground in economics, in the shape of agent-based computer models, which mimic real economies composed of millions of individuals making different decisions. Modern computational power makes it feasible to think of taking this approach to economic policy questions. On a smaller scale, however, the approach dates back to at least 1971, and a powerful explanation by Thomas Schelling of why neighborhoods seemed to sort themselves so readily into ethnically segregated areas. He assumed simply that everybody had a modest preference to have similar people nearby. Suppose that one in three neighbors is from the same group. Starting from a random distribution, step-by-step in-

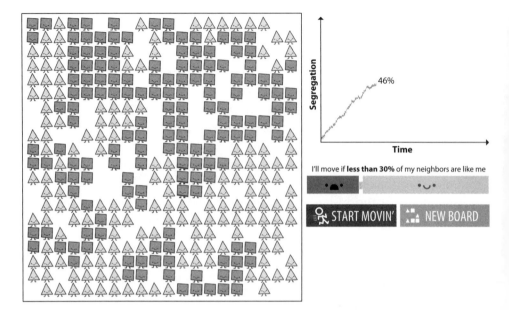

Figure 7.5. The parable of the polygons: An online example of Schelling's model. *Source*: www.ncase.me/polygons.

dividuals move, and within a short number of steps the neighborhood is almost wholly segregated (figure 7.5). This is a powerful model, although reality is of course more complicated. Online versions allow you to vary the parameters to see when any other outcome is possible. Soberingly, people only need to have very mild preferences to be near members of their own group, and once an area has segregated it is impossible to unsort. More encouragingly, if people also have a mild preference for some difference as well as some sameness, the segregation does not occur.

Schelling's insight was that simple rules of behavior can lead to striking outcomes, given the context for people's decisions. So thinking about designing the context can help achieve desirable outcomes. He gave traffic lights as an example. Almost everybody obeys the "red = stop" rule because it is in their own interest to do so; by disobeying, they risk death or injury. The more policies can be designed to be self-policing, the better. It should be noted that the design of the rule is not all that matters. India and the UK have very similar rules of the road, including traffic lights, but a road junction in an Indian city is a maelstrom of chaotic driving, with few people respecting the red lights. This illustrates the importance of social norms and the other issues discussed in chapter 4.

An alternative approach to public policy is to think about government in terms of its power to coordinate individual decisions by shaping the context in which people are making their choices, rather than government as a social engineer analyzing the context and trying to enforce specific behavior through taxes or regulation. Agent-based modeling is one approach; another is to think explicitly in game-theoretic terms about policymakers and the public. The challenge is then setting a framework that aligns individual choices so there is the best chance of achieving efficient outcomes. While this is certainly not easy, perhaps it is worth a try as every day brings examples of new government interventions that fail to achieve their aim or are even entirely counterproductive, usually because people change their behavior to work around them.

Conclusion

For all its political freight, public choice theory makes valid points about the incentives policymakers face. These incentives are most problematic when it is difficult for principals to monitor the behavior of agents and hold them accountable. Government failure and market failure should be seen as two sides of the same coin. Both kinds of failure arise from the context in which social organization inevitably has to occur, with asymmetries of information, economies of scale, and externalities, and where choices are made and decisions taken by humans rather than by ideal economic agents.

The aim of this chapter has been to show that government failure occurs precisely because governments are called on to provide services or impose regulations in contexts where there are market failures. The same characteristics—asymmetries of information, increasing returns to scale, and externalities, and humans mutually influencing each other through preferences and social norms instead of rational economic agents—explain both market and government failure. The collective action problem is difficult whenever any of the assumptions of the fundamental welfare theorems fail. That is pretty much always, as the assumptions of the theorems largely assume away social interaction, and conflicts of interest, and consider a collection of individuals. If the solutions to policy questions were easy, there would not be so much disagreement about policy among political rivals, or in different times and places.

This is not a counsel of despair about policy, however. The minimalist approach to policy, arguing for less government and more market, is itself a conclusion driven entirely by the assumption that people act as individuals whose choices have little impact on other people. If you make this assumption—in other words, assuming that externalities or increasing returns to scale are rare, public goods occur infrequently, and so on—then the circular conclusion that collective action is unnecessary is bound to follow. In fact, the tools of empirical economics offer a good deal of insight into policy questions—the subject of the next chapter.

Further Reading

Technical Follow-Up

Sanford Grossman and Oliver Hart (1983), "An Analysis of the Principal-Agent Problem," *Econometrica* 51: 7–46.

Oliver Hart, Andrei Shleifer, and Robert W. Vishny (1997), "The Proper Scope of Government: Theory and an Application to Prisons," *Quarterly Journal of Economics* 112, no. 4:1127–1161.

Jean-Jacques Laffont and Jean Tirole (1993), *A Theory of Incentives in Procurement and Regulation*, MIT Press.

Jean Tirole (1986), "Hierarchies and Bureaucracies: On the Role of Collusion in Organizations," *Journal of Law, Economics, and Organization* 2, no. 2 (October): 181–214.

Classics

James Buchanan and Gordon Tullock (1962), *The Calculus of Consent*, University of Michigan Press.

Mancur Olson (1971), *The Logic of Collective Action*, Harvard University Press.

George J. Stigler (1971), "The Theory of Economic Regulation," *Bell Journal of Economics and Management Science* 2 (Spring): 3–21.

Public Choice, Collective Action, and New Public Management

James Buchanan (1986), Nobel Prize lecture, http://www.nobelprize .org/nobel_prizes/economic-sciences/laureates/1986/buchanan-lecture .html.

Julian Le Grand (1997), "Knights, knaves or pawns," *Journal of Social Policy* 26, no. 2: 149–169, eprints.lse.ac.uk/3120/1/Knights,_Knaves_or _Pawns.pdf.

D. Mueller (1976), "Public Choice: A Survey," *Journal of Economic Literature* 14, no. 2: 395–433.

Sam Peltzman (1975), "The Effects of Automobile Safety Regulation," *Journal of Political Economy* 83, no. 4: 677–725.

Leon Robertson (1977), "A Critical Analysis of Peltzman's 'The Effects of Automobile Safety Regulation,'{~?~thinspace}" *Journal of Economic Issues* 11, no. 3: 587–600.

Regulatory Capture and Public Sector Capability

Ernesto Dal Bo (2006), "Regulatory Capture: A Review," *Oxford Review of Economic Policy* 22, no. 2: 203–225.

Bent Flyvbjerg (2014), "What You Should Know about Megaprojects and Why," *Project Management Journal* 45, no. 2: 6–19.

Anthony King and Ivor Crewe (2013), *The Blunders of Our Governments*, Oneworld.

Targets, Contracting Out, and Contestability

Gwyn Bevan and Christopher Hood (2006), "What's Measured Is What Matters: Targets and Gaming in the English Public Health Care System," *Public Administration* 84, no. 3: 517–538.

Gwyn Bevan and Deborah Wilson (2013), "Does 'Naming and Shaming' Work for Schools and Hospitals? Lessons from Natural Experiments Following Devolution in England and Wales," *Public Money & Management* 33, no. 4.

Chris Cook (2015), "New Public Management in English Schools," http://www.bbc.co.uk/news/uk-politics-31094670.

Eduardo Engel, Ronald D. Fischer, and Alexander Galetovic (2014), *The Economics of Public-Private Partnerships: A Basic Guide*, Cambridge University Press.

Tim Harford (2014), "Underperforming on Performance," http://timharford.com/2014/07/underperforming-on-performance/.

Steven Kelman (1987), "Public Choice and Public Spirit," *Public Affairs* (Spring), http://www.nationalaffairs.com/public_interest/detail/public-choice-and-public-spirit.

OECD (2017), "School Choice and School Vouchers: An OECD Perspective," http://www.oecd.org/edu/School-choice-and-school-vouchers-an-OECD-perspective.pdf.

Alternative Approaches

Kaushik Basu (2017), *The Republic of Beliefs: A New Approach to Law and Economics*, Princeton University Press.

David Colander and Roland Kupers (2014), *Complexity and the Art of Public Policy: Solving Society's Problems from the Bottom Up*, Princeton University Press.

CHAPTER 8

Evidence and Economic Policies

The government failures described in the last chapter make the point that implementing public policies is difficult, no matter how persuasive the policy analysis underpinning them might seem to be. So an obvious question is, How well is policy analysis actually implemented in practice? Do governments seek to learn lessons from the successes and failures of the past, or of other countries, and apply them in formulating new policies? This final chapter covers the vital topic of policy appraisal and evaluation: respectively, what are the practical questions the analysis should address beforehand in order to decide whether or not to implement a policy; and how well, looking back with hindsight, have specific interventions worked? At stake in either case is whether it is possible to give more or less objective answers to the economic questions. And what about difficult questions, such as how policy choices should reflect uncertainty, different beliefs, and preferences? What about the possibility that policy choices can be self-fulfilling?

The chapter considers the everyday tools at the disposal of policy economists. The workhorse approach to policy evaluation after the fact is econometric analysis using observational data on outcomes. Evaluation of policies in government is surprisingly rare, although academic researchers and some economists in think tanks do a good deal of this work. When it comes to looking ahead at whether to introduce a policy change, one of the most important tools is cost-benefit analysis (CBA), which has evolved as a workhorse method of policy appraisal. Long known and used by civil engineers, its wider use in economic policy was motivated in the first place by some major environmental disasters, and it is now used in many economic policy contexts in at least some countries. The chapter also discusses other, newer techniques to try out policies, particularly the use of randomized control trials and field experiments, important methodological innovations in empirical economics in recent years.

Taking into account the likely benefits and costs of government action is certainly desirable, yet there is always a danger that the available tools are either used too mechanically or not taken seriously enough but rather used as window dressing for political choices. CBA has limitations both in theory and in the way it is applied in practice, and these are covered too. The chapter concludes with the political economy challenges, and why policymakers may be reluctant to learn in a more systematic way from government failures.

The evaluation of economic and social policies is a growth industry—among researchers. The increasing availability of large datasets and improved econometric techniques has led to a renaissance in applied economics. On the other hand, it is relatively rare for governments and officials to evaluate specific economic policies in retrospect and only slightly less rare for them to be appraised in advance. This is not because officials are unaware of or uninterested in the vast amount of empirical evaluation of policies. It is that governments do not like to have their work marked all that quickly because of the political embarrassment if a policy turns out to have been a failure. Politicians are often unwilling to change their policies in light of evidence or analysis, if this runs counter either to their strongly held beliefs or to prior commitments that would be embarrassing or politically costly to ditch. What's more, although the use of economic appraisal and evaluation techniques has been slowly spreading in many countries, it is not clear this will continue. For in the context of strongly partisan politics, some politicians and commentators have taken to disparaging the role of experts and evidence altogether. Yet taxpayers and citizens could be much better served in terms of money saved and outcomes achieved if more policies were genuinely evidence-based, rather than tailored "evidence" being found to support favorite policies.

Evidence can be brought to bear in two ways: before a policy is introduced, to analyze the likely effects; and after it has been implemented, to evaluate whether it achieved its aims and/or had unintended consequences. These two approaches merge, as evidence about the past is one of the key inputs into thinking about the future. However, they are distinguished and referred to, respectively, as *evaluation* (of the past) and *appraisal* (of future policies). Academic and think tank researchers carry out extensive evaluation of the effects of policies using the full array of econometric techniques available to economists, in the kind of studies cited throughout this book. As this is not an econometrics textbook, this chapter is mainly about appraisal, the process of thinking through rigorously and in a manner supported by evidence whether or not a proposed policy is likely to increase economic welfare.

A Note on Evaluation

As just noted, governments themselves undertake far too little evaluation of past policies. A study commissioned by the UK's National Audit Office (the taxpayers' watchdog) found that government departments had carried out very few evaluations of policies; of the thirty-four studies the report looked at in detail, only fourteen had provided sufficient evidence of policy impact to be useful. Departments are required to refer to past evaluations in carrying out their "impact assessments" (or appraisals) of new policies, but only 15% of the impact assessments actually referred to past evidence. A similar report in 2017 by the US Government Accountability Office found that only two in five government managers were aware of any evaluation of any policy carried out in the previous five years. The UK has established several "What Works" centers—groups of researchers charged with evaluations in specific areas of policy (health care, education, criminal justice, early years interventions, old age care, local economic growth, well-being). These are slowly building up bodies of evidence so that past knowledge about the effects of different kinds of policies is not lost with every change of government. On the other hand, some senior politicians have taken to disparaging "experts," in particular economists. Nor is it apparent that evidence is carrying greater weight in political decision-making.

The UK is not particularly bad—on the contrary, the OECD reckons it is better than most governments at taking evidence into consideration in policy development. Looking at the record of US administrations in considering the effect of planned new regulations, Robert Hahn and Paul Tetlock wrote: "The quality of government economic analysis of regulations appears to fall far short of guidelines. . . . The quality of regulatory analysis in the US does not appear to have changed much over time." This may be changing, as in early 2019 the US signed into law a Foundations for Evidence-Based Policymaking Act, although it remains to be seen how well it will work.

The absence of evaluation of the past in government means most evaluation is carried out by academics. One of the most powerful tools available to economists is careful econometric evaluation. The past two or three decades have brought tremendous advances in the techniques for causal inference and in the availability of large-scale micro datasets. "Big data" is now arriving on the scene too, although how much it can be used for causal inference is still debated; it is mainly used to identify correlations and patterns. There has been a proliferation of research looking at the effectiveness of past policy interventions in many areas of social and economic policy, from early years support and education to pensions, from crime to health care, from immigration to energy policy. A recent study found that over three-quarters of the articles in academic journals now concern empirical research covering a large terrain of policy-relevant questions. This empirical turn has been enabled by the computer revolution, the subsequent availability of data, and tremendous improvements in econometric techniques.

By definition, econometric estimates need data and involve looking at past experience, but the results can provide useful information about the possible consequences of future policies as long as the contexts are sufficiently similar. Of more concern is the risk that too much weight is placed on econometric results that cannot really bear it. Three issues need careful attention before too much weight is placed on the estimates:

- *Statistical significance.* Economists often rely in a mechanical way on whether or not estimated regression coefficients are statistically significant, at the conventional 5% level. This has a formal meaning concerning the (un-)likelihood that the observed coefficient is the same as its value in the null hypothesis, given the variability in the sample. It is a test of precision, much affected by the variance of the observed sample. Given the convention for publishing journal articles—statistically significant regression results—many researchers knowingly or not adjust their specifications and estimation methods to deliver statistical significance. What Stephen Ziliak and Deirdre McCloskey have called the "cult of statistical significance" can distort results and lead economists to overlook economically significant (in the normal sense of the word) results that do not happen to pass the 5% threshold.

- *Causality.* As everyone who ever studies statistics knows, correlation does not imply causality. Unfortunately, in the economy, where there are many feedback loops of mutual influence between variables, it is difficult to establish causality. The favorite econometric tool for trying to do so is the *instrumental variables* (IV) technique. For example, how much a person earns depends on how long they stay in education, but the educational choice in turn depends on how much people can earn with different qualifications. To estimate the effect of education on earnings, it is necessary to find an "instrument" that is closely correlated with years of education but not with any other variables in the regression. Good instruments are hard to find; in this example, the cost of education (fees, student loan costs) might be a possibility. A recent paper suggested that the great effort put into IV estimation is wasted or worse, as the estimates are often falsely significant and sensitive to outliers in the data.

- *Power.* Another recent survey of a large number of empirical papers found that many lacked *power*, a technical statistical concept referring to the likelihood that a genuine effect will be identified—and a non-existent one will not be identified. In other words, where statistical power is high, there is a low risk of both false negatives and false positives. Few econometric studies even consider the power of the tests they report. The survey concluded: "Nearly 80% of the reported effects in these empirical economics literatures are exaggerated; typically, by a factor of two and with one-third inflated by a factor of four or more."

It is more important from the social welfare perspective for empirical economics to be right than to be publishable, but academics are mainly incentivized to publish as many studies as they can. As in other sciences such as psychology and indeed in statistics itself, there is a healthy process of introspection under way in economics about the validity of empirical results and the status of scientific knowledge.

Still, with all due caution, good econometric evidence is the gold standard form of evidence to inform a broad understanding of what kinds of government policy have been effective in what circumstances—and which have not. The Further Reading section includes some references to the literature on evaluation.

Getting the Basics of Appraisal Right

The first (and perhaps overly obvious) step in developing and implementing any public policy is to think it through properly. Officials and government economists are often excellent at the theoretical economic analysis; important as this is, thinking through should also involve more attention being paid to practical questions of implementation, as described in chapter 7.

The aim is to increase economic efficiency, figuring out what policy intervention is needed to maximize net social benefits. This is not simply a question of considering the market failure in question and how government action might fix it; rather, it is comparing the costs of the market failure with the costs of government failure, and its probability, should the government decide to act. As this book has tried to show, markets and governments tend to fail in the same contexts, because the challenges of collective action are hard whenever there are characteristics such as asymmetric information or externalities. The assessment of efficiency also ideally should account for uncertainty, transaction costs, cognitive costs, and likely behavioral responses. This includes incentives created for all the humans involved—public sector officials as well as private individuals and businesses.

Any policy intervention will have wider, unintended consequences. The history of government is littered with examples of policies that have been either ineffective or counterproductive, and with a cost that is not always taken into account. The cost has several components: the policy's direct financial cost, including administration, monitoring, and enforcement; the opportunity costs, comprising how else the public sector might have spent the attention and money; and the efficiency costs, imposed on the private sector when (in a second best world) regulations or taxes change their profit or utility-maximizing behavior. Officials have no excuse for not trying to think through how government action might fail, and whether no action—the zero option—is preferable to some action. It is their job, hard as this can be to sell to a politician who wants to "do something." In many countries, most policy officials try to do exactly this, as in the inspiring examples of public service Michael Lewis describes in *The Fifth Risk*.

All public policies create winners and losers. An initial appraisal should therefore also include distributional considerations, and whether the proposed policy needs supplementing with others to offset undesirable distributional consequences. Although whether to actually go ahead with a policy that causes some people to lose out always has to be political in the end—and there almost always are losers—economists cannot wash their hands of thinking about fairness and pointing out the distributional aspects of policies.

A further set of considerations is the political feasibility of a proposal. There is no point in advocating something that will never happen. Political calculation is for politicians, but a basic sense check is vital for the credibility of officials. It is an uncomfortable situation for economic advisers when the political decision makers have no interest in unfavorable economic evidence concerning their own preferred policy ideas—a more frequent occurrence, again, as politics becomes more sharply partisan and ideological.

The rest of this chapter concerns the many practical considerations: What constitutes good evidence? How in practice are the future costs and benefits of a policy to be calculated, how should the limits of an appraisal be drawn, what assumptions need to be made? What role is there for experimental methods in public policy? How should evidence from the evaluation of past and present policies inform decisions about new policies?

Cost-Benefit Analysis

The everyday tool of economists in government analyzing a potential policy—although unfortunately taught to economics students to a far more limited extent than econometrics—is *cost-benefit analysis* (CBA) (sometimes referred to as benefit-cost analysis, or BCA).

CBA is ubiquitous in life, although usually only implicitly. As every decision involves a choice, a road not taken (as the famous Robert Frost poem puts it), we are all constantly making mental CBA assessments. Should a small business invest in a new machine, or is the risk of not getting the sales to justify it too great? Should the local authority invest in a road upgrade, or improve school services instead? Should you cross the road to get to the shop, despite the risk of being hit by a vehicle?

The origins of CBA lie with a nineteenth-century French civil engineer, Jules Dupuit, who explicitly introduced (in 1848) the idea that public investment in transport projects, such as canals and bridges, should create maximum utility. Alfred Marshall, one of the leading economists at the beginning of the twentieth century, formalized this. The use of CBA in transportation was embedded further by the US Federal Navigation Act of 1936, which required benefits of a publicly funded project to exceed costs, leading the US Army Corps of Engineers to develop a technique for making this kind of assessment. Economists picked up on the engineers' work again in developing the modern approach to CBA.

More recently in public policy, the spread of CBA techniques far beyond infrastructure projects dates back to one of the biggest environmental disasters in US history, the spillage of over ten million gallons of oil by the Exxon Valdez container ship in the pristine Prince William Sound in Alaska on March 24, 1989. The question of compensation, involving legal action, prompted renewed attention to the empirical assessment of costs and benefits. In particular, how should figures be put on environmental benefits and damage, with no market for beauty or healthy seabirds, and potentially large externalities? The realization that there was no consensus about how to go about this led the US National Oceanic and Atmospheric Administration to establish a commission of eminent economists to consider how to improve the techniques. The commission, chaired by Nobel laureates Kenneth Arrow and Robert Solow, concluded in its 1993 report that—if done with due care—survey-based methods (known as *contingent valuation*, described below) would enable comparison of costs and benefits in such circumstances.

Much of the thinking about CBA since then has taken place in the context of environmental economics and policy. However, it has also spread further into the consideration of regulations in other domains, apart from environmental protection. Some governments now require a CBA to be carried out for big investments, such as infrastructure projects. The UK Treasury requires a CBA for all major government spending proposals (using techniques set out in its *Green Book*). The US federal government requires a CBA of proposed major regulations. CBA is applied to a wide range of government actions and policies, including transport projects, health spending, approval of new drugs and medicines, environmental protection, and safety regulations.

The principle is straightforward, but of course the practice is complicated. These are the steps:

- Determine the relevant policy options (introduce a new regulation, or leave things unchanged? Build a new bridge, or stick with the congested existing one?)

- Decide on the relevant scope (national or local? Take into account environmental or social externalities?)
- Set the relevant time horizon for the assessment (perhaps five to ten years for a consumer safety regulation; twenty years for an early years education proposal; fifty years for a bridge; one or two generations for climate change policies)
- Predict all relevant variables over that time period (number of pupils, likely traffic growth, consumer spending on the item in question, energy demand, and so on), which might require in turn forecasting other variables (income growth, population)
- Use these to forecast the economic benefits and costs of the proposal over the relevant time horizon—which among other things requires
   o Selecting prices to calculate values, usually market prices unless there are clearly important externalities (as there will be in environmental policies)
   o Remembering to include relevant opportunity costs
- Discount future costs and benefits over the selected period by using an appropriate discount rate for future values to calculate their net present value (NPV)
- Given the uncertainties and assumptions, conduct a sensitivity analysis by varying key variables and assumptions

At each step, there are judgments and choices to be made.

Setting the Scope of the CBA

The first three steps concern the scope of the analysis. A key challenge in carrying out a CBA in practice is contained in the word *relevant* in the first point above. What is the scope of the exercise? Where are the limits, including the time horizon, to be set on the costs and benefits being take into account? This is a matter of judgment.

The choice of time horizon should depend on when the benefits and costs are likely to fall, and particularly the benefits in the case of an investment project when much of the cost is incurred up front.

The units of time (months, years?) need to be made explicit. The time path matters too: for example, are the costs incurred early and few of the benefits until much later? This affects the calculation of net benefits over time when valued in today's money. There is no hard theory as to what time horizon to select, but it ought to depend clearly on the context.

Still less is there hard theory about where to set the analytical limits of an appraisal. For example, in considering a proposal to upgrade a road, the costs of building and maintaining it are relatively straightforward, and it is also obvious that there are costs for people who live next to a road that is going to become much busier and noisier. But should the assessment include the opportunity cost of not being able to go ahead with a planned housing development next to the wider road, or the loss of business in a shopping mall located next to a nearby road that will be much less frequented if the upgrade goes ahead? Or for that matter the environmental costs of making it easier for people to use cars rather than take the train? Similarly, the benefits should include the time saved by people who will have a less congested journey, but what about the potential additional economic activity in two towns linked by the upgraded road? Or the reduction in traffic noise on the nearby route? As in so many other areas of policy choice, such as competition policy (chapter 2), the selection of the right counterfactual is important.

These questions highlight an issue with all CBA exercises: although it is usually presented as a technocratic exercise, and indeed is usually highly technical to carry out, the net outcome involves distributional—and therefore political—choices. The assessment always involves winners and losers, and adds up their gains and losses. Yet CBA is a frequently used tool in public policy, presented as an objective technical assessment. But there is also an implicit distributional judgment involved in weighing each dollar or pound of loss and gain equally in the calculation. This is why controversial projects that will impose big costs on some individuals—perhaps they face a new major road at the end of their peaceful garden—are seen as political rather than economic or technocratic. Relying on the Pareto efficiency concept alone is no help in practical CBA assessments.

It is also tempting to say the scope of CBA exercises should be relatively narrow, or there will be no end to the "relevant" considerations. Yet there are plentiful examples of past major projects that would not have gone ahead if a conventional narrow CBA had been applied to them. Many Western economies are still using infrastructure built fifty or a hundred years ago—some parts of it (like the London Underground and Paris Metro) even Victorian. For example, the municipal engineer Joseph Bazalgette started constructing London's sewers in 1860, after a cholera epidemic and the Great Stink of 1858 caused by untreated sewage in the River Thames. It was a massive engineering exercise involving building the Embankment along the river as well as about 14,000 miles of underground tunnels in and around the capital (figure 8.1). By the time his network was completed in 1863, it had 150 years' worth of capacity—only now is the system is being upgraded for the first time since—and it cost the equivalent of over £200 billion at today's prices. Such projects would only pass a CBA hurdle if they have a visionary assessment of what the relevant scope or time horizon might be. But this does not mean they should never go ahead. Where would the modern world be without Victorian vision?

The challenge is all the more difficult if the project or regulation being appraised is likely to lead to substantial changes in people's incentives and behavior, as this makes predictions about future benefits (in particular) very difficult. The formula for conducting a CBA is only accurate when considering marginal, incremental changes (because it is a linear approximation to a more complicated formula, and therefore only valid when looking at small moves away from the current position). If the future involves non-linear (and so potentially big) changes, or discontinuities (step changes), the "true" net benefit might be very different from the calculated CBA figure. This is a particular problem in the context of environmental assessments, for instance, where tipping points are possible or likely (such as a species falling below its ecologically viable

Figure 8.1. Bazalgette's vision: building 150 years' worth of capacity. Photograph by Otto Herschan/Getty.

population level or a small further rise in global temperatures leading to big shifts in climate systems). But it is also a consideration in the context of big infrastructure projects that will clearly change people's behavior.

CBA Formulas

The decision rule for a CBA can be expressed in several equivalent ways. One is calculating the *net present value* (NPV), where NPV is equal to the sum of benefits minus costs over the relevant time horizon, each term adjusted by the discount factor $1/(1 + r)^t$, where r is the discount rate:

$$NPV = \sum_{t=0}^{T} \frac{B_t - C_t}{(1 + r)^t}$$

where the B_t are benefits at time t and C_t are costs at time t (the formula can be shown with a separate initial cost, C_0, and no benefits in time period 0). The decision rule is then asking whether the NPV is greater than zero, or alternatively ranking projects by their NPVs.

An equivalent way of expressing the rule is to look at the *benefit-cost ratio* (BCR): discount the future benefits and costs to get net present benefits and net present costs. A ratio greater than one implies that benefits exceed costs.

$$BCR = \frac{\sum_{t=0}^{T} B_t / (1 + r)^t}{\sum_{t=0}^{T} C_t / (1 + r)^t} \geq 1$$

Another alternative is to use the NPV formula above and set it equal to zero to calculate the *internal rate of return* (IRR), the discount rate that gives NPV = 0. Companies often take this approach for their investment decisions, going ahead only with those that exceed a set threshold, which in theory is linked to the cost of the capital they have to raise to invest (in principle, their *weighted average cost of capital*, but in practice often a set number such as 5% or 8%).

The formula for present values can also be rearranged to give annualized values of costs and benefits, converting a variable stream of figures into a constant stream. This is particularly the case when looking at costs alone—to assess cost-effectiveness—if there is any uncertainty or debate about the likely future benefits, or to compare two possible investments or projects with different expected lifetimes. If there are no initial costs at time zero, this gives the following formula for costs:

$$\text{Annualized costs} = \text{NPV of costs} * \frac{r(1 + r)^t}{(1 + r)^t - 1}$$

and similarly for the annualized benefits.

These are equivalent ways of calculating the net benefit of a project over a future period of time. The fact that the calculations involve the future means the choice of interest or discount rate used is a fundamental decision.

Choice of Discount Rate

The results of CBAs are usually extremely sensitive to the actual number used for the discount rate. Think about a project with a potential net benefit of $1 this year and $1 next year. The total net present value over two years is $1.96 at a 4% discount rate and $1.91 at a 10% discount rate ($1 plus $1/1.04 in the first case and $1 + $1/1.10 in the second). These seem small differences, but the power of compounding means the gap between the net benefit estimates using different discount rates grows quickly. After five years, the NPV is $4.17 for a 10% discount rate versus $4.62 for the 4% rate. There are large differences for long-run evaluations depending on the choice of discount rate. In addition, predictions of costs and benefits grow more uncertain as well, the farther into the future the calculation is looking. So factoring in a premium to account for the uncertainty leads evaluations to diverge even more.

The sensitivity of the calculation to different discount rates means there is much discussion about the appropriate rate to use. The choice of rate depends in part on the context. Financial market interest rates are inappropriate for most public sector contexts, not least because taxation needs to be taken into account: private investors will likely have to pay tax on their returns. In general, the public sector should choose a lower discount rate for several reasons. Public sector bodies or non-profit institutions are assumed to be more patient than private investors, or have a longer time horizon. The rate chosen should also reflect the opportunity cost of the money being used to finance an investment. Other considerations play into public sector projects too. One is whether the economy is growing, because if people are going to be much better off in the future, we poorer taxpayers might want to be better compensated now for an investment that will benefit them. We might also want to incorporate views about whether we care less about people in the future than we do about ourselves.

Sometimes the interest rate on long-term risk-free assets, such as government bonds, is used in CBAs. Generally, though, the ideal rate to be selected for government CBAs—especially for questions involving long horizons, such as environmental policies—is based on a 1928 formula for the *social discount rate* set out by Frank Ramsey and known as the Ramsey rule. It is

$$r_t = \delta + \eta * g_t$$

where

δ is the pure social time preference rate (this is lower the more patient the society to get a return on money invested now)

η is the elasticity of marginal utility of consumption (measuring how quickly utility falls as consumption increases over time, or in different places, or different states of the world, which is lower the more slowly this marginal utility declines)

g_t is the growth rate of consumption per capita at time t (measuring how much additional consumption there will be in future time periods)

The need for a social discount rate that differs from any private interest rates is due to several factors: observed market interest rates will not take an inter-generational perspective; future generations have no voice in current policy decisions; and long time horizons involve greater uncertainty. The formula, derived from Ramsey's work on optimal long-run economic growth, intuitively states that the optimal interest rate society will pay to deliver the amount of savings and investment that maximizes social output over time depends on the growth of consumption, how much extra utility the additional consumption brings, and how much people now care about the well-being of people in the future.

The selection of actual figures is much debated, however. For example, δ has a clear ethical dimension: Do we think future people are "worth" less than we are? If not, and we believe the same moral weight should be given to future people as people alive now, it should be set to zero or at least very low. Some economists prefer to take a "descriptive" approach and infer values for δ from observed behavior.

The g_t component depends on forecasts about future growth, for if people in the future will be richer because of economic growth between now and then, future net benefits can properly be discounted more heavily; after all, they will be enjoying higher levels of consumption than we are now. Sometimes it is reasonable to assume a figure similar to the average growth rate in the recent past, say, 0.02 (2% per annum per capita); but in some contexts the future could be different from the past. For instance, in the context of debating climate change and what measures to take to adapt to it or mitigate it, for example, some environmentalists argue that future growth will be zero or negative because of the possibly catastrophic consequences of our present inaction.

The η term adjusts additional future units of consumption according to their marginal utility. It seems reasonable to assume diminishing marginal utility of additional consumption, but it is hard to know what the figure should be. If $\eta = 1$, then a 1% increase in income is worth the same to everybody, whenever they live, regardless of their level of income. Sometimes the formula is set equal to a "safe" market interest rate in order to derive an estimate for one of the components, given the debate about each of them.

In practice, different economists, and governments, use different social discount rates. The UK recommends a discount rate of 3.5% for calculating NPVs over less than 30 years based on the following calibration of the Ramsey rule:

$$\delta = 1.5\%, g = 2.0\%, \text{ and } \eta = 1$$

For periods longer than 30 years, a declining discount rate is recommended: 3% for between 31 and 75 years; 2.5% for 76 to 125 years; 2% for 126 to 200 years, 1.5% for 201 to 300 years, and finally 1% for periods beyond 301 years. In France, since the 2005 *rapport Lebègue* the selection has been a 4% discount rate less than 30 years (based on $\delta = 0\%$, $g = 2\%$, and $\eta = 2$). For longer time horizons, a discount rate of 2% is used. In the United States, the Environmental Protection Agency recommends using 2%–3% but testing the outcome with 7%, while the Office for Management and Budget recommends using 7% and testing with 3%. So there is obviously no consensus, and given the sensitivity of CBA calculations to the choice, the only practical approach is to conduct sensitivity tests using a range of discount rates (box 8.1). Given how low interest rates on government debt have been for a decade now, though, the figures produced by using the Ramsey formula have sometimes been higher than the actual interest rate governments pay to borrow.

Box 8.1

The disagreement about what discount rate to select is sharpest in the context of environmental subjects. This disagreement was illustrated in the debate about the 2006 Stern Review, *The Economics of Climate Change*, a landmark UK Treasury report.* It argued for a social discount rate of 1.4% ($\delta = 0.1\%$, $g = 1.3\%$, and $\eta = 1$). A lower figure for the social discount rate makes the future net cost of environmental damage far greater, and likewise the net benefit of acting to avert it now. Other economists disputed these low numbers; William Nordhaus suggested $\delta = 1.5\%$ and $\eta = 2$, more than doubling

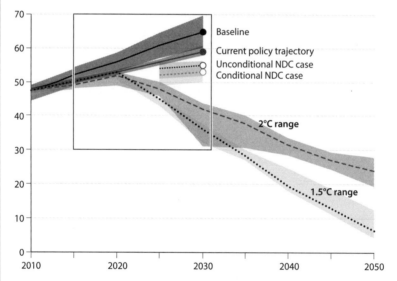

Global CO_2 emissions (GCO$_2$e). *Source*: UNEP 2018 Global Emissions Report. Figure shows the range of emissions in baseline forecast, range if current policies continue, range if "nationally determined conditions" (NDCs; i.e., pledges) are implemented, and what is needed to limit temperature increases as shown.

the Stern figure at the same forecast for growth. Partha Dasgupta suggested η should be up to 4, reflecting a greater concern for income inequality (including over time), even with a low δ that gives a much

(continued on next page)

(continued from previous page)

higher social discount rate than Stern suggested. A social discount rate of 1.4% rather than 6% would multiply sixfold the discounted value of future climate damage in a hundred years from now.** The calculations in the context of climate change are made all the more difficult by the uncertainties involved in predicting the economic and also scientific variables, including concentrations of CO_2 and other greenhouse gases. Economists and climate scientists use systems of equations, *integrated assessment models*, to try to capture the many relationships and feedbacks between the relevant economic and climate variables.*** There are several, known by acronyms such as DICE, PAGE (used in the Stern Review), and FUND. More complicated models try to incorporate additional influences, less amenable to prediction, such as technological innovation and changes in social preferences. Even so, all the models agree that to limit global temperature increases to 2°C or less, CO_2 emissions need to decline rapidly from now on.

* https://webarchive.nationalarchives.gov.uk/20100407172811tf_/http://www.hm-treasury.gov.uk/stern_review_report.htm.

** Partha Dasgupta (2006), "Comments on the Stern Review's Economics of Climate Change," Cambridge University Working Paper, http://www.econ.cam.ac.uk/people-files/emeritus/pd10000/publications/stern07.pdf.

*** John Weyant (2017), "Some Contributions of Integrated Assessment Models of Global Climate Change," *Review of Environmental Economics and Policy* 11, no. 1 (Winter): 115–137, https://doi.org/10.1093/reep/rew018.

Choice of Discounting Formula

The NPV formula uses standard exponential discounting, which implies people are indifferent between having $100 now, $110 in a year, and $121 in two years. The value of future net benefits falls by a constant proportion per period of delay. There is some evidence

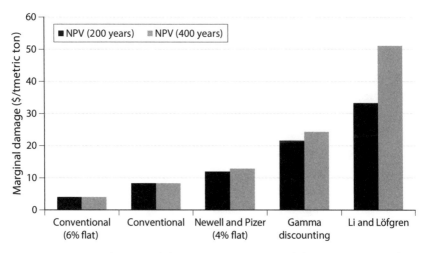

Figure 8.2. Estimated marginal damage per metric ton of CO_2 using various discount rates and methods. *Source*: David Pearce et al. (2003), "Valuing the Future: Recent Advances in Social Discounting," *World Economics* 4, no. 2 (April/June): 136.

(see chapter 5) that people find a form of hyperbolic discounting more intuitive, as in practice many people are more impatient about near-term sacrifices but more patient about the future than implied by the standard formula. As noted above, official government procedures often use step functions with discount rates that decline in steps over increasingly long time horizons, which goes some way to acknowledging this. When assessing estimates of something like the marginal damage from CO_2 emissions over periods as long as two hundred or four hundred years, the choice of technique makes a substantial difference. Using the standard formula, the present value of future net benefits falls to low values within a short time. Using a hyperbolic discounting formula (with appropriate parameter values), or incorporating uncertainty that increases over time, or disagreement about the right discount rate to use, or putting more weight on the opinions of those who are more concerned are all adjustments that give more weight to net costs and benefits in the more distant future. Figure 8.2 illustrates the difference the formula choice can make.

The first two sets of bars compare a higher and lower rate and show that with standard discounting the second two hundred years have no weight in the NPV estimate. Different discounting approaches increase all the estimates compared with the standard formula, and give varying degrees of additional weight to the more distant future.

Incorporating Nonlinearities in CBA Methodology

The differences resulting from choices of the discount rate and formula matter a good deal in some circumstances, and possibly in an asymmetric manner. For instance, if considering an investment to preserve an ecosystem, and looking at long-term costs and benefits, the possibility of a tipping point beyond which further depletion of a species will cause ecosystem collapse might make one inclined to err on the side of caution and use a lower discount rate—so, somewhat counterintuitively, being more cautious points to more dramatic action now. Whereas if considering a road improvement scheme over a ten-year horizon, the risks of making the "wrong" decision about the discount rate (placing too much or too little weight on the net benefits of the investment) are probably symmetric.

As noted earlier, the CBA formula is a linear approximation to a more complicated non-linear formula, so it is only likely to be close to an estimate of a true net benefit when considering marginal changes. Yet it is most important to have some structured method of appraising major policy changes or investment projects, not marginal ones. Environmental economists have been particularly interested in appraising non-linear, non-marginal changes, such as the potential acceleration of damage near tipping points, and have shown that the standard CBA methodology could be seriously misleading both in theory and practice. Taking into account possible non-linear, non-marginal changes is, needless to say, more complicated than the linear method used in everyday public policy; but it should be more widely adopted in relevant contexts, such as major infrastructure projects and environmental assessments.

Valuing Future Costs and Benefits: Revealed Preference and Stated Preference

Ideally, estimates of the future costs and benefits needed for a CBA would be available from econometric methods, such as estimating demand and supply functions given observations on past prices and quantities. For example, forecasting future passenger numbers on a new rail line can draw on elasticities of demand estimated econometrically from the existing rail network and its use, as well as other variables relevant to an economic model, such as incomes or employment. Even in a relatively straightforward case where the past seems a useful guide to the future, some care is needed, because it can cement unwanted characteristics in place. For example, in assessing the net benefits of public transport investments, it might seem obvious to use wage rates to value the time saved from a faster commute. But wage rates are higher where people are more productive, which might be because past public transport infrastructure is better than elsewhere. So the disparity could increase over time in a phenomenon known as the *Matthew effect* (from the Parable of the Talents, Matthew 25:29). This can be avoided by using national average wage rates rather than the local figure.

Unfortunately, CBA is often needed in circumstances that make it difficult to predict future benefits or costs. This is particularly so when environmental benefits and costs are involved because a lot of nature is free, and even if market prices are available, they would not reflect the many externalities. Similarly, sometimes it is also necessary to evaluate cultural or amenity values, such as the value of a historic site or the community spirit of a town. How should policymakers go about valuing the invaluable? Similar issues may arise in the context of zero-price digital goods, when policymakers may want to estimate the burden of a new regulation on a digital company that might cause it to withdraw a service.

If directly relevant data is not available, there are two approaches: *revealed preference* and *stated preference* (or *contingent valuation*). The aim is to elicit people's *willingness to pay* (WTP) for an amenity or *willingness to accept* (WTA) its loss, when market prices are unavailable or not all that informative because of externalities or non-price aspects of the decision.

Revealed Preference Methods

Looking at the actual choices people make in using a good or an amenity is an appealing way to estimate costs and benefits. For instance, the value people place on an amenity like a local nature reserve can be estimated by looking at the travel costs incurred (How many visitors are there and how far do they travel?) and the entry fees they pay. The value of the resource must exceed the total cost of travel and the admission price, otherwise people would not have bothered going. If you have ever been asked for your zip code or postal code when you enter a national park or museum, it might be to gather this kind of data for an econometric valuation exercise.

Such direct observation of relevant costs is not always possible, but another important revealed preference method is *hedonic valuation*, an indirect method. It involves using the market prices of other goods affected by the issue of interest. For example, environmental amenities (nearby parks) or disamenities (noise from traffic or aircraft, pollution) affect house prices (along with other factors, such as the quality of the house and other neighborhood characteristics). On-the-job dangers, such as exposure to toxins, affect wages, along with other variables. Multivariate regression techniques can provide estimates based on affected market prices (house prices and wage rates are the most commonly used). A further possibility is looking at defensive expenditures (box 8.2). Hedonic regressions are also used in the context of other types of public policy evaluation as well as CBA, discussed further below.

Stated Preference Methods

The stated preference or contingent value approach derives estimates from surveys or questionnaires (box 8.3). Although CBA techniques date back to the nineteenth century, the Exxon Valdez disaster on March 24, 1989, when almost 11 million gallons of crude oil spilled from the ship into a pristine Alaskan bay, was a

---

Box 8.2. Defensive expenditures

Sometimes *defensive* or *averting* expenditures can form the basis for empirical estimates. For example, willingness to pay to avoid pollution can be estimated by looking at spending on buying bottled water, air purifiers, or masks. This approach was used to look at the cost of a 1987 trichloroethylene spill, detected in groundwater near Perkasie in southern Pennsylvania. Local people spent $1 million a week for more than eighty weeks on bottled water, treatment systems, boiling water, and other measures to safeguard themselves.* A similar methodology was used to estimate that ten additional days of cleaner air in Chinese cities would reduce spending on face masks by US$187 million, so the value of reducing heavy pollution would be at least that amount.**

* C. Abdalla, B. Roach, and D. Epp (1992), "Valuing Environmental Quality Changes Using Averting Expenditures: An Application to Groundwater Contamination," *Land Economics* 68, no. 2: 163–169.

** Junjie Zhang and Quan Mu (2017), "Air Pollution and Defensive Expenditures: Evidence from Particulate-Filtering Facemasks" (July 20), http://dx.doi.org/10.2139/ssrn.2518032.

---

trigger for the development of the contingent valuation methods widely in use today. There were some straightforward cost elements, such as fishers' loss of livelihood. But much of the cost was clearly environmental damage, and there was also, equally clearly, going to be massive litigation seeking compensation from the oil company. How should these compensation claims be evaluated? The US National Oceanic and Atmospheric Agency's expert panel of economists considered how to go about the evaluation.

The expert panel, which reported its findings in 1993, noted that contingent valuation methods have a number of drawbacks, including the following:

- *Framing bias*: Answers depend on the exact wording of the questions, as well as differing between WTP and WTA.

Box 8.3. Elements of contingent valuation

WTP or WTA is sometimes thought of as having three elements:

Use value: the value you get now from using the resource

Option value: the value you get from having the option to use the resource in the future (similar to the way financial market options have value)

Non-use value: made up of various components, such as bequest value (the value you get from the idea of being able to leave it to future generations), existence or intrinsic value (how much you value just knowing it is there), or pure altruism (how much you value other people being able to use it)

- *Strategic bias*: Interviewees might give false values—overstating their WTP to ensure preservation, understating it to promote development.
- *Information bias*: If respondents have no knowledge/experience of the context, they cannot give an informed valuation.
- *Hypothetical bias*: The respondents do not actually have to pay the costs, so they may not consider their answer carefully. For instance, surveys in environmental contexts tend to report high values for species protection, but it is the construction companies that directly bear the costs.

These challenges in deriving and interpreting WTP and WTA estimates mean some economists are very critical of contingent valuation approaches, and in particular consider that they give implausibly large estimates. Yet they are widely used, especially in environmental economics (box 8.4), and there is a considerable scholarly literature exploring how to overcome the drawbacks. The Arrow panel's report set out some guidelines for carrying out a contingent valuation exercise:

- The survey must give an accurate outline of the issue.
- Survey interviews should be done in person, not by telephone (the report predated widespread internet use).

- The questions should be as specific and concrete as possible, and expressed in terms of actual prices.
- Respondents should be reminded that paying more for one thing leaves less money elsewhere.

These recommendations would make contingent valuation exercises very expensive, however, so they are rarely all followed in practice,

---

Box 8.4

An early example of contingent valuation methods in practice was a 1992 study looking at WTP for the preservation of the Northern spotted owl in the Pacific Northwest of the United States.* The owl's habitat was under threat because of the sale of forest timber. The question was whether certain forest areas should be withdrawn from commercial use. A survey was mailed to 1,000 households nationally, asking whether the respondent would be willing to pay more in taxes and higher prices to implement the conservation policy. It concluded that the benefits of preserving the owls exceed costs by at least 3:1 and perhaps as much as 43:1. Note, though, that a sample of the national population was asked about benefits, while the costs of not being able to harvest timber fell on the forestry company. There have since been many contingent valuation studies looking at endangered species. One recent survey of the literature found over one hundred studies mainly for the US and other rich economies, usually considering "charismatic" species, mainly mammals.** The range of estimates was wide, depending on location and species. What's more, it concluded: "Willingness to pay was generally found to be positively correlated with higher income, higher education level, lower age, and stronger pro-environmental attitudes." In other words, it is not a neutral tool.

* D. Hagen, J. Vincent, P. Welle (1992), "Benefits of Preserving Old Growth Forests and the Spotted Owl," *Contemporary Policy Issues* 10, no. 1: 13–26.
** Ram Pandit et al. (2015), "A Review of Non-market Valuation Studies of Threatened Species and Ecological Communities," Department of the Environment, Canberra, Australia.

particularly face-to-face interviewing. The subsequent literature has considered how to ensure *incentive compatibility*, in other words that the valuation reflects people's true preferences, testing for biases, calibrating results with different sources of evidence, and carefully designing the survey and the sample.

One common approach is to set up questionnaires in a far more structured way, known as *choice experiments* (box 8.5). This survey-based approach does not ask people directly about their WTP (or WTA). Instead, the respondents are given a set of hypothetical situations and asked to choose among alternatives, which are made as

---

Box 8.5. Choice experiments

One 1983 study gave respondents a choice of different bundles of diesel fuel odors from big trucks and transport costs (high/low, low/high);* the implicit WTP to avoid exposure to the fumes was about $75 per household per year. This compared to a cost per household per year of $3.60 to control truck emissions (although these costs would be born in the first instance by the trucking firms).

A similar approach has been used in a recent preliminary study of the value people place on digital goods for which they are not charged an explicit price, such as social media, online maps, and email.** Given the choice between different bundles of goods, including non-digital ones such as TV and breakfast cereals, the experiment found a median WTA loss of such goods ranging from $155 a year for instant messaging services to a hefty $17,530 for search engines. While these specific figures may turn out to be too high, the contingent valuation approach is one of the few options available for measuring the value of such zero-price goods.

*Thomas J. Lareau and Douglas A. Rae (1989), "Valuing WTP for Diesel Odor Reductions: An Application of Contingent Ranking Technique," *Southern Economic Journal* 55, no. 3: 728–742.

** Erik Brynjolfsson, Felix Eggers, and Avinash Gannamaneni (2018), "Using Massive Online Choice Experiments to Estimate Changes in Well Being," NBER Working Paper No. 24514, https://www.nber.org/papers/w24514.

Table 8.1. Summary of Alternative Valuation Methods for CBA

Method	Basis	Comments
Estimate supply, demand functions	Observed changes in prices/quantities	Requires good data and econometrics; ignores externalities
Revealed preference methods		
Hedonic prices	Market prices (e.g., house prices, wages)	Requires market data and data on relevant characteristics. Assumes prices respond to the characteristics of interest.
Direct costs	Travel time, distance, opportunity cost	Requires significant data. Looks at averages, not differences between people.
Stated preference methods		
Contingent valuation	Surveys of WTP/WTA	Biases in responses
Choice experiments	Survey-based estimates of marginal WTP/WTA	More complex questionnaires

concrete and familiar as possible. Researchers can then compare people's choices between different bundles of goods or outcomes, and so derive a marginal WTP.

Although widely used, the drawbacks to contingent valuation raise the question, "Is Some Number Better Than No Number?," the title of a well-known article by Peter Diamond and Jerry Hausman discussing its limitations. It tentatively concluded the answer is yes, but the number must be used with caution. CBA is an everyday tool of policy economists, with several approaches to estimating costs and benefits (table 8.1) but one whose use should be more heavily caveated than is often the case by the time it gets to political decision-making, particularly when the figures in the calculation are based on a contingent valuation approach.

Finally, it is worth noting that sometimes the sheer lack of data means that simpler rule-of-thumb alternatives are used. Benefit transfer takes the benefits estimated from one study and simply applies them to another context, which is cheap and easy but requires the contexts to be sufficiently similar. Cost-effectiveness is applied when a project is going ahead anyway and the task is to find the least-cost way of doing it.

The Value of a Statistical Life

Cost-benefit analysis should be applied in all kinds of contexts, from environmental policy to infrastructure investments to regulation. It is far more common in the first two cases, but the application of CBA to regulation is gradually becoming more widespread. In the US, for example, successive governments have increased the requirement for CBA of new regulations—Republican administrations because they believe there is too much red tape, Democratic ones because they believe benefits such as future environmental or safety gains have tended to be underestimated. In applying CBA to regulations, however, a particularly tricky issue is how to value human life. Although a human life is priceless, this does not help allocate funds for investment or health spending, or appraise proposed safety regulations to weigh the burden of regulation against the injuries and deaths averted. As in other areas of CBA, the cost side of the equation is relatively straightforward to calculate, but the benefit depends on valuing lives saved by incurring that cost. Uncomfortable as this feels, not thinking about the issue simply makes the calculation implicit rather than explicit.

The concept used is the (unfortunately named) *value of a statistical life* (VSL). It represents the change in individual WTP for small changes in mortality risks.

$$VSL = \Delta WTP / \Delta risk$$

For example, suppose a proposed safety regulation would reduce the risk of death from an activity from 1 in 100,000 people to 1 in 200,000 per year. If people are willing on average to pay an additional $5 a year for this reduced risk, then

$$VSL = \$5 \div (1/200,000) = \$1 \text{ million}$$

It is important to note this is different from what you would pay to prevent a certain death; it is a *marginal* concept, and uses measures of small changes in risk.

The WTP element can sometimes be estimated using hedonic wage studies, which measure the value people put on changes in risk by comparing market wage rates for occupations with different mortality risks (controlling for all other contributory factors including individual characteristics). Although this method is not ideal, there is every reason to expect stated preference methods would give upwardly biased estimates. Even so, past estimates of VSL using wage studies have produced high figures too: $1.4–$5 million for the UK; $10 million for Japan; $700,000–$900,000 for South Korea; and $3.5 million for the US (all figures in 1995 dollars).

The VSL concept has been criticized for several reasons. Some critics argue that people have absolute rights in some of the contexts where VSL is calculated—for example, an absolute right to clean air to breathe. Moreover, someone who dies from the failure to regulate traffic fumes (in this example) suffers an infinite loss, for which no compensation is possible. It is immoral to try to quantify this, some would argue. The counterargument is that life involves many risks and it would be immoral *not* to use CBA and VSL techniques to try to maximize the number of lives saved or extended, given the limited resources available.

An alternative approach to encourage CBA in such contexts is the use of microlives and micromorts. A *microlife* is one-millionth of an adult life span (about 1/2 hour), and a *micromort* is a one-in-a-million risk of sudden death. A micromort is calculated from aggregate sudden death statistics divided by total population. In the UK, the sudden death risk is 320 micromorts a year on average. Presenting VSL calculations in micro units appears to make them more palatable. The risk of different activities can be compared in terms of their micromorts or the loss of microlives—the difference being that micromorts do not accumulate but lost microlives (from lifestyle choices such as smoking) do. The National Institute for Health and Care Excellence (NICE), the UK body that carries out CBAs on medical interventions and drugs, suggests the NHS could pay up to £30,000 to prolong an individual's life by a year (17,500 microlives), making its estimate of the value of a microlife about £1.70. Across a number of extreme sports, such as sky diving or marathon running, people seem willing to take on a risk of up to 10 micromorts—the exception being base jumping, which involves an additional 430 micromorts a jump on average, or one death in every 2,300 jumps.

Public Value

It is evident that carrying out a CBA involves many judgments and assumptions, particularly in contexts where either the CBA is an assessment of an investment or regulation that could change people's behavior significantly or trigger non-linear or step-change effects, or where it involves intrinsically hard-to-value characteristics, including environmental or cultural ones. This raises an obvious question: Rather than obscuring the judgments in technical CBA calculations, why not make them explicit?

One technique that does this uses the concept of public value. It is similar to a CBA in systematically comparing costs and benefits, but differs in not trying to encapsulate all the benefits in a single monetary figure. Instead, it assesses different elements of cost and benefit separately, and considers the distributional trade-offs between the different groups affected. The public value approach has been used by many public bodies in the US and UK in local government, policing, the arts and creative sector, architecture, and heritage. With some variations, a public value assessment calculates costs in the same way as in a CBA, but it looks at benefits under separate headings:

- How many people will benefit?
- What will the quality of their experience be?
- Is the proposal likely to achieve its aims or have its proposed impact?

It is usually possible to give parts of the answers to these questions in numerical form, although not necessarily as monetary values. Other parts are qualitative or discursively answered. The point is that there is a reasoned argument so that others can understand why the ultimate decision went the way it did—even if they disagree with the judgment. The transparency of the decision-making in a public value assessment is important, because it gives legitimacy to decisions in contexts where there is uncertainty about the future and where different people's or groups' interests conflict. Public value was a fashionable concept in the 1990s and 2000s and is less so now, although still used by public bodies (box 8.6). It is perhaps a victim of the tyranny of numbers, which can make purely numerical or monetary calculations seem more scientific than is really the

---

Box 8.6. An example of public value in practice

The BBC Trust, the governing body of the BBC from 2006 to 2017, was a pioneer in the use of public value methods.* It used formal public value tests to approve new BBC services or major changes. The elements of public value considered for a new service, for instance, were

Reach: the projected usage of the service over a given period of time (for example, the number or percentage of adults who would use the service at least once in an average week)

Quality and distinctiveness: the quality of any content to be supplied by the service, or possibly technical issues, and the extent to which the proposal was distinctive from other existing or proposed services

Impact: the benefits users of the service would gain, as consumers, and as citizens (e.g., a better functioning democracy, or understanding and respect between different communities)

Cost and value for the money: the financial implications of supplying the new service or, conversely, not going ahead with it

Every test included a public consultation and the publication of interim and final reports.

* D. Coyle and C. Woolard (2010), "Public Value in Practice: Restoring the Ethos of Public Service," BBC Trust, http://downloads.bbc.co.uk/bbctrust/assets /files/pdf/regulatory_framework/pvt/public_value_practice.pdf.

case. A public value approach is really a form of CBA that is honest about the limitations of that technique and yet still gives some analytical structure to policy decisions.

Randomized Control Trials and Policy Experiments

One possible reason for growing interest in evidence on the effectiveness of economic policies is the use of randomized control trials (RCTs). Long used in medicine and many natural sciences, this is a relatively new technique in economics and other social sciences, dating from the early 2000s. Their use originated in the study of low-income economies, and there have now been hundreds of projects in many countries designed to assess specific policy interventions aimed at challenges such as reducing the incidence of malaria, increasing school attendance, and encouraging parents to get their children immunized. The number of RCTs has been increasing rapidly. They are being applied increasingly in high-income economies and to issues that once seemed off limits (such as policing and education). The size of the trials has grown much bigger (one was conducted in half the cities of France; another in the Indian state of Andhra Pradesh, which has the same population as Germany). The American Economic Association now maintains a registry of RCTs in economics (at https://www.socialscienceregistry.org/).

The initial rapid spread of RCTs in developing countries came about because aid donors, both governments and non-governmental bodies such as the Gates Foundation, have increasingly insisted on empirical evidence that their money is being spent well (box 8.7). This donor pressure has been absent in the rich economies, so the use of RCTs is more limited, albeit spreading slowly, often in the guise of pilot policies. Although taxpayers would surely like to know whether their money is being spent well, politicians are less keen to have their policy commitments tested experimentally. The idea of a pilot, which can be either embraced or disowned by politicians who do not have a lot at stake either way, is a welcome one for navigating the political economy of economic policy proposals. However, businesses are increasingly embracing RCTs, often to test

Box 8.7. RCTs in practice

There has been such strong growth in the use of randomized control trials in economics that their practitioners have earned a label: the randomistas. The trend started in the study of policies in developing countries, often projects funded by aid donors. Many policy areas are covered but with a focus on health, education, and access to finance, reflecting many of the priorities of the donors. One health RCT concerned anemia, which impacts 40% of children in Asia and Africa, affecting their physical and cognitive development. The proportion among the group studied in Delhi was higher: 69% of preschool children had anemia and 30% had intestinal worms. More than 2,300 children were randomly assigned to one of three groups to be given vitamin A and iron supplements and deworming treatments phased in at different times. The children in the treatment groups gained weight and attended school more often.*

Education is another policy domain where many RCTs have been conducted. For example, in western Kenya, dropout rates from primary school are high, and higher for girls than boys. Schools charge fees and money is needed for books and supplies as well. In a trial, 64 out of 127 schools were randomly invited to participate in a program that gave scholarships to sixth-grade girls who scored in the top 15% on official tests. The scholarships raised test scores for girls, including those who had not won scholarships, and also (by less) for boys, who were not even eligible. Nonetheless, only in one district was there an impact on student attendance. However, teacher attendance improved significantly.**

The use of RCTs is spreading rapidly to developed economies now. To give one example that caught the headlines, 5,000 resumes were randomly assigned either "black-sounding" or "white-sounding" names. The resumes were sent in response to 1,300 sales or administrative jobs advertised in Boston and Chicago. Two each of high-quality and low-quality resumes were sent to each employer. Success was judged by whether or not the candidate got a call back

(continued on next page)

(continued from previous page)

---

or an emailed invitation to interview. The study concluded: "Resumes with white-sounding names received 50% more callbacks than those with black names. But, regional differences are important to note— for example, in Chicago, employers located in black neighborhoods discriminate less against blacks. Based on researchers' estimates, a white name yielded as many more callbacks as an additional eight years of experience."***

* Gustavo Bobonis, Edward Miguel, and Charu Puri-Sharma (2006), "Anemia and School Participation," *Journal of Human Resources* 41, no. 4: 692–721.

** Michael Kremer, Edward Miguel, and Rebecca Thornton (2009), "Incentives to Learn," *Review of Economics and Statistics* 91, no. 3: 537–556.

*** Marianne Bertrand and Sendhil Mullainathan (2004), "Are Emily and Greg More Employable Than Lakisha and Jamal? A Field Experiment on Labor Market Discrimination," *American Economic Review* 94, no. 4: 991–1013.

See directory at https://www.povertyactionlab.org/evaluations.

---

different behavioral assumptions (as discussed in chapter 5)—digital businesses refer to this as *A/B testing*—and this might encourage greater use of the technique in public policy. There are signs this is happening. The MIT laboratory that introduced RCTs to development economics, J-PAL, has opened an office in North America this year. The new(ish) behavioral economics units in government in several countries, described in chapter 5 too, are also keen users of RCTs.

The use of RCTs has several advantages over other methods of evaluation:

- They overcome the lack of data needed for other methods because they generate their own data.
- They can assess small variations in policies by comparing different treatments for different groups.

- They can defuse some ideological conflicts when appropriately designed.
- They allow policy proposals to be tried on a small scale as pilot schemes before a big (and hard-to-reverse) commitment to them is made.

Needless to say, there are drawbacks too. There has been much debate about whether the results from RCTs generalize much, or at all. Does a small trial looking at how to boost immunization of children in Delhi have any information at all for policymakers looking to increase the use of vaccinations in Baltimore? However, while this is obviously a valid question, it does assume that other forms of evidence such as econometric estimates, generalize better, which might not always be the case.

More significant are the concerns about the design of RCTs and the ethical issues involved. Their use is being taken up so eagerly that not all the researchers are setting up careful and truly random tests. For instance, if people are told they are taking part in a trial this might change their behavior, which needs to be taken into account in the design. Ideally, people should not know they are in a trial at all. The design also needs to genuinely isolate the effects of the policy being tested, which can be tricky. The medical profession has strict ethical guidelines governing trials, and this ought to be the same for policy RCTs too. Although universities and the professional bodies do have ethics policies in place for any research involving humans, not all RCTs are conducted by academics. The policy world too needs a consensus set of ethical rules governing RCTs.

Economic policy would also benefit from the equivalent of Cochrane reviews in medicine. These are meta-studies systematically surveying and summarizing all the available evidence on different types of treatment. There has been a vast amount of empirical research on many areas of policy, countless CBAs conducted (although very few evaluated after the fact), and now a rapidly increasing number of results from RCTs. Economics must work out how to learn from past policy successes and mistakes, so future policymakers have a better chance of making decisions that increase society's economic welfare.

Conclusion

The subject of this chapter—how to assess how well economic policies might work or have worked in practice—is one of the most important practical aspects of policy economics. Yet it is all too often ignored in economics degrees, so many of the economics graduates who later work in public service have to learn about these techniques on the job. The application of econometrics or hedonic regressions or cost-benefit analysis is obviously more technical than the introduction in this chapter. The aim here has been to underline the importance of ensuring that policies deliver on their aims, and to highlight some limitations of the economic techniques currently available. Some number *is* better than no number, and government involving experts is better than government ignoring evidence. But, equally, the answer to a policy challenge or problem is never just a number; there is always judgment involved.

Once evidence exists, there is the issue of whether and how it will be used. The techniques described in this chapter obviously involve matters of judgment and are subject to uncertainty. It is easy for people with a firm political belief to ignore or dismiss contrary evidence. As Keynes once wrote: "There is nothing a government hates more than to be well-informed; for it makes the process of arriving at decisions much more complicated and difficult." It might be that politicians see economists as just one voice among many to take into account in weighing up their policy decisions. Economists advocate for economic efficiency, while politicians have all the other potential aims of policy in mind. The other side of the coin is that economists, or those whose political views are supported by certain economic evidence, sometimes claim undue certainty for their empirical assessments.

These are fraught times for claims about "facts." Equally, these are superb times for discovery given the ability to access more data, greater interdisciplinary working, and innovative tools for interpreting and presenting evidence. The aim of this book has been to make a case for the role of economics in public policy that is both ardent (because economics does bring distinctive insights into the way societies can make best use of the resources available) and modest (because organizing a society with due regard for complex contexts, conflicting interests, and uncertain knowledge is not easy). Simple answers are probably wrong; complicated answers are unappealing. But this challenge is one of the most important and stimulating facing us today, when so many countries are experiencing deep fractures; and I hope readers are inspired to pursue more of what they have read in this book.

Further Reading

Technical Follow-Up

Matthew D. Adler and Eric A. Posner (1999), "Rethinking Cost-Benefit Analysis," University of Chicago Law School, John M. Olin Law & Economics Working Paper No. 72 (April).

Joshua Angrist and Steffen Pischke (2015), *Mastering Metrics*, Princeton University Press.

Simon Dietz and Cameron Hepburn (2013), "Benefit-Cost Analysis of Non-marginal Climate and Energy Projects, *Energy Economics* 40: 61–71.

Christian Gollier (2013), *Pricing the Planet's Future*, Princeton University Press.

Jiehan Guo et al. (2006), "Discounting and the Social Cost of Carbon: A Closer Look at Uncertainty," *Environmental Science & Policy* 9: 205–216.

Classics

Robert K. Merton (1968), "The Matthew Effect in Science," *Science* 159, no. 3810: 56–63.

Frank Ramsey (1928), "A Mathematical Theory of Saving," *Economic Journal* 38, no. 152: 543–559.

CBA

Kenneth Arrow et al. (2012), "How Should Benefits and Costs Be Discounted in an Intergenerational Context?" Resources for the Future, http://www.rff.org/files/sharepoint/WorkImages/Download/RFF-DP-12-53.pdf.

Peter A. Diamond and Jerry A. Hausman (1994), "Contingent Valuation: Is Some Number Better Than No Number?," *Journal of Economic Perspectives*. 8, no. 4 (Autumn): 45–64.

Daniel Fujiwara and Ross Campbell (2011), "Valuation Techniques for Social Cost Benefit Analysis: A Discussion of the Current Issues," HM Treasury, UK Department of Work and Pensions (July), https://www.gov.uk/government/uploads/system/uploads/attachment_data/file/209107/greenbook_valuationtechniques.pdf.

Jerry Hausman (2012), "Contingent Valuation: From Dubious to Hopeless," *Journal of Economic Perspectives* 26, no. 4: 43–56.

HM Treasury (2018), *The Green Book: Central Government Guidance on Appraisal and Evaluation*, https://assets.publishing.service.gov.uk/government/uploads/system/uploads/attachment_data/file/685903/The_Green_Book.pdf.

John A. List, Paramita Sinha, and Michael H. Taylor (2006), "Using Choice Experiments to Value Non-market Goods and Services: Evidence from Field Experiments," *B.E. Journal of Economic Analysis and Policy 5*, no. 2.

David Pearce et al. (2003), "Valuing the Future: Recent Advances in Social Discounting," *World Economics* 4, no. 2 (Apr/Jun): 121–141.

US Environmental Protection Agency, "Guidelines for Preparing Economic Analyses" (chapter on discounting), https://yosemite.epa.gov/ee/epa/eerm.nsf/vwan/ee-0568-06.pdf/$file/ee-0568-06.pdf.

Policy Appraisal

Robert W. Hahn (2019), "Building on Foundations for Evidence-Based Policy," Science 364, no. 6440: 534–535.

Robert W. Hahn and Paul C. Tetlock (2008), "Has Economic Analysis Improved Regulatory Decisions?," *Journal of Economic Perspectives* 22, no. 1: 67–84, https://www.aeaweb.org/articles?id=10.1257/jep.22.1.67.

Dieter Helm and Colin Mayer (2016), "Infrastructure: Why It Is Underprovided and Badly Managed," *Oxford Review of Economic Policy* 32, no. 3: 343–359.

Catherine L. Kling, Daniel J. Phaneuf, and Jinhua Zhao (2012), "From Exxon to BP: Has Some Number Become Better Than No Number?," *Journal of Economic Perspectives* 26, no. 4: 3–26.

Sally Sadoff (2014), "The Role of Experimentation in Education Policy," *Oxford Review of Economic Policy* 30, no. 4: 597–620.

Cass Sunstein (2018), *The Cost-Benefit Revolution*, MIT Press.

RCTs and Experimental Methods

Abhijit Banerjee and Esther Duflo (2009), "The Experimental Approach to Development Economics," *Annual Review of Economics* 1, no. 1: 151–178.

Abhijit Banerjee and Esther Duflo (2011), *Poor Economics*, PublicAffairs.

Angus Deaton and Nancy Cartwright (2018), "Understanding and Misunderstanding Randomized Controlled Trials," *Social Science & Medicine*, 210: 2–21.

John A. List (2011), "Why Economists Should Conduct Field Experiments and 14 Tips for Pulling One Off," *Journal of Economic Perspectives* 25 (3): 3–16.

ACKNOWLEDGMENTS

This book builds on a course I taught in the economics department at the University of Manchester from 2014/15 to 2017/18, and I owe heartfelt thanks to my colleagues in the department there, particularly Martyn Andrews, Peter Backus, Ralf Becker, Rachel Griffith, Ed Manderson, and Dan Rigby. Also to the graduate TAs on the course, Bob Hindle, Cahal Moran, and Mohsen Veisi. I'm grateful to all the students who took Econ 20431 over those four years, for asking questions that made me think, for their feedback, and for their enthusiasm both for the economics and for the mission of public service. I'd like to thank my colleagues at the University of Cambridge, particularly Toke Aidt, Carolina Alves, Dennis Grube, Flavio Toxvaerd, and above all Michael Kenny for their welcome, their support, and their willingness to let me lecture on these topics on the MPhil in Public Policy. Special thanks to Don Ross and Alex Teytelboym for their comments on parts of this text. I have also greatly benefited from being one of the contributors to the CORE Economics project and thank Sam Bowles and Wendy Carlin in particular for their insights into how to make economics rigorous while at the same time subtle and relevant for the next generation.

Over many years I have also benefited from the experience of contributing to a number of areas of public policy in the UK, and from the insights of the many economists and officials I worked with over the years on the Competition Commission, the BBC Trust, the Migration Advisory Committee, the Natural Capital Committee, the Industrial Strategy Commission and Council, and the Digital Competition Expert Panel. I've learned a tremendous amount from Kate Barker, Jagjit Chada, John Fingleton, Jason Furman, Andy Haldane, Jonathan Haskel, Dieter Helm, David Metcalf, Gus O'Donnell, and Dave Ramsden, among others.

I especially want to mention Peter Sinclair, who was the first person to teach me any economics when I was a raw student at Brasenose College, Oxford, in the late 1970s. Peter is a wise, wide-ranging economist, and a gifted and inspiring teacher. He has launched many distinguished economists on their careers. I have tried, imperfectly, in this book to attain his clarity of exposition and his genius for finding intriguing and lively examples to bring theory to life. The late Paul Geroski, chairman of the Competition Commission, was another inspiration to me in my policy career; working with him was like taking a daily masterclass in applied economics.

My special thanks also to Julia Wdowin at the Bennett Institute, University of Cambridge, for her indefatigable research assistance. Also thanks to all the team at Princeton University Press for their superb help, particularly Sarah Caro, for her enthusiasm for this book

As ever, I owe a particular debt of gratitude to my husband, Rory, who put up with me writing this when on holiday and in all spare moments, and of course to Cabbage the dog for helping me think while taking her for walks.

Photograph by Rory Cellan-Jones.

APPENDIX: CONSUMER SURPLUS AND WILLINGNESS TO PAY/WILLINGNESS TO ACCEPT

Chapter 2 discussed the concept of consumer surplus. This is the amount consumers would have been willing to pay in excess of the price they actually had to pay for a good. The measures of willingness to pay (WTP) and willingness to accept (WTA) discussed in chapter 8 are related to consumer surplus, and so can be linked to economic welfare.

Consider a change in the relative price between the two goods, which changes the slope of the budget constraint (how many coconuts the individual can get for one pineapple). In figure A.1, pineapples (x-axis) become more expensive as the budget constraint shifts from the solid line to the dashed line reflecting the new prices.

Compensating variation is the amount an individual would be willing to accept in compensation for a relative price change—it is the amount of income that keeps them on the same indifference curve as at A when the price change has taken them to B ($= Y_1 - Y_0$ valued at the new prices).

Equivalent variation is the amount the individual would be willing to pay to avoid the change—it is the amount of income that would get them to the same indifference curve as at B if the price change had happened ($Y_1 - Y_0$ valued at the old prices).

These diagrams show an individual's indifference curves. When aggregated across individual utilities, the gains or losses in equivalent variation or compensating variation are measures of consumer surplus (the area under the demand curve in excess of market price—see chapter 2). They differ from each other because they are measured at different relative prices; this is the point made in chapter 1 about the difference between evaluating a policy change from the perspective of the winners or the losers. Whose perspective you

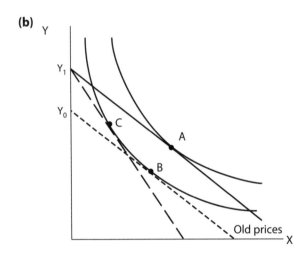

Figure A.1. Compensating and equivalent variation.

take—in other words, which relative prices are used to evaluate the change—determines the measure of the welfare gain.

Changes in compensating variation and equivalent variation are related to the WTP and WTA measures discussed in chapter 8 in the following ways:

A positive change in compensating variation is the maximum a person is willing to pay to obtain the increase in utility arising from the change in the state of the world. A negative change in equivalent variation is the maximum willingness to pay to prevent a utility-decreasing change.

A negative change in compensating variation is the minimum compensation the person is willing to accept for a utility-decreasing change. A positive change in equivalent variation is the minimum the person is willing to accept in compensation for forgoing a utility-increasing change.

WTP and WTA can also be evaluated for changes in incomes or amounts of a (non-market) good rather than changes in prices. The choice of which one to use depends on the allocation of property rights: Is somebody actually being asked about giving up something to which they already have a right? In that case, it is the WTA.

Willingness to pay for something is usually slightly lower than willingness to accept compensation for its absence or loss, which is not surprising as the two are evaluated at different relative prices: without the change and with the change. There is also an income effect in the sense that someone's view about how much they can afford to pay is naturally less than how much they would like to receive in compensation. In practice, the gap between the two can be larger than one might expect. It is sometimes suggested that this reflects the effect of negative versus positive framing effects (chapter 5). There is some evidence the discrepancy is bigger for non-market or public goods; for instance, the WTA figure exceeds the WTP figure by more for a new road through a rural beauty spot than for a housing development in an urban area. The divergence between the two tends to be higher when there are no close substitutes for the good or amenity in question.

GLOSSARY OF TECHNICAL TERMS

Adverse selection: A situation that occurs because of asymmetric information, which leads to distortions in market allocations. Either the buyer or seller holds more information about the expected value of the transaction, which they do not reveal, leading to increased risk.

Allocative efficiency: A situation in which the last unit of every good or service produced has a marginal benefit to consumers equal to the marginal cost of supply. The output level of production is equal to its marginal cost and meets consumer preferences.

Benefit-cost ratio (BCR): An indicator used in cost-benefit analyses; if greater than one, expected benefits exceed expected costs.

Choice architecture: The recognition that the framing, layout, and design of alternative choices to be selected from can influence individual decision-making.

Club goods: Goods that are excludable but non-rival in nature.

Collective action problem: A situation where conflicting interests and incentives to free ride between individuals means that benefits from cooperation toward reaching a common goal or acquiring public goods are forgone.

Compensating variation: The amount that would return a consumer to their initial utility level following a price change in a good or service.

Competition policy: Policies to enable new entry and make markets function better, encourage innovation, and improve efficiency in individual markets, with the ultimate aim of greater consumer welfare. Policy acts in areas related to anti-trust and cartels, market liberalization, state aid control, and merger control.

Concentration ratios: The combined revenue share of a number of the largest firms (say, the top five of ten) in the market to total revenues in the market.

Conduct regulation: Regulation concerning the desired or expected conduct of regulators and regulatory entities.

Contestability: The ease with which new providers can enter a market.

Contract curve: The set of points of mutually beneficial trade between market participants, reflecting different initial distributions of resources.

Creative destruction: Schumpeter's term for the dynamic birth of innovative firms and death of inefficient ones in a market economy.

Deadweight loss: The absolute loss of economic efficiency when a market is not perfectly competitive.

Deferred acceptance: An algorithm for efficient matching of supply and demand in contexts such as job markets or dating markets.

Edgeworth box: A tool for representing the possibilities of distribution of two goods between two entities.

Entry barriers: Obstacles that can make it difficult for new firms to enter a given market. These can include licensing requirements, regulations, fixed or start-up costs. skill shortages, and access to materials.

Envelopment: A tactic often used in digital markets when a platform expands into activities beyond its original ones using the customer base it has built.

Equity: Fairness.

Equivalent variation: The amount that would take a consumer to the new utility level if a price change in a good or service were to occur.

Externality: A benefit or cost that accrues to a third party as a consequence of production or consumption activity.

Free riding: Benefiting from public goods without paying for them.

General equilibrium: The simultaneous equilibrium of all the markets making up the economy.

Hedonic valuation: A model linking price to internal characteristics of the good being sold.

Herfindahl-Hirschman index: A measure of the market concentration of a certain industry, and an indicator of the amount of competition between firms in that industry.

Heuristics: Rules of thumb.

Incentive compatibility: The situation when every individual's incentives are compatible with those of all the others.

Indifference curve: Points on a graph that show combinations of different quantities of two goods between which a consumer is indifferent in terms of the utility they receive.

Information asymmetries: A situation where one party (in a transaction or deal) has more or better information than the other party involved.

Innovation rents: The higher profits a firm can make as a result of an innovative product or service, often protected by a patent.

Internal rate of return (IRR): The expected rate of return in terms of net present value generated by an investment project, often compared to a threshold level.

Intrinsic motivation: The non-economic motivations for economic decisions, such as public service or altruism.

Isoquants: The set of points on a graph that show the different combinations of inputs that would result in the same level of output.

Land value tax: A tax leveled on the value of land (before any buildings or improvements).

Marginal rate of substitution (MRS): The rate at which a consumer is willing to give up a given amount of one good in exchange for one unit more of another good.

Marginal rate of technical substitution (MRTS): The rate at which one input into production can be substituted for another, keeping the level of output constant.

Market definition: The boundaries of a market in terms of what goods or services can substitute for each other in either production or demand, used in competition policy to assess which firms compete effectively with each other.

Market design: Tools—often algorithms—for redesigning the rules by which transactions occur and the infrastructure that enables the transactions, in order to provide practical solutions to real-world problems.

Market failure: A situation in which the free market allocation of resources is not efficient. This can arise due to negative externalities, monopolies, or lack in provision of public goods. There is an overall social welfare loss associated with market failure.

Microlives: A measured unit of thirty minutes of life expectancy.

Micromorts: A measured unit of risk of a one-in-a-million chance of sudden death.

Monopoly rent: The above-normal profit earned from having market power and producing below-competitive quantities at above-competitive prices.

Moral hazard: A tendency to change behavior, namely, to act in a more risky way, once the individual/party is insured against the costs of bad decision-making.

Natural monopoly: A type of monopoly that arises when one is the most efficient number of firms in the given industry. This is normally the case when there are extremely high fixed or start-up costs, unique raw materials, or technology involved.

Net present value (NPV): The value of future costs or benefits discounted by an interest rate to put them in terms of today's dollars or euros.

Network effects: The value that an additional user of a good or service adds to the benefit other users gain from the good or service.

Occupational licensing: A way in which government regulates the number of those able to practice a certain profession, establishing a limit to the amount of licenses that can be distributed to those who wish to work in certain occupations.

Pareto efficient: A state in the economy where resources are allocated in such a way that they cannot be reallocated in any other way to make at least one individual better off without making at least one individual worse off.

Pareto improvement: A reallocation such that at least one individual can be made better off, without any individual being made worse off.

Partial equilibrium: The determination of price and quantity in one given part of an economy, isolating its operation from other remaining sectors.

Peak loading: A period of time when demand for a product or service over a certain sustained period is significantly higher than otherwise average demand levels.

Positional goods: Goods that are valued highly because of their relative scarcity, which reveal some information about the consumer's relative social standing.

Price elasticity of demand: A measure of how demand responds to a change in the price of a given product.

Price inelastic: When consumer demand is (relatively) unresponsive to changes in the price of a given good or service, often the case with essential goods such as elecricity.

Process innovation: A new or improved production or delivery method that aims to lead to greater efficiency for a firm.

Product innovation: The process by which a new or improved version of a good or service enters a market.

Product mix efficiency: The mixture of goods and service in the economy that is on the production possibility frontier and best reflects the preferences of consumers.

Production possibility frontier: All combinations of maximum possible output in an economy of two goods or services when all available resources are used efficiently.

Productive efficiency: A state in which all goods and services in an economy are being produced at their lowest cost. In this case, it is not possible to produce any more of a given good or service without producing less of another.

Projection bias: An observed feature of human cognition whereby tastes and preferences are assumed to stay the same, not changing over time.

Prospect theory: A set of regularities about how people make decisions between alternative options that involve risk and uncertainty, involving reference point, risk aversion, and asymmetric preferences as between gains and losses.

Public good: A good that is neither excludable nor rivalrous. That is, individuals cannot be excluded from its use nor does use by one individual reduce the benefit that another individual can gain from its consumption.

Regulatory arbitrage: Seeking ways to legally circumvent costly regulations.

Regulatory asset base (RAB): The assets owned by a utility company whose pricing and/or rate of return is governed by regulation.

Regulatory capture: Regulation in the interests of the regulated industry.

Rent seeking: The pursuit of gain (in excess of costs) by an individual or firm that has no economic welfare benefit for society.

Revealed preference: Consumer preferences revealed by actual behavior, rather than claimed or stated preferences.

Risk compensation: The tendency for people to change their behavior according to the level of risk they perceive in a given situation. When risk is perceived to be lower, people will behave less cautiously.

Social capital: The institutions and relationships that broadly underpin economic transactions with trust and reduce free riding.

Social discount rate: A rate that aims to put a present value from society's perspective on future costs and benefits; particularly useful for cost-benefit analyses with long time horizons needing to take future generations into account.

Social welfare functions: An aggregation of individual utility functions enabling the ranking of different economic outcomes.

Stated preference: Consumer preferences as stated, for example, in surveys.

Tragedy of the commons: A situation where individuals seek to maximize their own benefit gained from using a shared resource, which results in overexploitation of the resource.

Value of a statistical life (VSL): A metric of how much an individual is willing to pay to reduce their risk of death, which differs from the valuation of a life. The metric may be used in the context of risk of death in different environmental, occupational, or locational settings.

Weighted average cost of capital: A measurement of the cost of capital in a firm, combining their different sources of finance according to how much they raise from each source.

Welfare economics: A branch of economics concerned with the analysis of economic efficiency and social welfare.

Willingness to accept (WTA): The lowest amount a consumer must be paid to give up a good or put up with a bad such as pollution.

Willingness to pay (WTP): The highest amount a consumer will spend on one unit of a good or service.

Winner's curse: The over-paying in an auction by the successful bidder, when the amount bid exceeds the value of the asset, owing to incomplete information or emotional engagement in the contest, for example.

X-inefficiency: When a lack of competitive pressure within a market or industry results in fewer efficiency improvements or cost reductions over time than in a competitive environment.

INDEX

Page numbers in *italics* refer to figures and tables.